Growing Up with LITERATURE

Growing Up with LITERATURE

Walter Sawyer, EdD
Russell Sage College
and
Diana E. Comer
Becker Junior College

Foreword by Francis P. Hodge
Illustrations by Sally Newcomb

DELMAR PUBLISHERS INC.®

NOTICE TO THE READER

Cover illustration by Dahl Taylor

Delmar Staff

     Administrative Editor: Jay Whitney
     Project Supervisor: Marlene McHugh Pratt
     Production Coordinator: Bruce Sherwin
     Design Supervisor: Susan C. Mathews

For information address Delmar Publishers Inc.
2 Computer Drive West, Box 15–015
Albany, New York 12212

COPYRIGHT © 1991 BY DELMAR PUBLISHERS INC.

Printed in the United States of America
Published simultaneously in Canada
by Nelson Canada,
a division of The Thomson Corporation

10 9 8 7 6 5 4 3 2 1

Library of Congress Cataloging-in-Publication Data

Sawyer, Walter.
    Growing up with literature/Walter Sawyer and Diana E. Comer;
foreword by Francis P. Hodge; illustrations by Sally Newcomb.
       p. cm.
    Includes bibliographical references and index.
    ISBN 0-8273-3440-0
    1. Children—Books and reading.   2. Children's literature—Study
and teaching (Preschool)—United States.   3. Early childhood
education—United States.   4. Early childhood education—United
States—Curricula.   I. Comer, Diana E. (Diana Elizabeth)
II. Title.
LB1140.5.L3S28   1991
372.21′0973—dc20   90–46418
                                                           CIP

Table of Contents

Foreword by Francis P. Hodge

This volume, *Growing Up with LITERATURE,* is long overdue in the educational marketplace. Many texts are available emphasizing classroom instruction in literature at all grade levels. Many texts also are on the market offering guidance to parents about the importance of books in the development of young children. This text takes the best of the aforementioned examples and treats the continuity of one to the other. This feature distinguishes *Growing Up with LITERATURE* from many other contemporary literature-related texts.

Dr. Walter Sawyer, writing instructor at Russell Sage College, and Diana Comer, director of early childhood programs at Becker Junior College, are eminently qualified to address this topic. I have known Dr. Sawyer, who is both a father and an educator, for nearly twenty years. He has worked diligently with his own children in their development as literate human beings. He has studied and guided school programs aimed at improving literary facility among school children, particularly at the elementary level. Ms. Comer also has a distinguished career as a parent and as an educator working in early childhood education.

Dr. Sawyer's and Ms. Comer's approach is truly grassroots in origin. They start with the WHYS and carefully lead the early childhood educator and the parent along the road to the WHAT WITHS and the HOWS. Their approach is a carefully conceived road map of operational ideas and suggestions. Their points have been tested and have proven successful in numerous cases. They offer alternatives, suggesting titles that might be utilized; they indicate areas of concern; and, significantly, they advise caution and thoughtful planning by both parents and teachers.

Encouraging a love for literature, developing good readers, and making reading an integral part of everyday life are so important for young readers. Without a foundation from home and early childhood, children often experience difficulty in school, especially in mastery of reading skills. Working through the suggestions and recommendations offered by Dr. Sawyer and Ms. Comer in *Growing Up with LITERATURE* can instill in young readers a love for and understanding of literature.

Dedication

To Jean C. Sawyer, who truly understands the beauty and power of literature.

W.S.

To all the caring, professional teachers who give unselfishly of themselves and their expertise to uplift and offer hope of a better tomorrow to the children in their charge.

D.E.C.

Preface

Growing Up with LITERATURE is a book that celebrates the interaction that can take place when quality children's literature is shared with youngsters. It is a comprehensive guide for the individual wishing to learn how to use children's books effectively in early childhood programs. Sections are included on selecting appropriate books, motivating children to participate in the experience, integrating literature into a program, and managing the process. While its primary audience is practitioners in early childhood education programs, parents will find a wealth of information as well.

The philosophy of the book is to present literature as an integrated part of an educational program rather than as an isolated feature used only at storytime. This approach is supported by much of the current thinking, theory, and research on the development of literacy. While the foundation of the book rests on firm conceptual ground, the practical aspects of working with children are at the forefront of the presentation. It is a hands-on tool for both short- and long-range program planning. It explains such concepts as whole language, the role of computer technology and emerging literacy in easily understood terms that are easily translated into classroom practice.

The text makes a valuable contribution to the field of early childhood education. There are few practical books on using literature in early childhood programs which are based upon the current thinking and theory on emerging literacy. *Growing Up with LITERATURE* provides a wealth of practical ideas and strategies which can be implemented in the classroom. The clear concise explanations describing the process of implementation ensures their transfer. In addition, hundreds of books appropriate for young readers are cited. A wide range of titles is used to familiarize the reader with the variety of books available. The citations range from classics to the latest contemporary publications.

Many special features are included. First, and most important, is the approach stressed within the book. The focus is on integrating literature as an integral part of education throughout all areas of the curriculum. Each chapter includes both references for further reading and a set of questions for thought and discussion. The questions tend not to seek rote types of answers. Rather, they require a more careful analysis of the material in the chapter in order to give a thoughtful and logical response. An instructor's guide is also available.

Walter Sawyer is a graduate of Siena College, Assumption College, and the State University of New York at Albany. He holds B.A., M.A., and EdD degrees. He is certified in and has worked at all levels of education from nursery school through graduate school. Currently he is an administrator for the Waterford-Halfmoon School District in upstate New York and teaches graduate courses in writing and reading at Russell Sage College. He has been an active member at all levels of the International Reading Association, and is past president of a local reading council.

He has a deep personal interest in storytelling and has published over forty articles, papers, and book chapters in the field of literacy.

Diana Comer is the Director of Early Childhood Education at Becker Junior
College. She holds a B.S. degree from Worcester State College and an M.S.
degree from Cambridge College. She has many years of experience as both a
teacher and a teacher educator in the field of early childhood education.

The authors would like to extend an acknowledgement to several key people
in this endeavor: To Jean Sawyer who listened to and provided critical feedback on
many of the chapters in addition to watching the children. To Andrew and Emily
Sawyer who shared so many of the cited children's books in family read aloud
sessions. To Frank Hodge for the Foreword to this book and for guiding us all
down the right road. To our editor Jay Whitney for all of his support and encouragement. To our reviewers, Colin K. Ducolon, Professor, Early Childhood Education, Champlain College; Mary Ann Gordon, ECE Teaching Master, Lambton
College; and Margot Keller, M.S., Assistant Professor, Early Childhood Development, Lima Technical College, for the perceptive feedback and useful comments
which made *Growing Up with LITERATURE* a better book.

W.S.

D.E.C.

About the Illustrator

The illustrator for *Growing Up with LITERATURE,* Sally Newcomb, has been snipping since she could first hold a pair of scissors. Illustration is a new enthusiasm. "I found myself grinning a lot when I worked on these pictures," she said.

A portrait silhouette artist since 1956, she is one of the very few moderns who specialize in full-length silhouettes, as well as family groups, pets, and equestrian subjects. With a B.A. and M.A. (in English) from Rutgers University, she has also lectured widely on the history of silhouette—especially the British-American connection.

Her portrait work takes her on yearly migrations from as far west as Kansas City to as far east as Edinburgh, Scotland. She has made regular visits to Saks Fifth Avenue, Bloomingdale's, Dillard's, Jacobson's and Marshall Field's. Her work was mentioned in the September, 1987 issue of *House Beautiful* magazine.

The first "Artist in Residence" in the House of Seven Gables, Mrs. Newcomb has demonstrated her work at Greenfield Village, Erie Canal Village, Boscobel Restoration, the Nantucket Historical Association, and Heritage Plantation in Sandwich, Massachusetts.

Growing Up with LITERATURE

1

What's So Special about Literature?

o say that literature has a special place in the development of the young child is an understatement. Literature, shared aloud in a warm atmosphere and at an appropriate pace, can be the vehicle through which children learn about their world.

The technology of television, telecommunications, and computer science allows information to come to us today at an ever increasing speed and in greater abundance than ever before. However, people are not always capable of processing this information in any meaningful way. This is true for adults and it is also true for children. When the amount of information is too great and the speed too rapid, the full meaning is lost. The nuances are not noticed. The subtle humor slips past. The message becomes devoid of emotion.

There has been an abundance of research over the past quarter of a century which stresses the importance of books and literature as part of a child's development. When children come to school already reading or with a deep interest in reading, critical facts can often be found in their preschool experiences. They usually had books in the home. They observed adults reading. They were read to by adults. They had someone to talk to about books, reading, and literature.

While experience is a powerful teacher for a young child, books and literature can have a profound influence as well. Early in life, children strive for meaning. They try to find out how things work. They attempt to learn how people respond to them and what control they have over their environment. Bruno Bettelheim, a well-known child psychologist and holocaust survivor, contends that finding meaning in life is the greatest need any human being possesses. He believes that finding this meaning is also the most difficult achievement for anyone at any age.[1] The purpose of literature and education is to help people arrive at this meaning. Given this, a broad exposure to literature is a critical component of child development.

Have education and family life succeeded in fulfilling the need to find meaning in life? The answer is partly yes. Despite the large amount of television viewing that young people engage in, sales of children's books are rapidly increasing. Most writers and many successful adults confirm the importance of books and being read to in their early years. On the other

---

[1] Bruno Bettelheim, *The Uses of Enchantment: The Meaning and Importance of Fairy Tales* (New York: Alfred Knopf, 1976).

hand, our nation has an alarmingly high secondary school dropout rate. Our level of adult illiteracy is high in comparison to other industrialized countries. More importantly, we tend to be a nation of people who choose not to read. Jim Trelease cites statistics that indicate that *TV Guide* is the most widely purchased weekly publication in the country. His work has uncovered the fact that when we do read, it is both infrequent and lacking in quality.[2]

Clearly, it is imperative that young children are encouraged to develop interests and attitudes toward reading and literature that will stay with them throughout their lives. Such attributes can help children become competent students and thoughtful adults. More importantly, literature will enrich their lives and help them find meaning in their existence. Before beginning to understand how to develop these attitudes in young children, it is important to have a fuller understanding of the importance of literature and reading. This chapter further discusses the value of reading, the relationship of literature to reading, and the concept of the magic of reading.

THE VALUE OF LITERATURE

Literature serves many needs and imparts many values which may not be immediately discernible. Literature may not appear as spectacular as a computer game or television program, but it provides something different.

Children and adults often need time to reflect on their experiences. Allowing time to think results in deeper learning and understanding. One can always go back to a book to reread an enjoyable, confusing, or important part. This often cannot be done with other media. For example, a child's first experience with snow and playing in the snow can be thrilling. To make it even more meaningful and memorable, one might share Wendy Watson's *Has Winter Come?*

If a child seems reluctant about playing in the snow, one might read Emily Arnold McCully's *First Snow.* Told entirely in illustrations, it is the story of the smallest member of a mouse family who overcomes a hesitancy to play in the snow. Each of these books can be shared over and over again with a child.

The issue is not a matter of literature being positive and technology being negative. Rather, it is more a problem of balance. Both may be used for helping children develop in appropriate ways. There is certainly a need for children to be aware of the technology of their world. It will be an important part of their lives. However, it is equally important for books and literature to be an integral part of living. Literature can help children comprehend their world, build positive attitudes, and make a connection with their humanity.

Learning about the World

Through books, children can both learn about and make sense of their world. They learn about their world when books inform or explain various parts of it. By doing this, books can also arouse the curiosity of children. After reading about some-

[2] Jim Trelease, *The New Read-Aloud Handbook* (New York: Viking Penguin, 1989).

thing, youngsters will often seek to learn more about it. They may request similar books. They may recreate scenes from the book.

Children can understand their world better through the information provided in books. They may have experienced or seen something they do not fully understand. By learning more about it in books, they are often better able to achieve an accurate understanding. This can happen the other way around as well. If one knows that children are going to see or experience something, books about the topic can be shared prior to the experience. If one anticipates a trip to a fair or a zoo, sharing books about the experience will make the experience more meaningful. One might choose books such as *Angelina at the Fair* by Katherine Holabird, *A Koala Grows Up* by Rita Golden Gelman or *Have You Seen My Duckling?* by Nancy Tafuri. These books will enable children to have a more meaningful experience when it does occur. Learning is a process of relating new things to things that are already known. Since the pages of books can be studied, reread, and thought about over time, books are ideal tools for helping children learn and understand.

Building Positive Attitudes

Besides learning about their world, it is critically important that children develop positive attitudes about many things. They need to develop positive self-esteem and to see themselves as competent human beings capable of caring and of being loved. They need to develop tolerance for others who may not share their beliefs or who may be different than themselves. They need to develop a curiosity about learning and life. Books and literature can become primary tools for satisfying that curiosity.

Self-Esteem. Reading good literature can help children develop positive self images in a stressful world. Economic hardships, crime, drugs, and conflicts in the world are readily apparent. While one might wish to shield youngsters from some of these, the information is so prevalent that children are usually aware of them. Family and health problems may be factors children are dealing with as well. Parental love is strong and usually exists even when there is tremendous hardship. The concept of parental love can be reinforced with books such as *Don't Worry, I'll Find You* by Anna Grossnickle Hines and *Some Things Go Together* by Charlotte Zolotow. Through books, children can identify with others like themselves. They can see how others deal with similar problems. By sharing a story with an adult, children can talk about some of these issues.

Literature can help children define their feelings and develop a sense of self. Literature that mirrors the child's situation or is merely related to the situation can be chosen by a perceptive adult. Reading about others who are attempting to make sense of a similar situation can bring hope. Learning that some feelings are normal can enable children to understand that they themselves are normal. They can learn that there is no need for guilt or a lowered sense of self-esteem.

There is a substantial selection of books that explore the idea of self-concept. Many address this concept as an issue of developing relationships among siblings and peers. Watty Piper's classic, *The Little Engine that Could,* has long been used in this way. A more recent story that deals with the problem with subtle humor is *Chicken* by Tricia Tusa. Books that specifically relate to developing a sense of self within a set of siblings include *Jenny's Baby Brother* by Peter Smith and *A Lion for Lewis* by Rosemary Wells.

Tolerance of Others. Good literature can help children understand how they fit in and how important it is to relate to others. Adults who are successful in working well with others can provide good role models. They tend to know how to have their needs met in society while pleasing others at the same time. Besides providing a role model, parents and teachers also work to set realistic goals and limits for group interaction. Providing examples of appropriate human behavior is a powerful instructional tool.

Literature, through its art, imagery, humor, and empathetic characters, provides a good teaching tool for developing tolerance of others. By learning how characters in stories develop solutions to social problems, children can begin to assume a role in goal and limit setting for their own behavior.

There are wonderful books that can explore the nature of differences among people and the acceptance of others. *Watch Out for the Chicken Feet in Your Soup* by Tomie dePaola explores the acceptance by a young boy of his grandmother and her old world habits. *Aunt Armadillo* by Robin Baird Lewis celebrates the relationship of a little girl and her eccentric aunt.

Curiosity about Life. Children possess a curiosity about the world around them. They want to know about things and places. They want to know who different people are. They are proud of the things they have learned. Keeping this sense of wonder alive through a literacy program that includes a sound read aloud program will help to encourage success in later schooling and in life.

It is true, of course, that many young children can learn to memorize the alphabet, numbers, names of states, and so forth. It is also true that some children, through intensive flashcard drills, can begin to learn a reading sight vocabulary. Just because children can learn some of these things at a very young age, however, does not mean that it is a good idea for them to do so.

If children are to succeed in later schooling, it is critical that they want to learn and succeed. While children can be forced to learn bits and pieces of isolated reading skills, no amount of pressure can force children beyond their capability. Exerting this kind of pressure on young children can be totally destructive to their desire to learn and read. Pressure cannot force them to be curious and enthusiastic about books and literature once they have decided that reading is tedious, dull, and boring. Once the desire to better understand oneself and life is lost, it is an incredibly difficult task to revive it. It is far better for parents and teachers to focus on sharing appropriate stories that foster self-esteem, a tolerance for others, and a curiosity about life.

The Human Connection

A good story can do many things for a child. The act of reading a book with a child can do many things for child and reader alike. The sharing that emerges from the

Interest and enjoyment in reading can be enhanced by the good feelings shared when an older child reads to a younger one. Courtesy Diana Comer.

relationship creates an important human connection. There is a personal interaction between the child and reader that is absent from most other media experiences. There is time for the reader to react to the child's delight, confusion, anger, or fear. There is a feeling of warmth and safety for the child in the physical presence of the reader. The reader can assure the child that all is well and detect unasked questions. The book can be stopped or reread. Discussion can take place at any point without destroying the overall experience of the story.

The book in this situation becomes much more than a set of papers with markings and illustrations. The sound and rhythm of language can be slowed down, speeded up, made louder, or made to express emotions the story suggests. The beauty of the language and the story can be developed in a manner appropriate to the children. The illustrations and photographs in the book can be touched, studied, discussed, and returned to as the story goes along. All of this is done within the relationship developed by the child and the reader.

EMERGING LITERACY AND LITERATURE

All parents and teachers want their children to learn to read. However, there has been substantial debate as to when the teaching of reading should begin. Should reading skills be taught to preschool children? Should formal reading instruction be delayed until the child reaches seven years of age? Should the first grade curriculum be pushed down into the kindergarten? Should children who have not mastered kindergarten readiness skills enter a transitional program between kindergarten and first grade until they have mastered the skills?

The answers to these questions depend on what is actually meant by the word "reading." In the context of this book, reading refers to the acquisition of meaning from a written text. The focus is on meaning. In view of this, children begin the process of learning to read from the moment of birth. They are engaged in learning to read when they first begin to listen for the voice of a parent, the rhythm of a story, or the soothing sounds of a lullaby. Some may argue that the very young child is only using listening, but this distinction between listening and reading is an artificial one. The two are inextricably related to each other; each supports the other.

Viewing grade levels as distinct is also an inadequate way of thinking about the way children learn to read. The grade levels in schools are for the convenience of adults rather than children. They enable adults to sort children based on age, ability, cultural awareness and reading level. Children develop at widely varying rates and learn to read at different times in their development. Expecting all children to learn to read at a certain level at a certain age or grade is hopelessly naive. Children tend to send signals when they are ready for new challenges. It is up to the adults to do a better job of reading these signals and responding appropriately to them.

There is a need to be aware of how literacy emerges and the role that literature can play in that emergence. To develop this awareness, one needs to develop a concept of what is contained in a real literacy curriculum and couple it with a realistic understanding of the place of reading skills. This view must then be combined with a set of realistic expectations for individual children.

A Literacy Curriculum

Over the past few decades there has been an abundance of research on how young children develop literacy. While it may sound obvious, literacy develops best in a literate environment. Given the view taken in this book, a literate environment possesses certain features. These features are the experiences and materials that will best enhance the ability of children to derive meaning from what they are doing. Jerome Harste and Virginia Woodward have studied early literacy programs for many years. Their research identifies three key aspects of a literate environment:

1. Supporting the success of the learner;
2. Focusing on learning language; and
3. Allowing the learner to explore language.[3]

Each of their points needs to be considered.

---

[3] Jerome Harste and Virginia Woodward, "Fostering needed change in early literacy programs," in Dorothy Strickland and Leslie Morrow (eds.), *Emerging Literacy: Young Children Learning to Read and Write,* Chapter 12 (Newark, Delaware: International Reading Association, 1989).

Supporting the Success of the Learner. This concept holds that children tend to learn best from first hand experiences. The environment should be filled with a variety of printed material. Storytime should have a prominent role in a program. Many opportunities should be available for children to read, write, and draw. The physical area should have a variety of centers set up in such areas as housekeeping, art, music, mathematics, and literature. Finally, the program should make use of the community by both exploring it on field trips and by inviting visitors in.

Focusing on Learning Language. Given the assumption that children develop literacy skills at different points in their development, one must be willing to invite them to read and write on their own level. Literature should be seen as a vehicle for exploring the world rather than as a tool for teaching reading skills. Reading and writing should be seen as devices for sharing meaning and clarifying thought.

Exploring Language. Language is a very complex thing and mastering it can take a lifetime. More and more sophisticated strategies are required to fully master language and use it effectively. When there is an abundance of reading and writing opportunities and experiences, children learn to be more strategic in their attempts at reading and writing. By having parents, teachers, and visitors as models, children can more easily attempt more complex language skills. By providing extensive opportunities for them to expand their communication through storytimes, discussions, and centers, children can develop a sense of authorship. Authorship is the idea of putting some of their own unique selves into a story or a communication. Children may begin to do this by listening, creating, interpreting, reenacting, dramatizing, and discussing stories.

Reading Skills

Learning to read is important and necessary for all children. A variety of reading skills are needed to be a competent reader. Some say that a phonetic approach in which children focus on learning the sounds of the letters is best. Others contend that a look-say approach that focuses on learning whole words is the superior approach. While there has been a long simmering debate over whether phonics or a look-say approach is best, advocates from each side largely ignore the more important issues. They tend to believe that their position represents the focus of reading. They ignore the fact that reading is more than sounding out words or identifying a list of words. Reading has to do with finding meaning in written text.

Children eventually need to develop both phonetic skills and a store of words that they can recognize on sight. However, they also need to understand other features of language such as semantics, syntactics, and pragmatics. Semantics refers to the meanings that words possess. Since the purpose of reading is to get meaning, understanding the word meanings is critical to true reading. Syntax refers to the parts of speech. Nouns are different from verbs and verbs are different from adjectives. They each do something different in a sentence. What they do in combination is to give a sentence meaning. Pragmatics refers to the practical functions of language. Such things as tone of voice, the degree of formality, and idioms might be grouped under this area. Each lends another key to the true meaning of the message.

The final point on reading skills concerns how and when they are taught to or learned by children. Traditionally, both word attack and comprehension skills have been taught in isolation. That is, the skills are taught through word lists, parts of words, sentences, and brief paragraphs developed to teach a particular skill. They may or may not then be tried out in an assigned piece of text. The belief is that if children are taught all of the little pieces of the "reading puzzle" they are then able to put the puzzle together.

A contemporary wholistic approach to teaching beginning reading uses real words in real books written by real authors. The skills of reading are taught in the context of literature. There are no reading skills that were traditionally taught in isolation that cannot be meaningfully taught in the context of literature. Such an approach provides far more opportunities to also teach the semantics, syntactics, and pragmatics of language.

Realistic Expectations

Children need realistic expectations. Goals, when they are reached, can provide satisfaction and a sense of self-worth. If they are set too high they can lead to frustration, anger, and a sense of failure. If set too low they can encourage a lack of effort and a tendency to be satisfied with mediocrity.

Who sets the expectations? In education, it is generally the teachers and parents who set expectations. Perhaps this system should be questioned. Children may need to become more involved in developing expectations. When someone else sets the goals, there is a lack of emotional involvement by those who must strive to attain those goals. This does not mean that children should have total control. They need the security of knowing that adults can be depended on to provide appropriate guidance and to set reasonable limits.

When expectations are set too uniformly or too high, serious problems can occur. This is already happening in education. It is probably impossible to determine exactly what happened first, but the net effect is often demoralizing to children. In any case, accountability movements in education can be used as a starting point. As the population demanded improved education, legislatures responded with cost-effective devices. They tended to include such things as more rigorous standards for becoming a teacher and increased competency tests in reading, writing, and other basic skills for children. In order for children to be ready for the tests, the curriculum in elementary schools has sometimes been pushed downward.

Prospective kindergarteners are now routinely screened for readiness to enter school. Kindergarteners are now frequently retained for a second year of kindergarten or placed in transitional first grades. Some school districts have two levels of kindergarten, one for those who are "ready," and one for those who supposedly need more time to become "ready." There are various rationales presented for each of these policies. They usually sound well-intentioned, often citing a need to give children more "time to be ready." Basically, however, this is a program designed to categorize children on the basis of such factors as intelligence, cultural background, and language skills. All of these policies may be misguided. By separating more able children, it is likely that the expectations for them will be raised to an even more frustrating level. This separation also deprives them of the opportunity to share their skills with, and to develop an acceptance of, those who are less able. Separating less able children deprives them of a group of good language models and may also crush their sense of self-worth.

A true literacy program can accommodate nearly all children whether they are gifted, average, culturally deprived, or handicapped. This is accomplished by providing a rich language environment, accepting children with the skills they possess, and countering some of the narrow views of literacy that still exist.

THE MAGIC OF READING

Making reading a joyful experience for children lies at the heart of this book. Introduced correctly, literature can be seen throughout life as the friend and companion it deserves to be. In order for this to happen, the adults who work with young children need to foster this relationship with literature in their own lives. It is a mistake to think that one can teach children to love reading and literature without possessing that same love oneself. Children are quite perceptive; they can often spot false enthusiasm in a second.

Some of the best books written today are written for children. The books available for children are a wonderful place to begin or to extend a love for literature. The success of the strategies suggested in this book will depend on this love.

Organization of the Book

The chapters of the book are arranged in an order that provides a logical development to understanding an early childhood literature program. They may, however, be read in any order that suits the needs of the reader. Chapter 2 describes a variety of physical environments for enhancing the sharing of literature. Chapters 3 and 4 focus on literature itself. They describe criteria for selecting quality books and strategies for using various types of literature with children.

Chapters 5 and 6 describe a variety of procedures for the motivational and creative sharing of literature. Chapter 7 explores the critical aspect of integrating literature with all parts of the curriculum. It provides a variety of approaches and suggestions for developing units. Chapter 8 addresses ways of using books to assist children with their emotional understanding of the world through bibliotherapy. Chapter 9 discusses the influence of television and other media on literature and how both can be used effectively with children. Finally, Chapter 10 summarizes the concept of using the community in conjunction with a literature program for children.

Authors and Illustrators

The people who write and illustrate books for children often rely heavily on their own childhood for ideas. They tend to be careful observers of youngsters they see

Books such as this can be used to talk about reading as an adventure. Courtesy Delmar Publishers Inc.

around them. As such, they are quite in tune with much of childhood. Learning about the personal life and thoughts of an author or illustrator can be a powerful motivation factor. Therefore, it is important to be aware of the lives of authors. The knowledge can be shared with children at various points surrounding the reading of a book. Some books even allow one to see how authors develop and books are born. *The Art Lesson* by Tomie dePaola is an autobiographical depiction of a young child who later becomes an author/illustrator of children's books. *How a Book Is Made* by Aliki clearly and accurately depicts the actual creation of a children's book. Information about authors can be found on book jackets, in reference books

Sketch by Dick Bruna. A visit with an illustrator can be a most exciting time. Courtesy Dick Bruna.

in the children's sections of libraries, in the stories themselves, and by writing to publishers. If resources are available, sponsoring a day with an author can be a tremendously rewarding experience for children and adults alike.

SUMMARY

The basic assumption of this book is that literature has tremendous value for young children. Literature is different from other informational media in that it usually includes another human being with whom the story is being shared. Literature derives its value from three things: First, it informs and excites children about the world in which they live. Secondly, it contributes to developing a positive self-image and the acceptance of others. Finally, literature serves to help children connect to both the people sharing a story and the people within the story.

Literature has a definite place within a wholistic literacy curriculum. It serves as a major part of the material in which children explore language. Children do this through such things as listening to, reenacting and interpreting the story. Within the literacy curriculum one must determine the appropriate place of reading skills and how they will be learned. Within the program, realistic expectations must be formed with each individual child's needs in mind.

Finally, literature should be a joyful experience. It is really about the wonders of life. One of the ways literature can be made more meaningful is to help children make the connection between the people who write and illustrate children's books and themselves.

QUESTIONS FOR THOUGHT AND DISCUSSION

1. How does the transfer of information from a book differ from the transfer of information from a television program?
2. Defend or refute: The United States is a "nation that reads."
3. How can literature help young children learn about their world?
4. Can a child's self-esteem be addressed through literature?
5. Defend or refute: Preschool children who are capable of learning the alphabet and word lists should learn them at that time.
6. What does the term "reading" really mean?
7. How can elementary school reading competency tests have a negative effect on the preschool or kindergarten child?
8. According to Harste and Woodward, what three key features should be present in a literacy curriculum?
9. Why aren't phonics enough to help a child learn to read?
10. How do traditional and wholistic approaches to teaching beginning reading differ?

CHILDREN'S BOOKS CITED

Aliki (Brandenberg), *How a Book Is Made* (New York: Harper and Row, 1986).

Tomie dePaola, *The Art Lesson* (New York: G. P. Putnam's Sons, 1989).

Tomie dePaola, *Watch Out for the Chicken Feet in Your Soup* (New York: Simon and Schuster, 1974).

Rita Golden Gelman, *A Koala Grows Up* (New York: Scholastic, 1986).

Anna Grossnickle Hines, *Dont Worry, I'll Find You* (New York: E. P. Dutton, 1986).

Katharine Holabird, *Angelina at the Fair* (New York: Viking Penguin, 1985).

Robin Baird Lewis, *Aunt Armadillo* (Scarborough, Ontario, Canada: Annick Press, 1985).

Emily Arnold McCully, *First Snow* (New York: Harper and Row, 1985).

Watty Piper, *The Little Engine that Could* (New York: Platt and Munk, 1930).

Peter Smith, *Jenny's Baby Brother* (New York: Viking Penguin, 1988).

Nancy Tafuri, *Have You Seen My Duckling?* (New York: Viking Penguin, 1984).

Tricia Tusa, *Chicken* (New York: Macmillan, 1986).

Wendy Watson, *Has Winter Come?* (New York: Philomel, 1978).

Rosemary Wells, *A Lion for Lewis* (New York: Dial, 1982).

Charlotte Zolotow, *Some Things Go Together* (New York: Harper and Row, 1969).

SELECTED REFERENCES

Berry T. Brazelton, *What Every Baby Knows* (Reading, Massachusetts: Addison Wesley, 1987)

Betty Browman, *The Early Years in Childhood Education* (Boston, Massachusetts: Houghton Mifflin, 1982).

Kathryn Williams Browne and Ann Gordon, *Beginnings and Beyond: Foundations in Early Childhood Education* (Albany, New York: Delmar Publishers, 1985).

Rosalind Charlesworth, *Understanding Child Development—For Adults Who Work with Children* (Albany, New York: Delmar Publishers, 1987).

John Dopyera and Margaret Lay-Dropera, *Becoming a Teacher of Young Children* (New York: Random House: 1987).

Joseph Chilton Pearce, *Magical Child* (New York: E. P. Dutton, 1977).

2 Planning for Success

Whenever one reads to a young child, the experience is enhanced when some planning has taken place. The same is true for developing a reading area. A reading environment is more than just ambience. It sets the tone for the entire reading experience. A teacher's manner and presentation are a part of the reading environment. If the teacher is hurried and unprepared, the children may sense this. As a result they may be unable to relax and benefit from the story. If the youngsters are all seated at desks in rows, the environment is too stiff and formal. Such an approach does not reflect a knowledge of child development. The teacher must develop understandings, patterns, and plans for a successful reading encounter.

Each age has different needs, interests, and preferences that can be used to encourage children to interact with the story. There are several questions a teacher might ask when planning a reading:

- Is the material age-appropriate?
- Did I read the story first so that I am familiar with it?
- How will I motivate the children to want to be involved with the story?
- Where and when will we read the story?
- Why am I reading this particular story?
- How can I make this story most meaningful to the children?

A great deal of material needs to be considered before these questions can be answered. Knowing the answers will be beneficial to both the teacher and the children each time a story is planned.

CREATING A GOOD ENVIRONMENT FOR INFANTS

There are many theories and sources of information concerning how infants grow and develop. It is not necessary to review all of the research here. However, it is necessary to review some of the general concepts upon which the ideas presented here are based. This review will form a foundation for understanding the relationship between child development and emerging literacy.

The most important factor in the language acquisition process is the interaction of adult with child. It is the sound of soft soothing words that helps the infant respond when frightened or upset. These sounds may be a parent's voice, the sounds and rhythm of a lullaby, or the words of a pleasant rhyme.

While there are rival theories about just how children develop language, there is substantial agreement that even very young infants listen to and respond to the sounds of language. In the beginning, infants respond by making sounds of their own. The sounds help them make their needs known and express emotions. For example, during the first three months infants learn to cry in different ways to indicate hunger, discomfort, and other feelings. Toward the end of the three months, cooing sounds are used to indicate pleasure. At about six months, infants add babbling sounds to their repertoire.[1]

Emerging Language

It is not until about the age of one year that language truly begins. The term language, as used here, means that words are meaningful to the child. For some advanced children, this can occur at eight months. For some handicapped children this might not occur until age three or even later.[2] Children often comprehend some language that they have not yet begun to speak. At one year of age, children use an average of three words meaningfully. The rate of language acquisition grows slowly at first, but then increases rapidly. At age two, children use approximately 272 words meaningfully. The rate then accelerates into thousands of words over the next few years.[3]

Throughout this period, there is a need for adults to provide language to children through talk and through contact with the environment. Adults should provide encouragement and opportunities for infants to experience their environment. Part of this exploration will be the investigation of language and its uses. Children will explore how it sounds, what it does, and how it can be used.

Linking Language to Literature

Singing songs, reading stories, doing simple fingerplays, and playing games with a high amount of adult/child interaction is the best way to initiate a connection with literature. Traditional rhymes, Mother Goose stories, and poetry are easy to memorize and recite. Infants enjoy this whether they are being cuddled, rocked, or just resting in a crib.

From about six months on, holding an object and telling a story about it is pleasurable for the infant. For example, one might hold a small stuffed kitten up to the child. While letting the child touch or pet the toy kitten, one can recite the three little kittens rhyme. With infants of eight to fifteen months of age, learning the sounds that things make is a great motivation. As they develop, babies enjoy making the sounds of an object. They do this well before they are able to name the object. Familiar objects to use for this activity include a car, truck, airplane, train, and boat. One can further encourage children's language acquisition and under-

[1] David McNeil, *The Acquisition of Language: The Study of Developmental Psycholinguistics* (New York: Harper and Row, 1970).

[2] Dorothea McCarthy, "Language Development," *Encyclopedia of Educational Research;* ed. W. S. Monroe (New York: Macmillan, 1950), 165–172.

[3] Werner F. Leopold, "Semantic Learning in Infant Language," *Child Language: A Book of Readings;* ed. A. Bar-Adon and W. F. Leopold (Englewood Cliffs, New Jersey: Prentice-Hall, 1971).

standing of the words by reinforcing and accepting their approximations of the sounds. This lets children know that others understand their developing language patterns.

Reading to Infants

Each month that books are not read to infants is a month that is lost forever. Books can and should be read to infants from the moment they are born. The books should, of course, be durable if the child is going to handle them. Hard cover books, board books, and plastic books are good beginning books. The pictures used in the books should be simple, as very young children, even when they do begin to look at the pages, are not able to focus on busy pictures.

One important aspect to consider with the use of books at the infant stage is the attitude of the adults toward books. Books should be treated as something special. They are not something that one eats. The concept of respecting books can be constantly modeled. Paperback books are more difficult to use with infants as they do not hold up well with the touching that most infants do with books. This does not mean that one should avoid such books. Rather, the teacher must maintain more control over the book itself. There is nothing wrong with saying that the book is going to be kept by the teacher. It can always be shared again. This approach allows the teacher to use many books with children.

When reading books with infants, one may wish to include the use of props such as toys with the reading. Effective utilization of puppets, toy cars, and other objects which may be featured in the story can enhance the reading experience. The object connects the infant with the story in a positive, hands-on manner.

Reading Areas for Infants

In setting up a reading area for infants, the teacher must remember that infants sit on laps, crawl about, and listen in various positions and in various places. Ideally, the reading area should be on the floor. Colorful pillows, quilts and mats are inviting and comfortable. Adding a few stuffed toys makes it a special place.

Mobiles, wall hangings, and soft sculptures can also be added to enhance the setting. Cardboard boxes can be used to make story-related cars, boats, and trains. This will help to stimulate the children's imaginations by creating a concrete representation of the story. Recreating the story in play is an important part of language development. Through recreating the story, children are dealing with and making sense of language. In this case, they are replicating the language of the author.

Dorothy Kunhardt's *Pat the Bunny* is great fun to read with infants. As the book progresses, the reader has the opportunity to touch the cotton tail of the bunny, smell some flowers, look in a mirror, play peek-a-boo, and engage in other similar activities. One can re-create the reading and language experience by using the ideas from the book within the reading area. For example, one can include in the reading area a peek-a-boo game, a mirror activity, and scented flowers. The book is most interesting for infants. Both children and adults enjoy reading it over and over again.

Enjoyable books should be read as often as infants respond to them. Children will usually point to their favorites even before they can ask for them verbally. It is important to remember to continuously share the beauty of the language through repeated readings of favorite stories. Whether it is spoken or written, language should be shared in a warm, pleasant environment. Books will naturally become an important part of children's lives if the interest and enjoyment are started and shared from a young age.

Creating an Environment for Toddlers

Picture a tornado roaring through a summer sky with touchdowns of mayhem every few miles. This provides some idea of a toddler's day. Ever curious, toddlers seem determined to fit years of exploration and discovery into each day. The attention of toddlers may quickly jump from object to object. On the other hand, they can sustain attention in a particular pursuit if motivated and involved. Most toddlers do enjoy completing tasks. However, the tasks must be age appropriate in order for toddlers to achieve success without becoming frustrated.

Toddlers are more able to assert themselves and their independence. The word "no" is more than a word for many of them; sometimes it seems to be a creed. For this reason, care must be taken when encouraging toddlers to stay on a task when they feel they have completed it. "Me done!" is rarely spoken by a toddler without the exclamation mark at the end.

Motivations are important in planning environments for toddlers. They want to hear stories and look at books if they feel the activity is exciting. The storyteller or reader must provide effective presentations of the tale and show enjoyment in the activity. The closeness and warmth of the reading experience is still a desirable part of the setting. Toddlers like to point to and touch books as they are read. They like to feel a part of the experience. Teachers need to plan for this when choosing books.

Using Language. At this stage, one can observe toddlers making many attempts to use language. They use it to satisfy their needs, to make themselves understood, and to understand their world. They may understand much language before they are able to say those same words, sentences, and paragraphs.[4] They make intelligent generalizations with language based on what language rules they already use. For example, a child might say, "I hurt-ed myself," or "Me go."

While it might not appear so, the beginning stages of writing emerge at this stage. From the first time a child touches a crayon to a paper, or even thinks about doing it, writing has begun. It will take several years to develop, but all of the pictures and attempts to put something meaningful in a visual form are part of the child's developing writing ability.

During this period of life, adults must provide time, opportunities, models, encouragement, and acceptance. Children are drawn to whatever language is available. They like its sounds and rhythm. Good language models and a wide

[4] John B. Carroll, "Words, Meanings and Concepts," *Harvard Educational Review* 34 (Spring, 1964), 178–202.

variety of experiences should be provided. On the other hand, this is not the time for punitive correction of incorrect language structures by children. The same is true for drawing and writing attempts. Children need acceptance of their honest attempts to create meaning. They need someone to listen to them and someone to tell about their drawings.

Toddler Humor. During this time, children develop senses of humor. This humor begins with simple substitution in which the toddler is aware that the substitution has been made. For example, a child knows that "Mama" is the sound for mother and "Gaga" is the sound for daddy. When mother asks in the name game "Who Am I?" the child responds with "Gaga" while looking at mother, and then bursts out laughing. The child has made a joke. More jokes will be attempted, especially if they are encouraged by the laughter of the child's audience.

There are many picture books and stories which provide humor for toddlers. Examples include Judith Barrett's and Charles B. Slackman's *I Hate to Take a Bath,* John Burningham's *Mr. Grumpy's Outing* and Pat Hutchins's *Rosie's Walk. Rosie's Walk* is especially appropriate. Toddlers will interact with the story by trying to warn the hen of the coming danger. It is great fun to read.

Many nursery rhymes also provide humor. For example, have you ever really seen a dish run away with a spoon? Have you ever seen kittens washing mittens? Do people really live in pumpkins? Picturing the absurdity is half the fun of listening or reciting these rhymes. Nursery rhymes also lend themselves to wonderful art activities and dramatic presentations which toddlers can easily enjoy. Blanche Fisher Wright's *The Real Mother Goose Husky Book One* and *The Real Mother Goose Husky Book Two* is a terrific set of books with which to start such stories with toddlers. The illustrations are effective and the books are sturdy. The repetitive parts of most stories are easy for toddlers to repeat. They can often join in reciting some of the repeated lines.

Toddler Interests. Toddlers have an interest in all of the objects and events around them. They want to know the sounds of everything and the "whats" of everything else. They want to know who everyone is and what they do. Tana Hoban's books are wonderful for explaining many of these early concepts. In *Push-Pull, Empty-Full,* she uses photographs to clearly demonstrate concepts. Lois Lenski's stories are written in a style that is appealing to toddlers. The children can actually hold a book that is just their size. The stories range from *Debbie and Her Family* to tales about *The Little Sailboat* and *Cowboy Small.*

Other books and authors have specifically addressed the interests of toddlers as well. Helen Oxenbury's books can be used to demonstrate many basic concepts. The illustrations are clear and simple, telling the story without any text. *Good Night, Good Morning,* for example, tells the story of the day's cycle for a toddler. The child character goes through the book doing all of the same things that the toddler reader might do on a typical day. Jan Ormerod's *Making Friends* is a delightful book with large print text. It is brief, contains age-appropriate sentences and includes appealing illustrations. Jan Ormerod has addressed the topics of exercise, sunshine, and babies in other books.The First Little

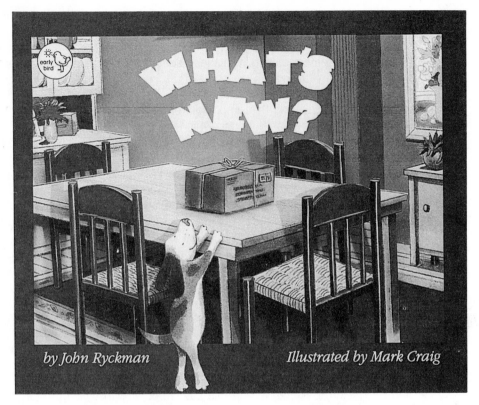

Books such as this touch on the curiosity of toddlers with warmth and fun.
Courtesy Delmar Publishers Inc.

Golden Book series of books develops many concepts. For example, Stephanie Calmenson's *My Book of Seasons* helps the reader come to know the seasons by using the five senses to experience each one. These bright, colorful books are endearing and full of fun.

Eric Carle's writing is exceptional for toddlers. The illustrations are excitingly colorful. They possess a visual texture not often found elsewhere. Each book has a special attraction. For example, *The Very Hungry Caterpillar* shows caterpillars and what they might eat. In fact, the caterpillar eats right through the illustrations. This book is always a favorite.

Reading Areas for Toddlers. A reading area for toddlers must be exciting. The area should be on the floor, but a low loft-type structure might also be used. Toddlers love to climb. To add comfort and fun, placing large pillows and stuffed toys in the area is still appealing. A large stuffed toy for the toddlers to sit on can also be a creative addition. Rocking chairs are a nice touch in any reading area. The motion is soothing and a rocker is usually large enough for a reader and a couple of toddlers to sit together to share a story. Carpeting should be used with any wooden loft or stairway loft.

Reading is special no matter where it is done. Inexpensive props can greatly enhance the reading experience. Courtesy Diana Comer.

Decorated walls and mobiles are an easy accent that can be changed often. They keep the interest level high. Visibility is important with toddlers as their social skills are still limited. The walls or dividers within the area should be low.

Boxes and large climbing structures with pillow centers also make a reading area a special place. Many windows should be cut in the large boxes if they are used. The boxes can be decorated with white paint to make an igloo. Windows can be cut to suggest a spaceship. Boxes can be painted brown to make a jungle hut. The books that parallel the topic the box represents can be placed inside the box. The children's interest is heightened when they participate in creating and changing the reading area and its props.

Creating an Environment for Preschoolers

The child of three and four years of age never seems to stop asking why. These questions are both the bane and the bonus of the preschool teacher's planning. Preschool children are very interested in themselves and their families. They are fascinated by the world around them, but now realize that it includes others outside their immediate environment. It is a time of incredible stretching and growth of knowledge. Preschoolers seem to be sponges for information, always wanting to know how, why, and where.

Using Language. At the preschool level, children continue their rapid development of language skills and vocabulary growth. They are now able to use language as a tool for understanding themselves and their surroundings. They are able to correctly use a variety of grammatical structures and sentences.[5]

The writings of preschoolers generally consist of drawings, which are attempts at self-expression. Whether or not adults can tell what the child has drawn, the artwork does have definite meanings to the child. The role of the adult at this time is to provide much interaction for the child in the form of listening, answering questions, asking questions, providing language models, and sharing a variety of experiences.

Preschool Humor. The child's sense of humor at this point is beyond simple word substitutions. These are more sophisticated children who don't laugh as readily at dishes running away with spoons. The preschool child's humor requires a semblance of possibility. *Curious George* by H. A. Rey demonstrates the enjoyment children have for this more sophisticated humor. George, a well loved character, gets into all sorts of mischief by circumstances rather than by design. The humorous aspects of the plot are possible, yet highly improbable. Therein lies the humor. For example, when George plays with the telephone, he mistakenly rings the fire department. This causes a hilarious chain of events.

There are other aspects of the humor appreciated by this age group. Three and four year olds still laugh at certain words, but are more likely to substitute a possible rather than an impossible term. Fantasy is still important for these children. Preschoolers love to play house and act out roles as well. At this age, "Little Red Riding Hood" is no longer just a story. It is an event that can be acted out both seriously and humorously with only a few props.

Preschooler Interests. Values are often included in many of the stories intended for preschoolers. Children at this age are concerned with themselves and their feelings. Don Freeman's *Corduroy* tells of a teddy bear which is rejected by children because it is missing a button. Eventually it is acquired by a little girl who loves it anyway. The story is reassuring to preschoolers because it demonstrates the value of love over perfection.

Dr. Seuss's books often reinforce values while providing great fun through illustrations and language. Horton the elephant makes difficult decisions which, in the end, reinforce the correctness of the honest choices made. The Grinch shows how love can change people. The Lorax challenges children to think about the environment. Each book has a special style. In *Horton Hatches the Egg,* Horton sits on a bird's egg through terrible trials and tribulations. The egg hatches eventually and the reader is treated to an amazing conclusion to the story. Children will sit through this lengthy book over and over again. They do so because they can empathize with the story from beginning to end.

Preschoolers are fascinated with differences. They notice differences of sex, size, handicapping conditions, houses, and so forth. As might be expected, they

[5] Philip S. Dale, *Language Development* (New York: Holt, Rinehart and Winston, 1976).

want to know why these differences exist. Susan Lapsley's *I Am Adopted,* Myrtle Shay's *What Happens When You Go to the Hospital?* and Stan and Jan Berenstain's *He Bear, She Bear* are books that address some of these differences in positive and reassuring ways. Their tone is quite appropriate for preschoolers.

Preschoolers also have fears which should not be ignored. Realizing that others have similar fears can alleviate much of the stress created by these fears. Fears can include being alone, dealing with an older sibling, anger, frustration, the darkness, and so on. Some titles and authors on these topics include Bernard Waber's *Ira Sleeps Over,* Judith Viorst's *Alexander and the Terrible, Horrible, No Good, Very Bad Day,* Maurice Sendak's *Where the Wild Things Are* and Erica Frost's *Jonathan's Amazing Adventure.*

Reading Areas for Preschoolers. The reading area should be more adventurous. Lofts, mattress tents, and truck tires with pillows are good choices. Lighting becomes more important with this age group because the children will be looking more closely at the words and some may be beginning to read. Daylight should be used when possible. Therefore, locating the reading area near a window is recommended.

Recognizing the need of this age group to understand the "why" of things makes good sense in creating a reading area. One might include informative mobiles of seasons, plants, and stars. Posters illustrating what is inside such things as bodies, mountains, and the earth are good choices for walls. Locating real animals near the reading area is a fine idea, particularly when focusing on animal stories.

Obviously, these ideas take careful planning. However, including them as part of the lesson helps motivate the children. The availability of props after the book is read will encourage the children to recreate or reconstruct the book through talk and play. For example, after reading Jimmy Kennedy's *The Teddy Bear Picnic,* place a teddy bear and the book in the reading area on a rocking chair. In most cases, one will soon see children in the chair, leafing through the book and hugging the teddy bear. Making the reading area easy to change will help both the teacher and the children to continue to have creative interactions with books.

Creating an Environment for Kindergarteners

Kindergarteners are successful in many tasks. Their skills often show a good deal of self-reliance. Supervision by adults need not be as direct as it was for the earlier stages of development. Kindergarteners are active and enjoy active outdoor play. There is more cooperation in play both at home and in school. On the other hand, the mix of five and six year-olds can present a wide range of skills and abilities. Also, kindergarteners take note of what their friends say and do. This concern for what others think can lead to a reluctance to join in activities unless others are involved first. Teachers must sometimes involve these children in activities almost before they know it. The activities and stories must be chosen to maintain the active interests of these children.

The Power of Language. During the ages of five and six, children begin to experience the power of language. They come to understand how language can be used to express ideas and emotions, to create stories and meanings and to experience life. For some time now, they have been aware that they are surrounded by print. At this stage, children use complex sentence structures, compare words with greater ease, tell stories, and recognize words in print.[6] While they may read some words in print, they also attempt to include words within their drawings.

The role of adults at this stage of language development is to take advantage of the many opportunities that children present. Adults must use these opportunities to support the development of literacy. One can encourage children to understand that the printed word can represent all of the meanings and feelings that oral language can contain. The focus should be on meaning rather than on the correct form. A child's invented spellings (e.g., "I lik mi kat." for "I like my cat.") should be accepted without negative comment. The child will come in contact with correct spellings over and over again. The discovery of the correct forms will occur naturally and be incorporated into the child's original writing.

Kindergarten Interests. The powerful and the mystical are of great interest to kindergarten children. The classic stories of "Cinderella," "Sleeping Beauty," and "Rapunzel" are wonderful for reading aloud to five and six year olds. They respond to the epic adventures where, through enchantment and strength, the hero overcomes evil. The more overwhelming the odds, the better the story. There are many lesser known fairy tales and stories which can be used to both keep children's interest and to compare with more popular versions. For example, children can discover that Snow White had a sister named Rose Red in other tales. Reading several versions of the same story can be used to help children compare stories. Kindergarteners enjoy giving their opinions.

Anderson's Fairy Tales, retold by Rose Dobbs and *Household Stories* by the Grimm Brothers are collections with few illustrations but an abundance of stories. Many classic tales are also told in single books with wonderful illustrations. A favorite is *Beauty and the Beast* illustrated by Karen Milone. The jealous sisters in this book are so ugly that the beast is not so scary in comparison. The ending is pure fairy tale.

Kindergarten children are very involved with learning about their bodies and social interactions. At times they may find it difficult to play and interact because of the increased need to fit in with their peers. It is healthy to discover that these mixed feelings occur with other children as well. Beverly Cleary's books about Ramona Quimby are wonderfully reassuring to kindergarteners. They are finely crafted works and always popular. Ramona often acts impulsively and then regrets it just as many kindergarteners do at times. *Ramona the Pest* is a particular favorite of this age group, because she is in kindergarten when the story takes place.

Troubling issues greatly affect the kindergartener. The same issues that cause conflict for adults can be agonizing to a child. When the adults in a child's life are going through the emotional stress of a death, divorce, separation, unem-

---

[6] Philip S. Dale, *Language Development.*

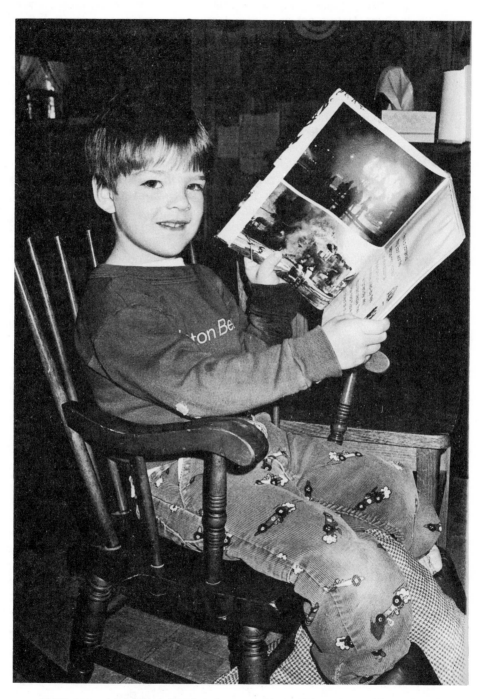

Children want to read well before they are able to. They enjoy making sense of their world. Courtesy Diana Comer.

ployment, or other personal difficulties, they often seek to protect the children from the hurt. Unfortunately, this seldom works. Children feel the pain anyway. When this occurs, they can also feel excluded. Being isolated or feeling isolated rarely helps anyone through a difficult time. Sharing is an outlet that allows the release of pain and the beginning of the healing process. Reading books on the topic can help the child to come to an understanding of what is happening.

Other issues that kindergarteners are concerned with include adoption and handicapped children. One often hears that youngsters can be cruel to other children who are different. While such behavior can occur, most children will act kindly and supportively to such children when given the opportunity to learn about the differences. For many, it is the fear of an impediment or situation and the accompanying ignorance which provokes unkind behaviors. Books such as *Why Was I Adopted?* by Carole Livingston and *My Brother Steven Is Retarded* by Harriet Sobol explain these concepts with clarity and sensitivity. Such books put to rest fears and beliefs such as, "I'll get adopted if I misbehave . . . This is catching . . . He's just trying to get attention." Dealing with these concepts honestly through literature can replace ignorance with truth and understanding. Understanding often leads to caring and acceptance.

Our world is undergoing an information explosion and kindergarteners are involved in this phenomenon. They enjoy books such as *My Visit to the Dinosaurs* by Aliki and *Rockets and Satellites* by Franklyn M. Branley. These content books and others like them can provide much information for children who thirst for knowing the what, why, and how of things.

Interest in reading grows for kindergarteners. ABC books and I Can Read books have an increasing attraction as the year progresses. Whether one is a proponent of early reading instructional programs or not, ABC books can be delightful. There are a great many available, each different, with a variety of illustration styles. Norman Bridwell's *Clifford's ABC,* Susanna Gretz's *Teddybear's ABC,* Anno's *Anno's Alphabet,* Vincent Jefferds's *Disney's Elegant ABC,* Deborah Niland's *ABC of Monsters* and Richard Scarry's *Find Your ABC's* are just a few of the favorites.

Reading Areas for Kindergarteners. Setting up a reading area for kindergarteners should be a group project. Involve the children in the planning, constructing, and changing of the area. Start the year with just the space set aside in the room. Bring in materials and discuss how the reading area can be created. The more children are involved in the planning, the greater their emotional commitment to the reading area and to reading. Most ideas, even if they initially seem impossible, can become a reality to some extent. With some imagination, one can create gardens, planets, caves, jungles, and treehouses for a classroom reading area.

PRACTICAL CONSIDERATIONS FOR READING AREAS

The reading area is a section of the room set aside for reading, sharing, and interacting with books. It may also be referred to as the reading corner, reading nook, or reading center. The reading area and the time spent there with children both need to reflect the teacher's attitude toward books, reading, literacy, and children. The best attitude is a relaxed approach toward all four. Children need to experience, listen to, interact with and enjoy the ideas in books. A reading area should give the feeling that books are an open invitation. They are to be enjoyed. The size of the space set aside for the reading area is not particularly important as long as it can comfortably contain the people using it at one time. What is important is the effective use of the space by the children. The visual and aesthetic appeal of the reading area promotes its effective use. This is achieved by making the space appropriate for the age of the children and warmly inviting.

Where to Put a Reading Area

A reading area can be placed almost anywhere. However, every room is set up differently. Any room arrangement has both strengths and weaknesses. A reading area may be set up in a corner, along a wall, or in a loft. When initially planning an area, one should keep in mind traffic patterns and lighting.

Traffic patterns are important in a classroom. One can move tables and screens to create large and small spaces within the room. Large spaces encourage movement. This is important for some activities, of course. Large spaces can also be distracting and chaotic, however. Small spaces are useful for separating children into interest areas for smaller projects. However, small spaces used to channel children through a room can be busy and noisy. The reading area, therefore, is best located off the beaten path, away from both large and small traffic areas. One may wish to locate a reading area near a dress-up or music area. In this way, books and ideas can spill over into play in these other areas. It is necessary to try a variety of arrangements to see which works best with a particular class and program. Limits can be set on the number of children allowed in the reading area at one time.

Lighting is an important consideration for a reading area. Poor lighting or inappropriate lighting can cause problems that are easily avoided. Since it is soft and easy on the eyes, natural lighting is preferred by most teachers. Obviously, this means that the reading area must be near a window. A location near the window can be helpful since it will allow for such reading related activities as daydreaming, bird watching, and cloud gazing.

It is not always possible to use natural lighting. There should be a back-up plan for cloudy days, dark mornings, and late afternoon hours. Many schools have fluorescent lighting for the whole room. However, some situations might call for a dark room with only a small lamp for reading. Lamps are preferred for the softer glow they emit. In addition, some find fluorescent light hard on the eyes. This is especially true when it creates a glare on glossy pages and chalkboards. Lamp bulbs should be a minimum of 60 watts when used for reading. Soft white bulbs are superior to regular lamp bulbs as they reduce the glare factor.

What kind of lamps should be used? Heavy lamps sitting on tables should definitely be avoided. They can tip over too easily, resulting in injury to children. Hanging lamps, wall lamps, and undercounter lamps avoid these tipping dangers.

Cords are a hazard in areas that encourage lounging, crawling, and snuggling. They can be chewed on and tripped over. Lamps which are securely attached to walls or ceilings are not in the way. They cannot be knocked over and the cords can be covered or discreetly tucked out of the way.

For those difficult spots such as lofts, cubby areas, and cloakrooms, undercounter lights are inexpensive, safe, and easily installed. They offer a good source of light. Any lamp used should be properly installed, carry the Underwriters Laboratory stamp of approval and have no frayed or uncovered wires. It is wise not to exceed the wattage listing.

After space and lighting have been selected, one needs to consider the furnishings of the reading area. Will a couch or carpeting be used? Will it be a theme space? A loft? These decisions depend on the size of the space, creativity, and materials available. The possibilities, nevertheless, can be endless.

Costs of a Reading Area

Cost is a factor in any planning. Day care centers and schools need to know that a reading area need not be expensive, but it is a necessity. While schools and centers should include the cost of reading areas in their budgets, alternative funding and sources of supplies can also be considered. Sources of free materials include stores, families, friends, yard sales, and social service agencies. Once the reading area is planned, one should make a list of materials needed. The list can be shared with all of the potential sources of free materials. Handwritten thank you notes for donations are appropriate. They also set up a friendly contact for future classroom endeavors. Positive public relations are provided for both the school and the donor when the school or town newspaper publishes a story about the donations.

Kinds of Materials Needed

A reading area needs places to shelve books and places for people. It needs dividers, props, and decorations. Audiovisual equipment such as tape players and filmstrip projectors and screens may be used in the reading area, but can be kept elsewhere. These audiovisual items are generally shared with or loaned to other areas within the school or center. They are only borrowed or loaned for specific activities.

Places to Display Books. Education catalogs often display wire racks or front-facing bookcases. They are best for displaying children's books because they allow the book covers to be seen. They are generally constructed of sturdy metal or hardwood. They are good long-term investments as they will give many years of use. The two sizes ordinarily used are shorter tabletop models and taller floor models. Both types can be costly, however. Someone with basic carpentry skills may be able to provide a comparable display at a more reasonable cost.

Second-hand bookcases are also a source for book storage and display furniture. Stores that are refurbishing or going out of business may be able to provide display units that are appropriate for books. One center used this approach to purchase a sturdy case with four lower drawers and a pegboard on the back. The five foot unit, costing fifteen dollars, now serves as a pegboard, room divider, storage unit, and shelving area for children's books and other materials.

Retail stores can also provide displays made of heavy cardboard. Most often these displays are discarded after they are used for a limited amount of time. When stores are finished using diplays, they are often willing to give them away. They work fine for most children's books. One such display, a styrofoam turkey from a liquor store, was used for several years in a center for a variety of purposes. One must think creatively to see the possibilities in these store displays.

Other unconventional items may also be used for book storage and display. These include plastic dishpans, apple baskets, laundry baskets, milk crates, wicker baskets, metal laundry tubs, kitchen cabinets, and plastic wastebaskets. With some construction skills, one can create inexpensive and sturdy shelving with pine boards and concrete blocks from a lumber yard.

Places for People

"A gentle rain pattering on the window . . . a warm quilt wrapped around you . . . nestled in Dad's lap for a story." This is an image of a great place to be for a story. It is cozy, warm, and comfortable. Comfort is a key word for a reading area. One should keep in mind the age and size of the children when planning the best way to use the space available for a reading area. Children love to snuggle into reading. They move around. They sometimes wriggle. They sometimes sit perfectly still. The seating in a reading area should be on the floor or a mattress for the greatest protection against falls.

There are additional ideas for seating that can be considered. Small bean bag chairs as well as regular size stuffed chairs might be used. Care should be taken when using furniture with hard wooden arm rests. Furniture legs can be cut off or removed to make the size of the pieces more appropriate for children. Sofa cushions and mattresses can be used on the floor as seating areas. Tent covers for a mattress can turn the area into a boat, automobile, or a cave. A child's swimming pool can be filled with pillows and stuffed toys as a seating area. Small chairs, rocking chairs, and stools might also be used in a reading area.

Besides the obvious choices, other ideas may be helpful. Old truck tires can often be acquired for the asking from construction and transportation companies. Before using them in a reading area, they should be cleaned thoroughly with detergent and water. Grill brushes and degreaser may be needed as well. The tires can be painted or covered with blankets to make them comfortable.

A loft makes a wonderful reading area for young children. If choosing a loft, have a knowledgeable person construct it. It should be carpeted, no higher than four feet from the floor, and sturdily built. If slats or railings are used, they should have spaces no larger than two inches wide so that children will not become stuck between the rails. Avoid pillows and other items that could cause a fall from the loft. When using carpeting as a seating surface, inspect the best carpets before making a decision on which to use. Wool carpets can be hot and itchy. Indoor-outdoor carpet is very durable. Nylon carpet cleans easily. Remnants from carpet distributors can be bound for a minimal price, eliminating any ragged edges. With large needles and upholstery thread, one can create a patchwork carpet out of carpet samples. An advantage of the patchwork carpet is that the finished rug contains various patterns, textures and types of carpeting. It can become a tactile masterpiece and define each child's space.

Wall Dividers. A reading area should be apart from the flow of traffic within the classroom. Room dividers can help create a space where there seems to be none available. Dividers which allow for maximum flexibility include wide book-cases, bulletin boards, pegboards, stand-up flannelboards, and chalkboards. Furniture can form part of the boundary of the reading area. The back of a sofa, a row of chairs, and a row of cushions can all serve as dividers. While one can purchase room dividers and supports from commercial supply companies, they can also be constructed from large cardboard boxes or four foot by eight foot sheets of plywood. Dividers need only be three to four feet in height to provide privacy. This height allows the teacher to retain visibility of the rest of the classroom.

Creating a Reading Area

It is the extras that often make a difference in almost anything. Attention to details can make a good thing better. So it is with reading areas. One should think of the reading area as an expressive part of the classroom. It should include items that reflect children's work and creativity. Part of the wall can include a bulletin board that changes as the seasons pass. Themes in the classroom can be reflected in the reading area. Puppets or stuffed toys in the area can reflect reading and favorite stories.

During "Dinosaur Week" books such as Syd Hoff's *Danny the Dinosaur* and Bernard Most's *If the Dinosaurs Came Back* could be read. A mobile of children's renderings of favorite dinosaurs could be hung up. A stuffed dinosaur or an inflat-able dinosaur could be added to the other animals in the reading area. A dinosaur chart might be placed on the wall. One could even place red vinyl balls in the area as dinosaur eggs. Sources of all of these items include education supply compa-nies, yard sales, relatives, and friends. In addition, bookstores increasingly stock stuffed characters from books.

Other innovative ideas for decorating include using large boxes to create special environments from telephone booths to ships. Adding a branch of a tree is an aesthetically pleasing feature of a reading area. It can be decorated for each passing season. Decorations could range from crepe paper leaves to cot-ton balls to cut out snowflakes. The children can add these to aid in their begin-ning conceptualization of seasonal change. Nontoxic live plants are always pleasing and popular in reading areas. They should be kept out of reach of small infants and toddlers.

Puzzles, sequence cards, big books, filmstrips, and cassettes can add another dimension to the reading area. It then becomes an active and interactive

Figure 1.   Sample reading areas. Reading areas can vary in size and content, but all should share a feeling of warmth and welcome. Courtesy Diana Comer.

environment rather than merely a place to flip through the pages of a book. Children can and should contribute to the aesthetic surroundings of the reading area. Constructing books and posters is personally rewarding to children. When displayed, these items surround the area with an aura of positive self-esteem. The children become aware that their contributions are as important as the other books and materials in the reading area.

PUTTING IT ALL TOGETHER

In order to see the "big picture" of a reading area, one should sketch out all of the parts of the area on paper. Seeing all of these components together in an illustration enables one to get a feel for the total package. Figure 1 illustrates a few ideas for a reading area.

Naturally, one adds extras as one's individual preferences and the needs of the children dictate. The ideas illustrated in Figure 1 are a sampling of the many ideas a teacher could use for a reading area. Figure 2 contains photographs of actual classroom reading areas. Note the similarities and differences.

Keep in mind that the more involved children are in the design and makeup of the area, the more comfortable they are within the center as readers, listeners, and sharers of the exciting world found in books and stories.

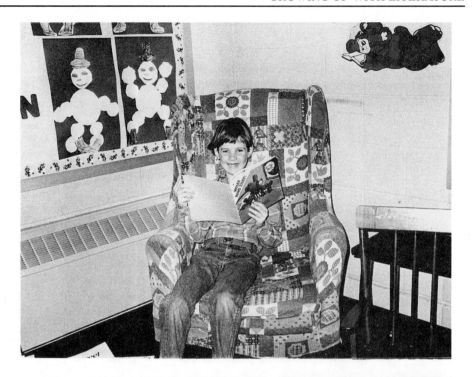

Figure 2.   Reading areas in use. A successful reading area is one that children are comfortable with and use freely. Courtesy Diana Comer.

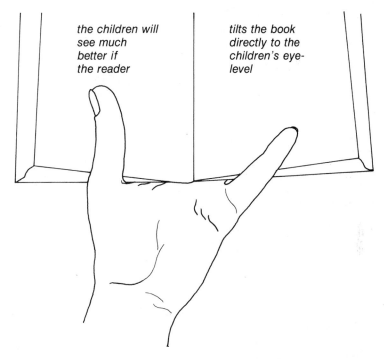

the children will see much better if the reader

tilts the book directly to the children's eye-level

Holding a book so that children can see the words and pictures may take a little practice, but it is an important part of sharing stories. Courtesy Diana Comer.

Holding a Book for Storytime

Many fail to grasp the significance of the small details in successfully reading a story to children. Reading to children is more than just picking up a book and reading it aloud. The setting is important. The choice of materials is important. The way the book is held is important. The book should be firmly grasped by the reader and held at eye level for the group of children.

After or during the reading of each page, the book should be moved from side to side. This will ensure that all of the children will see the pictures and the text. If the children cannot see the illustrations, they may become bored or frustrated. If this happens, it is highly likely that they will lose interest in the story itself.

If the teacher is familiar with the story text, then holding the book in this fashion will cause no problems in the flow of the narrative. If the children are seated next to the teacher or on the teacher's lap, the easiest manner to hold the book is to keep the thumb in the center of the pages and the book open in front of the group. One need not move the book as the children should be able to see quite well from their seated position.

Choosing a Place

The place the teacher chooses for reading a book to a group depends on the size of the group and the space used to accommodate the group. With larger groups of children, the teacher will generally select a circle-time area. With smaller groups, the reading area of a small corner will work well. Naptime is a good opportunity for reading aloud. A story at that time provides a soothing listening experience for the children as they begin their quiet time.

In general, several factors can contribute to a positive reading experience. One should, of course, always select a comfortable spot where the lighting is adequate but not in anyone's eyes. Make certain there is plenty of room for wriggling so the children will not be bumping into each other. Figure 3 illustrates several successful seating patterns.

Choose a place without immediate distractions. The housekeeping corner of the room or a spot next to the class gerbil may be too busy for a reading spot. When reading out of doors, check for anthills, damp ground, and insects that could turn reading time into first-aid time. One might have the children warm up for the story with a related fingerplay or song. This will provide both motivation and personal involvement in the story. Make sure all of the children are seated in such a way that they will be able to see the illustrations. Finally, one should always know the story before attempting to read or share it with others.

Finding Good Books

A later chapter will address the criteria for choosing good books. This section will focus on places to find good quality books. Books are an important part of any classroom's inventory, but they can be expensive. Adding to the classroom library within a budget can be a difficult problem. Once the teacher has decided which books are needed for the classroom library, the problem becomes one of finding the books.

Libraries. If the classroom is housed in a public or private school, the school library is the first source for borrowing needed books. Most librarians welcome suggestions by teachers concerning book selection for the school library. Librarians are terrific at helping the teacher find the right books to complement themes, units, and special classroom projects. The public library is an additional source of books for use in the classroom. Every classroom should also have its own permanent collection as well. To find these books one might search in yard sales, book stores, catalogs, book clubs, library discard sales, book fairs, estate sales, and moving sales.

A question that should be addressed before purchasing any materials is whether or not paperback books should be part of the classroom library. For reading aloud by the teacher, a paperback offers the same story as a hard cover edition, but at a lower cost. Teachers might disagree over whether paperback books are viable for classroom use. There are valid points to each side of the argument.

Paperback Books. There are many excellent editions of both classic and contemporary award-winning books available in paperback. Technology has improved the quality and durability of many paperbacks.

For the price of one hardcover book, one can purchase several paperback books. With the cost so much lower, a teacher can buy more books now rather than buying only a few copies each year. In this way, the variety of books found in the classroom library increases more rapidly.

Hardcover Books. These are more expensive, but they stand up better to the wear and tear of everyday classroom use. Although the initial cost is higher, it is more likely that the books will not need to be replaced as often. Since most books are printed initially in hard cover, a wider variety of titles is usually available.

The answer to the paperback versus hardcover argument is probably that both have a legitimate place in a classroom library. The classroom teacher can take advantage of both kinds by buying some paperbacks to increase the variety and some hardcover books to enhance the durability of the collection. If necessary, paperback books can be limited to teacher or short-term child use so that their life can be lengthened.

Since infants and toddlers need a hands-on experience with books, one might wish to limit their paperback book use to the teacher only. On the other hand, literacy development demands that books get into the hands of children as soon as it can be done meaningfully. Plastic books with rounded edges and posterboard books of sturdy quality are best for babies and very young children.

Book clubs can offer the teacher an effective means to buy books. The clubs offer an inexpensive way to purchase good quality contemporary and classic books. The regular offerings are usually in paperback, but bonus points can be earned. The bonus points can be used to purchase hardcover editions, filmstrips, cassettes, and posters. Each month the classroom is usually given free posters, books, and stickers as well. Caldecott Award winners are often offered by the clubs. In addition, the clubs can be used by parents of the children as a convenient way to increase home libraries. Of course, one should never make parents or their children feel that they must participate in a book club. The club offerings should always be optional. Clubs that offer books appropriate for young children include Scholastic's Firefly and SeeSaw Book Clubs, Troll Book Club, Weekly Reader Children's Book Club, Parents Magazine Read-Aloud Book Club, Grolier's Dr. Seuss and His Friends Book Club, Trumpet Book Club, Walt Disney Music Company and Western Publishing's Sesame Street Book Club. The addresses for each of these are found in Appendix A.

Publishers' book catalogs often offer excellent starter sets of books for classroom libraries. Sets may be purchased by subject area as well as by grade level.

Big books are also becoming more available. Big books are large size editions that enable children to more easily share the reading experience with the teacher. Some big books are tradebook stories reprinted in a larger format. Others are stories made specifically for a big book. These latter stories tend to be predictable in terms of repeated phrases and sentences throughout. This allows children to recognize some of the print and join in the actual reading. Publishers that distribute big book editions include Random House, Learning Well, Scholastic, Western Publishing, and The Wright Group. The addresses for each of these are

The single line is good for small groups.

When reading alone with one or two children, it may be most comfortable to sit in a chair with the child(ren) on your lap.

The traditional semi-circle is always an effective pattern for medium-sized groups from three to twenty children. It provides good visibility.

Figure 3.   Basic successful seating patterns. Courtesy Diana Comer.

Large groups of more than fifteen can be difficult. Having half of the children sit on the floor and half sit on small chairs can be an effective seating pattern.

Larger groupings can be made more visually effective by staggering the pattern of seating or by seating the children on a stage or stairway.

found in Appendix A. When writing to publishers, it is usually helpful to indicate the age or grade level you are interested in.

Teachers as Storytellers

Clara Thompson, a turn of the century educator, said that nothing in human nature had changed in education since she first taught in a one-room schoolhouse. Education is only as good as the individuals working within it. Children learn when one is able to reach them and bring them into the process of education.

Despite recent developments in technology and learning aids, the primary source of learning remains the teacher. If supplies and materlals don't arrive in time . . . if the video breaks down . . . if the teacher's manual burns . . . the effective teacher still teaches. The effective teacher can still motivate and teach the children. The most important tool of the trade—the resources within the teacher—is still there. The knowledge, creativity, and enthusiasm with which the teacher brings children into the learning process is what real teaching is all about.

The teacher must remember that body language and preparation impart nuances that young children perceive. When one is prepared effectively to share a story or teach a lesson, there is an air of confidence. Children notice this and respond to it. The enthusiasm is increased when the teacher feels confident and at ease. One becomes natural and less inhibited in the telling of the tale when this confidence is present.

Communicating a Message. Telling a story is more than simply reading it. One must share the message and the emotion that exists between the lines and within the illustrations.

The first thing to do in planning a reading is to know the story well. It is impossible to plan a story experience if the plot and the story are unknown to the teacher.

When reading or retelling, don't start until the children are listening. One can use a transition activity and a motivation to bring the children into a story mood that will help them to want to listen to the story.

The reader must speak clearly. It helps to speak a little slower and more distinctly than when using a normal speaking voice. This helps all to understand the words.

Use of Voice. The reader must use his or her voice effectively. A powerful and adaptive tool in storytelling, the reader's voice can be soft, loud, teasing, brash, or soothing. Different voices for different characters and varied pitches and tones of voice all help create and maintain interest in the story.

The reader must maintain the rhythm of the story. This means reading louder and faster for some parts of the story, while other parts of the story may require a slow whispering voice.

Body Language. Body language is also a part of storytelling. To eliminate the need to shift and move, get a comfortable position before beginning the tale. With just a bit of exaggeration, one's face can be used as a mirror of the story's action. Subtlety is necessary here. Maintaining eye-to-eye contact is important for keeping the children's attention on the story. Pausing before plot shifts adds to the excitement. One might even pause at a suspenseful point and ask an open-ended question about what might happen next. Finally, one should demonstrate enjoyment in the telling of the story. Choose good books that both the teacher and children will enjoy. Be discriminating. Never use a book just because it's available or because it's the book that was used last year. Make each book a special memory.

SUMMARY

In this chapter, it was found that the environment in which literature is shared with children is critical. Planning the setting for storytelling and sharing books is an important part of any early education program. Children respond to setting. They also respond to the opportunity to be involved in the planning of the setting.

The reading environment should be carefully designed to reflect age-appropriate approaches to the children. Therefore, it is necessary to have some understanding of various aspects of literacy development in infants, toddlers, preschoolers and kindergarteners. This information will assist the teacher in designing reading areas.

The reading area sends many messages to children about the importance of reading, the joy of reading and the role of the child in reading and literature. Children should come to understand that they are active participants rather than passive recipients.

The teacher is the primary tool needed to transfer the information from the book to the child. Storytelling skills may not be natural to everyone, but they can be developed with practice and forethought. The effective use of body language and voice can greatly enhance the reading process. Planning the storytelling experience is an absolutely essential part of sharing a story with children.

QUESTIONS FOR THOUGHT AND DISCUSSION

1. What concerns should one have when planning a story?
2. When do infants begin to associate sounds with meaning?
3. Describe a possible reading area for children.
4. What are some of the characteristics of a toddler that a story reader might want to take into consideration?
5. What should one look for in an illustration designed for infants and toddlers?
6. How does humor seem to manifest itself in a preschooler?
7. What changes might one make in converting a toddler reading area into one suitable for preschoolers?
8. What social changes seem to occur as children go from the preschool stage to the kindergarten years?

9. Kindergarteners are too young to be involved in contemporary social issues. Defend or refute this statement.
10. How might one change a preschool reading area into one that is suitable for kindergarteners?
11. What should one consider when choosing a site for a reading area?
12. Discuss various ways to display books so that children will be encouraged to use them.
13. Describe various ways of seating children for reading and identify the circumstances under which each would be used.

CHILDREN'S BOOKS CITED

Aliki (Brandenberg), *My Visit to the Dinosaurs* (New York: Crowell, 1969).

Anno (Mitsumasa), *Anno's Alphabet* (New York: Crowell, 1975).

Judith Barrett and Charles S. Blackman, *I Hate to Take a Bath* (New York: Scholastic, 1975).

Stan and Jan Berenstain, *He Bear, She Bear* (New York: Random House, 1974).

Franklyn M. Branley, *Rockets and Satellites* (New York: Crowell, 1970).

Norman Bridwell, *Clifford's ABC* (New York: Scholastic, 1986).

John Burningham, *Mr. Grumpy's Outing* (New York: Holt, Rinehart and Winston, 1971).

Stephanie Calmenson, *My Book of Seasons* (Racine, Wisconsin: Western, 1982).

Eric Carle, *The Very Hungry Caterpillar* (New York: Philomel, 1981).

Beverly Cleary, *Ramona the Pest* (New York: Dell, 1976).

Rose Dobbs (trans.), *Anderson's Fairy Tales* (New York: Random House, 1958).

Don Freeman, *Corduroy* (New York: Viking, 1968).

Erica Frost, *Jonathan's Amazing Adventure* (Mahwah, New Jersey: Troll, 1986).

Susanna Gretz, *Teddybear's ABC* (New York: Follett, 1975).

Grimm Brothers, *Household Stories* (New York: McGraw-Hill, 1966).

Tana Hoban, *Push-Pull, Empty-Full* (New York: Macmillan, 1972).

Syd Hoff, *Danny the Dinosaur* (New York: Harper and Row, 1958).

Pat Hutchins, *Rosie's Walk* (New York: Macmillan, 1968).

Vincent Jefferds, *Disney's Elegant ABC* (New York: Little Simon, 1983).

Jimmy Kennedy, *The Teddy Bear Picnic* (LaJolla, California: Green Tiger, 1983).

Dorothy Kunhardt, *Pat the Bunny* (Racine, Wisconsin: Western, 1962).

Susan Lapsley, *I Am Adopted* (New York: Bradbury, 1975).

Lois Lenski, *Cowboy Small* (New York: Walck, 1949).

Lois Lenski, *Debbie and Her Family* (New York, Walck, 1969).

Lois Lenski, *The Little Sailboat* (New York: Walck, 1965).

Carole Livingston, *Why Was I Adopted?* (Secaucus, New Jersey: Lyle Stuart, 1978).

Karen Milone (illus.), *Beauty and the Beast* (Mahwah, New Jersey: Troll, 1981).

Bernard Most, *If the Dinosaurs Came Back* (New York: Harcourt, Brace and Jovanovich, 1984).

Deborah Niland, *ABC of Monsters* (New York: McGraw, 1978).

Jan Ormerod, *Making Friends* (New York: Lothrop, Lee and Shepard, 1987).

Helen Oxenbury, *Good Night, Good Morning* (New York: Dial, 1982).

H. A. Rey, *Curious George* (Boston: Houghton-Mifflin, 1963).

Richard Scarry, *Find Your ABC's* (New York: Random House, 1973).

Maurice Sendak, *Where the Wild Things Are* (New York: Harper and Row, 1963).

Dr. Seuss (pseud. for Theodor Geisel), *Horton Hatches the Egg,* (New York: Random House, 1940).

Myrtle Shay, *What Happens When You Go to the Hospital?* (Chicago: Reilly and Lee, 1969).

Harriet Sobol, *My Brother Steven Is Retarded* (New York: MacMillan, 1977).

Judith Viorst, *Alexander and the Terrible, Horrible, No Good, Very Bad Day* (New York: Atheneum, 1972).

Bernard Waber, *Ira Sleeps Over* (Boston: Houghton-Mifflin, 1972).

Blanche Fisher Wright, *The Real Mother Goose Husky Book One* (Chicago: Rand McNally, 1983).

Blanche Fisher Wright, *The Real Mother Goose Husky Book Two* (Chicago: Rand McNally, 1983).

SELECTED REFERENCES

T. Berry Brazelton, *Infants and Mothers: Differences in Development* (New York: Dell, 1983).

David Elkind, *The Hurried Child* (Reading, Massachusetts: Addison-Wesley, 1981).

Stanley Greenspan, MD, *First Feelings* (New York: Simon and Schuster, 1973).

Arthur Jovan, *The Feeling Child* (New York: Simon and Schuster, 1973).

3 Choosing the Best Literature

his is an age of tremendous choice for consumers. Nearly everything purchased or selected requires decisions about the model, color, style, or type. This is true for cars, jewelry, food, stereos, and even the tools used to write this sentence. Choosing books for young children is no different. Every year approximately 2,400 new books for children are published. If those are added to the previous several decades' worth of books that are available, simple multiplication suggests that the choices number in the tens of thousands. If an early childhood educator reads or presents to the class only three books per day, over 700 books would be needed each year. Even a kindergarten teacher who might use two books per day over a 180 day school year would need 360 books per year.

The task of selecting a limited number of books from the tens of thousands available is not a simple procedure. While the choices are astounding, the right choices for a specific group of students require sensitivity and thought. The teacher must consider both the curriculum and the needs of the children, then match those considerations to the books available. It is at that point that the quality of the books themselves becomes important. A great book might not be right for a particular group. A tedious and boring book, even if it fits the curriculum perfectly, is of little value to the teacher or any group of children.

In addition, one needs to consider the purpose of using a particular book with children. Is it to use the illustrations and photographs as part of an instructional unit? Is it to help children understand the topic being studied? If children are motivated to learn more about a specific topic such as knights, dragons, or dinosaurs, the high interest these topics generate will help children increase their attention span while a longer piece is read. For this reason, it is not unusual for young children to have an amazing knowledge of the names and characteristics of several different dinosaurs.

This chapter examines the way to begin, by discussing aspects of good literature and the manner in which books are presented or put together. A summary is included of the various types of literature and some of the honors awarded to them.

HOW TO BEGIN

The best way to get started is to become an expert observer of children. This is not meant in the psychological sense of coding children's activities on a chart or checklist. Rather, the teacher must actively attend to the actions, language, and social interactions of children. One must always wonder what a child means by saying or doing a particular thing, as well as why the child said it or did it in that way. By becoming a child-watcher, the teacher will enter the world of children and learn what has meaning for them. This is critical because the most important characteristic about language is that it carries meaning. A book by a famous author, full of dazzling illustrations and gorgeous print, is useless unless or until it has meaning to the child. Cascardi[1] contends that, "There is no one kind of best book—there are good books of each kind and there are individual children with different interests who may find one category more appealing than another . . . that every child can benefit from exposure to the widest possible range of books."

By understanding individual children, the teacher will be able to respond by selecting books that are meaningful to them. This is more difficult than it may seem. It is important for the teacher to consider books that go beyond the teacher's personal interests and preferences. While everyone has such preferences, it is important to not transfer this personal bias to the class. Choosing books that reflect the interests of the class helps both the teacher and the children to grow.

One must consider the age of the listener or reader. However, children will often listen with understanding to books they cannot read by themselves. Lists of books grouped according to developmental levels are often distributed by libraries. These lists may provide a starting point for the new teacher or supply additional titles for the experienced teacher.

Mother Goose stories and fairy tales can be used with very young children along with a variety of other materials. Books with large text, colorful print, simple subjects, touchable surfaces, and rhythmical language are quite pleasing. Young children are also interested in books about topics such as themselves, self-help skills, their families, and objects from their surroundings. The teacher should be sensitive to individual problems and concerns within the class. Some characters and topics can be frightening to some children. On the other hand, a child who has experienced the death of a pet may be quite consoled by a book on that topic.

Betsy Hearne[2] has stated that, "Children's books are the place for powerful emotions, powerful language, powerful art. If the book you're reading seems boring, toss it. The book probably is boring, and there are thousands that aren't." As drastic as this approach may seem, it does have validity. Children should not be bored by the books and stories read to them. The teacher's role is to instill a desire to know, to imagine, and to read. A child who is wiggling and bored by the third page of a 32 page book is not inspired to do anything but escape.

The teacher must take into account the interests of the class when making a selection. Even if the book meets all selection criteria, it may not capture the attention of a specific group of children. If this happens, it should be put aside, or perhaps presented again at a later time.

---

[1] Andrea Cascardi, *Good Books to Grow Up On* (New York: Warner Books, 1985).
[2] Betsy Hearne, *Choosing Books for Children: A Common Sense Guide* (New York: Delacorte Press, 1985).

After knowing some things about the children one is working with, one can begin to think about the books themselves. With bookstores, libraries, and children's book clubs available in most communities, access to books is not usually a major problem. Talking to librarians, educators, and others associated with children is a good beginning source of information to develop a listing of potential books. They may also suggest additional sources such as *School Library Journal, The Horn Book Magazine,* and its parent newsletter *Why Children's Books?*

ASPECTS OF GOOD CHILDREN'S LITERATURE

Are the things that make a book good for children different from the things that make a book a good piece of literature for adults? Probably not. Of course with adults authors can write longer pieces with more complex topics, but these are differences in quantity. The quality of literature can and should be similar for both children and adults. The reader who spends much time reading literature written for children will soon discover that those who write successfully for children possess much talent. They are every bit as competent as those who write for adults. This does not mean that there are only good children's books. There are both good and poor books written for children just as there are good and poor books written for adults.

When an appropriate match has been made for the book, the children, and the curriculum, certain aspects of literature can be considered as well. These will include characterization, setting, plot, and theme. The adequate development of these elements is found in nearly all high quality literature. Depending on the piece, one element might be emphasized more than the others, but all are present.

Characterization

Every story has at least one character and usually there are more. While characters may be animals, people, objects, or imaginary beings, there should not be more characters than are necessary to tell the story. Above all, they must be real to children. The characters from literature who stand the test of time are those who feel real, act realistically and have real emotions. They give a glimpse of the reader's own self. The reader has a sense of "Yes, I know that feeling or that situation." In short, the reader cares about the character because of an emotional bond that is shared.

Characters Must Be Credible. Characters must be true and honest to their role or nature. A good author will let the reader know the personality and motivations of the character through the individual's thoughts, words, actions, language, and expressions. The author must be accurate with each of these in order for the reader to believe in the character. *Thy Friend, Obadiah* by Brinton Turkle is a story of a six year old boy set in colonial Nantucket. Dressed in colonial garb and speaking in historically accurate language, the child's reality transcends the time gap between colonial and modern times.

Mother Bear and Father Bear. Courtesy Stan and Jan Berenstain.

In their series of books about the Stupid Family *(The Stupids Die, The Stupids Step Out, The Stupids Have a Ball),* the writer/illustrator team of Harry Allard and James Marshall creates characters who are credible in spite of their incredibleness. The Stupids are a family who do everything . . . well, stupidly. The children mow the rug with a lawn mower and water the house plants with a garden sprinkler. Mrs. Stupid makes a dress out of live chickens, while Mr. Stupid eats eggs in the shower. Only the cat and dog seem to have any common sense. It is the fact that these characters are accurate to themselves that endears them to readers. Readers relate to the Stupids because everybody has done something foolish just like them. James Marshall explores this foolishness still further in his series of books beginning with the wonderful *George and Martha.*

Characters Must Be Consistent. The character may change and grow, but the basic portrayal must remain intact. That is, the character should not become a totally different character as a result of the experience in the story. In Munro Leaf's *The Story of Ferdinand,* circumstances change about the famous bull, but Ferdinand remains a pacifist. In *Curious George,* H. A. and Margaret Rey's monkey character learns from his mistakes but doesn't lose his personality or monkey qualities. Sometimes characters don't grow or learn from their mistakes. In Norman Bridwell's books about Clifford, the big red dog, the dog is always consistent in his ability to cause problems with his size. Children can count on that.

Characters can grow in several ways at once while remaining consistent. Such is the case of the main character in Robert Munsch's *Love You Forever.* In this touching story, a newborn baby and his mother grow over time to where the child becomes a young man with a child of his own while the mother becomes old and frail. The reader follows the child as he grows both physically and emotionally through childhood, adolescence, and adulthood. The underlying goodness and love that the two share triumph at the end, showing the consistency of the love the generations share.

Memorable characters from literature possess personalities that render them unique. Their personalities do not necessarily have to be overpowering. Rather, they are based on real aspects of humanity that make them special. Perhaps the character acts or speaks in a way that reminds readers of themselves. Perhaps the character does these things in a way readers wish they could. Few children are unaware of Dr. Seuss and Mercer Mayer characters, even though most don't know exactly what the characters are. The strong interaction between the reader and the personality is based on the strength of the personality and the believability of the character. Virginia Lee Burton draws the reader into the personality and emotional feelings of a building in *The Little House,* while Shel Silverstein does the same thing with a tree in *The Giving Tree.* Silverstein brings readers into the heart of the tree, feeling the changing seasons and the sensitivity of the relationship between the tree and the boy.

Child characters who are not stereotypical are frequently found in books for young children. In *William's Doll* by Charlotte Zolotow, readers meet a boy who, more than anything else in the world, wants a doll of his own. Others in the story don't understand why a boy would want a doll until his grandmother skillfully shows how natural a toy a doll can be for any child. In Tomie dePaola's autobiographical story *The Art Lesson,* the main character's personality and creativity continually shine through as he struggles with the rigid requirements of the school art curriculum.

The characters of Madeline by Ludwig Bemelmans, Little Tim by Edward Ardizzone, Max by Rosemary Wells, Amelia Bedelia by Peggy Parish, and Frog and Toad by Arnold Lobel stay with the reader for a lifetime. These characters touch the reader personally with whimsy, humor, empathy, and the stirrings of the need for independence.

Animal Characters. Animal characterizations are an important part of children's literature. Beatrix Potter gave her animals personality, but kept them in their delightful animal roles. She allowed them to continue to follow their natural instincts. Her drawings depicted them with clothing and human aspects as they went about stealing vegetables from a garden and living in a mouse hole. Each character is believable, yet retains the charm of its animal nature. Else Holmelund Minarik accomplishes the same thing with her Little Bear books as do Jan and Stan Berenstain in their Berenstain Bears series. In the latter series, the actions, emotions and situations are all human, but the bears do not appear to have just stepped out of the woods. Instead, they have a human-like home in the form of a tailored tree house.

Stories combining humans and animals provide a unique bridge between the two types of characters. In *Perfect the Pig* by Susan Jeschke, a human befriends a handicapped pig. Perfect was born the runt of the litter, but possessed wings that enabled her to fly. Cast out by her family because of this imperfection, she wanders through a series of adventures, meeting good and evil along the way. In *Beast* by Susan Meddaugh, a little girl refuses to allow the fear of the unknown deter her from investigating the captured beast in the family barn. The result is a satisfying friendship for both girl and beast. In Arthur Yorinks's *Louis the Fish,* the main human character gets his wish to live out his days as a fish. Raised by his parents to inherit the family meat market, Louis always felt like a ''fish out of water.'' He disliked the taste of meat and saw fish in everything he did. Even his customers seemed to look like fish to Louis. After struggling with this all his life, Louis's personality is at peace when he finally has his own aquarium to live in.

Portraying animals in a variety of character roles is quite valid and can be a positive and enjoyable experience for the reader. Difficult topics can be approached through animal characters with less traumatic reactions from children who may see themselves living or feeling the situation in the book. Topics such as new babies, moving, hospitals, divorce, and death are distanced through the use of animal characters. The safety surrounding such an approach can be the necessary support a child needs to deal with a topic.

Children often learn about animals and their habits from animal characters in books. They will sometimes correct or question a story when an animal character is not true to its animal roots. Even when this occurs, it does not lessen enjoyment

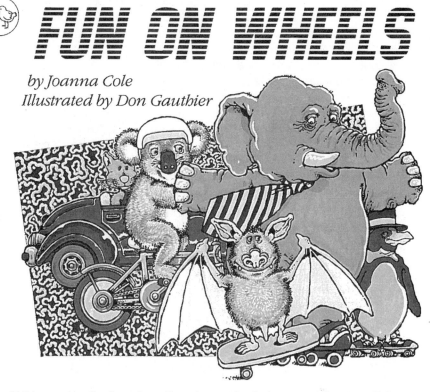

Children enjoy the fun of reading about animal characters. Courtesy Delmar Publishers Inc.

of fantasy or human-like animals. It demonstrates the great interest in animals that most children have during their early years. The author who includes well-defined animal characters will demonstrate a skillful blending of true animal characteristics and human behaviors.

Setting

The term "setting" usually makes the reader think about where and when a story takes place. This is partly correct, but a setting is often much more. Besides the actual location and time period of the story, the setting may include the way the characters live and the cultural aspects of the environment. While a story may take place in a small town at the time of the Civil War, it would make a difference if the town were located in the North or the South. The geography might not have much of an effect, but the moral tone would be quite different. A story is also affected by whether the characters are living in poverty or wealth.

The possibilities of setting are numerous, and each possibility has the potential to change the moral, ethical, and social tone of the story. This is true because the characters are closely connected to the setting. Characters do not act in a vacuum; they act in a specific place, time, and social environment. Just as people in real life do, characters in stories act in certain ways depending on their setting. For example people who are very hungry will behave differently depending on whether they are in a classroom, church, or restaurant. That is the expectation, but of course, in stories and in real life, individuals who don't quite conform to expectations can create interest and excitement.

The setting in children's books varies widely. It can be in a specific place, such as Boston Gardens in Robert McCloskey's *Make Way for Ducklings.* The setting can be a deliberately vague small town, farm, or forest, as in *The Biggest Bear* by Lynd Ward. The setting can jump from place to place depending on the story's needs. David McPhail's book, *Snow Lion,* is a good example of this. The lion has discovered snow on a mountain top and wishes to share it with his friends back in the jungle. As a result, the action bounces back and forth between the cold, snowy hills and the steamy jungle. Another example is Barbara Cooney's *Miss Rumphius.* In this touching story, also illustrated by the author, a young girl begins and ends her life on the coast of Maine. In the middle of the story, however, the setting shifts as she travels around the world. Cooney uses the reason for the girl's travels to neatly tie the various settings into a unified tale.

A setting can be implied rather than specifically described in the text or depicted in the illustrations. Jungle animals and descriptions of their homes would enable the reader to detect that the setting is a jungle or zoo.

Setting can reinforce the underlying theme of a story. In *Goodnight Moon* by Margaret Wise Brown, the setting of the bunny's moonlit bedroom reinforces the theme of the warmth, safety, and security that a child finds when settling down for a good night's sleep. In another story that takes place in a child's bedroom, *Where the Wild Things Are* by Maurice Sendak, the author cleverly confines the entire action to the room. Through the child's and the reader's imagination, the setting changes to the sea and finally to a faraway island where the wild things live. The reader is carried along with the dream. The child's anger at being sent to his room in the first place is balanced by the love symbolized by the hot dinner found upon returning from the imaginary, anger-filled journey. The dinner, left there by his mother, demonstrates that he is cherished. The setting changes enhance the character's feelings as the story proceeds.

Home Settings. The setting of a home can also be used to create a sense of anxiety, humor, or sadness when the unexpected happens. In *George Shrinks* by William Joyce, everyday household objects take on entirely new meanings when the main character wakes up to find himself only a few inches tall. In Tomie dePaola's *Nana Upstairs and Nana Downstairs,* a child's familiar world is made bewildering and sad when he experiences the death of a grandparent. It is only through the interaction of the child's creative character and the setting that the problem of the story is resolved. Terror turns to proud satisfaction for Louanne Pig in *Witch Lady* by Nancy Carlson. When she hurts her leg and is taken into a "haunted house" by the old witch, Louanne discovers that the witch is merely a kindly but eccentric elderly lady. Judith Barrett's *Old MacDonald Had an Apartment House* changes the idea of a home in a hilarious manner. Mr. MacDonald, the building super, always wanted to have a farm. He starts with one tomato plant, but soon the entire building is sprouting with vegetable plants and animals. What promises to be a tragic ending is averted by a clever use of the absurd setting.

School Settings. Stories set in schools are popular because children easily relate to them. Patricia Reilly Giff's Ronald Morgan series *(Today Was a Terrible Day; Watch Out, Ronald Morgan; Happy Birthday, Ronald Morgan)* has a wide audience. Ronald always seems to have problems in the school setting. He has a poor self-concept and is often unaware of things going on around him. His teacher, in the best teacher tradition, helps Ronald by encouraging him and helping him to discover by himself that he really can do many things.

Nature Settings. Romantic settings such as the mountains and the ocean are popular as well. Cynthia Rylant's *When I Was Young in the Mountains* provides a nostalgic look at being a child living in an extended family in the mountains of West Virginia. Being wealthy wasn't important, because the mountain setting and family provided all that was needed for happiness. In *Great Cat,* written and illustrated by David McPhail, it is only in the setting of an island in the ocean that the man and his gigantic pet cat can find peace and happiness. Another beautiful book about living near the ocean is Alvin Tresselt's *Hide and Seek Fog.* While the fog creates problems for the adults, the children make superb use of this change in their usual setting. Roger Duvoisin's illustrations of the fog-enshrouded town are so vivid the reader almost feels the moisture hanging in the air.

Plot

The plot can be seen as a kind of road map to a story. An author plans a plot to help the reader make sense out of the story. While the plot may unfold in chronological order, this does not always happen.

Plot is an artificial rather than a natural element with the purpose of simplifying life. The author does this by selecting some events, some characters, and some emotions. There are a limited number of episodes, and only those that are necessary to the story are included.

Plot focuses with character and setting in mind. That is, given the characters in a certain setting, what would tend to naturally occur? Thrall, Hibbard, and Holman[3] state that from this viewpoint, the function of plot is to translate character into action. In Aliki's *We Are Best Friends,* Peter and Robert are pals who are suddenly faced with the fact that Peter must move away. The reader is taken with wit and humor through a range of emotions and adjustments from anger, loneliness, and boredom to happiness and new friendships.

One might view plot as containing a beginning, middle, and end. The beginning should quickly set up interest for the reader. Younger children have shorter attention spans, so this is even more important. Interest is established by using

[3] William Flint Thrall and Addison Hibbard, *A Handbook to Literature* (New York: Odyssey Press, 1960), 358.

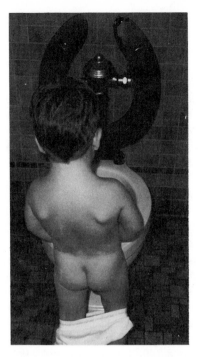

Even the topic of potty training is addressed in current children's literature.
Courtesy Diana Comer.

characters and a conflict that the reader can relate to and care about. The
conflict should grab the attention of the reader and create a desire to find out
what happens. In *Lizzy's Invitation* by Holly Keller, Lizzy is faced with the fact
that she is not invited to another child's birthday party. Keller sets up another
serious childhood problem, the death of a pet, in another of her books, *Goodbye, Max.* In *Ira Sleeps Over* by Bernard Waber, Ira's happiness at being invited
to sleep over at a friend's house is shaken when his big sister asks him if he will
be bringing his teddy bear along. He must then deal with the contrasting
problems of wanting to be more grown up, yet still desiring the security of
childhood comfort objects. Finally, Robert Munsch's witty book, *I Have to Go,*
begins on page one with the parents and child involved in the problems of toilet
training.

   In the middle of the plot, the conflict or problem may become more defined.
The rising action created by the interaction of the characters helps the reader
become more emotionally involved with the plot. The resolution of the conflict or
even the recognition of who or what is the cause of the conflict should not be too
obvious at this point. If the reader knows what happens now, there is little point to
finishing the story. Rather, the reader should feel more and more drawn into the
story. The quickening pace and the building of tension should continue as the
reader approaches the ending. By creating twists in the plot through new problems
and by suggesting false endings, the author intrigues and motivates the reader to

reach the ending. In Barbara Shook Hazen's *Tight Times,* the child and his already impoverished family spend much time dealing with the desire to have a pet at a time when the father has just lost his job. Nancy Carlson, in *Arnie and the Stolen Markers,* develops the conflicting emotions of desire and guilt throughout the story by exploring the main character's inner thoughts.

The ending contains the climax and the resolution of the plot. The climax is the highest point in dramatic tension, the point where everyone is quiet and sitting on the edge of their seats. The resolution is the final outcome of the problem or conflict. Even if the ending is happy, it can have an unexpected twist. In Dr. Seuss's *Horton Hatches the Egg,* children delight in the elephant-bird who hatches for the faithful Horton. In Dr. Seuss's *The Lorax,* children are given an unexpected last-minute reprieve from the pollution mess.

When the plot includes a child attempting to resolve a conflict, it is most appropriate if the child solves the problem without interference from adults in the story. In Nancy Evans Cooney's book, *The Blanket that Had to Go,* the child develops a satisfying solution concerning her fear of going to her first day at kindergarten without her security blanket. Marlene Fanta Shyer, in *Here I Am, an Only Child,* allows the child to come to his own acceptance of the fact that he does not have any brothers or sisters with whom to play.

The plot should be clear and believable even if the author asks the reader to travel into a world of fantasy. It should move from part to part with ease and consistency in order to maintain understanding and interest. Plots that are transparent or confusing will be boring to the young child. If a child is confused, it will be difficult to maintain interest. If the teacher can tell the final outcome on page one, chances are good that the child will be able to do this as well. The real answer is to use books with genuine and creative plots.

Theme

The theme of a story is an abstract concept the author has embedded in the story. The theme may include such ideas as the strength of friendship, the fragility of life, family life, or becoming independent. It is made concrete through other parts of the story such as characterization, setting, and plot. The theme often teaches a lesson or persuades the reader of something.

Illustrations enhance the theme as well. In *The Polar Express,* Chris Van Allsburg sets the tone of the theme with the bleak gray snow scenes of the home and the child. The full color illustrations fit perfectly with the theme of Verna Aardema's, *Why Mosquitoes Buzz in People's Ears,* which was illustrated by Leo and Diane Dillon. Each illustrator finds a unique way to reflect the theme and to blend the text and illustrations.

Identifying Themes. The theme can be an overview or an underlying part of the book. There can be one or several themes or subthemes in a story. The theme often reveals the author's purpose in writing the book. The author may use the story to help children understand or develop sensitivity to some issue or event. Even simple books for toddlers have underlying themes such as pride in self and independence. For example, toddlers relate to the activities involved in dressing by oneself.

Marie Hall Ets's book, *Play with Me,* may appear to be a simple book about a child trying to catch meadow animals. Its theme, however, concerns the need to enjoy the quiet observation of nature rather than trying to capture and possess it. A story from the humorous George and Martha series by James Marshall tells of an awful meal that Martha had prepared for George. Through the telling of the tale, the underlying themes of friendship and honesty become clear to the young reader. As the story proceeds, George's dilemma is handled in a positive and humorous way.

Charlotte Zolotow is the author of several books about relating to others. *Big Sister and Little Sister* tells of a big sister teasing a little sister. The themes of teasing, suffering from teasing, and the need for peace among siblings all emerge.

A theme should not be too obvious; it should unfold for the reader. Most well-written stories have layers of reasons or themes that add depth and dimension to the plot. *Mufaro's Beautiful Daughters* by John Steptoe is an African tale which can be read as a simple story in which the virtuous daughter is rewarded. It can also be read for its themes of kindness toward others, jealousy, bravery, and accepting consequences for one's actions. Many lessons can be learned from this one story about life and human nature. The illustrations, which won the Caldecott Honor Medal, provide a refreshing complement to the story.

The four areas of character, plot, setting, and theme are integrated in a successful story. Keeping a file of books that meet the criteria for each characteristic is an effective organizational tool. A full page or half page summary could be developed for each book to accomplish this. Items that should be included on the summary are:

Title
Author
Concepts in book
Short summary of story
Does it meet the criteria for characterization?
Does it meet the criteria for setting?
Does it meet the criteria for plot?
Does it meet the criteria for theme?

The file of books can grow over the years as new titles are published, increasing its value with each passing year.

PRESENTATION

The presentation of the story relates to the aspects of a book that are less a part of the thoughts and ideas of the author than those presented in the plot, setting, characterization, and theme. It is difficult to separate the aspects of presentation since a good book will integrate them into a whole work that is greater than the sum of the individual parts. They are separated here for discussion purposes only.

The four parts of the presentation discussed include: 1.) text style used in the printing; 2.) narrative style; 3.) the illustrations or photographs used; and 4.) anti-bias factors within the book.

Text Style

The style of print used in the text is important to the appearance of the finished book. Text style also contributes to the success of the unity between the text and the illustrations. Hundreds of type settings can be set or created for children's books. The size of the print must fit the purpose and feeling created by the narrative.

Print Size. Roger Duvoisin's *Veronica* uses tiny standard print set against humorously huge illustrations of the hippopotamus, making her look even more gigantic. Jean de Brunhoff's *Babar and the King* is set with a script that appears similar to a child's early cursive penmanship. While the book is easily read, few children's books use cursive rather than manuscript print. de Brunhoff's book places the illustrations at the bottom of the page, often taking up the entire page. Sometimes the text is placed between the boxed off illustrations where it fits the story best. The simple expressive illustrations blend with the cursive style of print without conflict.

Dr. Seuss's *Hop on Pop* is meant to help beginning readers. He has chosen a standard script found in many reading books, but the size is much larger. Standard print is about one-quarter of a centimeter tall. In Dr. Seuss's book, emphasized words are a full centimeter tall, while the words in the rest of the sentence are three-quarters of a centimeter tall. This fits the purpose and style of the book and is a good contrast with the zany pictures.

Dorothy Kunhardt's *Pat the Bunny* has very little print. What print there is, however, is a half centimeter tall and done in a child's manuscript. In *Life in the Forest,* Eileen Curran uses a bolder thickness of a half centimeter standard size print. The text on the pages runs right into the illustrations. As a result, each double page looks like a painting of a forest without any disruption. Yet, the words within the paintings are easily visible.

In *The Grouchy Ladybug* by Eric Carle, the print starts as one size and grows with the story. Carle's use of small pages building to larger and larger pages as the ladybug encounters ever bigger animals is enhanced by the effective use of print size. The print reaches whale size at the conclusion of the book. Virginia Lee Burton also uses this change of type size in her book, *Choo Choo: The Story of a Little Engine Who Ran Away.* Throughout the story, the train's name continues to appear in print. Every time it appears, it does so in larger print, standing out clearly within the text. The frequency of the large printed name grows along with the rising action of the story.

Print Color. Color is another key choice for print. Tana Hoban uses bold white block print set against a black background in *A Children's Zoo.* Robert McCloskey chooses a standard print in the same sepia color as the illustrations in *Make Way*

COMPUTER OUTLINE   D CPP 309   No. 0731
14 point
ABCDEFGHIJKLMNOPQRSTUVWXYZ&
1234567890
(.,:;'"*?¿!¡)%¢$/ÇÉíÑ
24 point
TYPOGRAPHY IS THE SELECTION

ITC LSC Condensed®   D CPP 012   No. 0170

ABCDEFGHIJKLMNOPQRSTUVWXYZ&
abcdefghijklmnopqrstuvwxyz1234567890
(.,:;'"*?¿!¡)%¢$ ÇÑçéíñß

Typography is the selection of a congruous typeface

ITC LSC Condensed Italic   D CPP 059   No. 0171

ABCDEFGHIJKLMNOPQRSTUVWXYZ&
abcdefghijklmnopqrstuvwxyz1234567890
(.,:;'"*?¿!¡)%¢$ ÇÑçéíñß

Typography is the selection of a congruous typ

Congress Regular   T/D CPP 256   No. 2293
FONTS Congress under license from Ingrama. S.A.
ABCDEFGHIJKLMNOPQRSTUVWXYZ&
abcdefghijklmnopqrstuvwxyz1234567890
(.,:;'"*?¿!¡)%¢$/ÇÑçéíñß
10 on 11 point
TASTE IN PRINTING DETERMINES THE FORM TYPOGRAPHY IS TO TAKE. THE SEL
ection of a congruous typeface, the quality and suitability for its purpose of the
paper to be used, the care and labor, time and cost of materials devoted to its

Congress Italic   T/D CPP 253   No. 2294

ABCDEFGHIJKLMNOPQRSTUVWXYZ&
abcdefghijklmnopqrstuvwxyz1234567890
(.,:;'"*?¿!¡)%¢$/ÇÑçéíñß

TASTE IN PRINTING DETERMINES WHAT FORM TYPOGRAPHY SHALL TAKE. THE
selection of a congruous typeface, the quality and suitability for its purpose of
the paper to be used, the care and labor, time and cost of materials devoted

Congress Medium   T/D CPP 268   No. 2295

ABCDEFGHIJKLMNOPQRSTUVWXYZ&
abcdefghijklmnopqrstuvwxyz1234567890
(.,:;'"*?¿!¡)%¢$/ÇÑçéíñß

TASTE IN PRINTING DETERMINES THE FORM TYPOGRAPHY IS TO TAKE. THE
selection of a congruous typeface, the quality and suitability for its purpose
of the paper to be used, the care and labor, time and cost of materials devot

COMPUGRAPHIC CORPORATION

Types of print. Courtesy Compugraphic Corporation.

for Ducklings. Other books have used color in additional creative ways depending on the needs and purpose of the story.

Print Location. Print can be placed in various locations on the page. It can be spaced as in poetry. While most of the words can be placed in paragraph form, variations can also be used.

In summary, the choice of print can enhance or diminish the effect of the narrative and its illustrations. In a quality book, the choice of print is always a consideration that shows.

Narrative Style

Each author has an individual style which is demonstrated by how the author tells the tale. Style is reflected in the choice of words, the figures of speech, the rhythmic pattern of the language, sentence structures, and rhetorical devices. Style differences create a wide diversity in children's books. For example, Steven Kellogg uses exaggerated illustrations in *Much Bigger than Martin.* In this story, Martin's little brother fantasizes about being larger than and in charge of his bossy older brother. The storyline captures the heart and soul of children's feelings with humor and hyperbole (which occurs when the author uses a tremendous exaggeration of fact). Kellogg's style is quite different from that of Tasha Tudor, for example. Her gentle, country-like stories are filled with whimsical children at play and in action.

Poetic Style. A. A. Milne uses poetry in the Christopher Robin stories to bring the reader into the world of Christopher and Pooh. The rhythm is bouncy and fun, hinting to the reader that the stories will be likewise.

The Brothers Grimm alternate narrative with poetry in a character's dialogue for a special effect that is well remembered: "Queen, you are full fair, 'tis true, But Snow White fairer is than you," from "Snow White and the Seven Dwarfs"; and, "Little tree, little tree, shake over me, That silver and gold may come down and cover me," from "Aschenputtel."

Lewis Carroll uses a mixture of narrative, short stories, limericks, and poetry within the classic *Alice's Adventures in Wonderland.* This combination keeps the action ever changing and ever enchanting.

Repetitive Style. Repetition is used to create a delightful tale in *Millions of Cats* by Wanda Gag. By the time the reader gets to "trillions of cats," children are eagerly anticipating and joining in the repetition.

Ludwig Bemelmans's short, rhyming narrative fits well with the stories of the twelve little girls in the ever popular Madeline series. The adventures in the series always begin with the same opening lines which, for hundreds of children, have come to mean that enjoyment will surely follow.

Margaret Wise Brown has a natural touch with her books for children. *Goodnight Moon* is one of the most popular bedtime stories with preschoolers because the simple script is a reassuring ritual played out in almost every child's house each night.

Judith Viorst uses a running narrative with a repetition that exposes the thoughts and the focus in *Alexander and the Terrible, Horrible, No Good, Very Bad Day*. The title itself is the repetition line. The illustrations aptly show just how the events of the narrative are making Alexander feel. This book causes laughter because all readers can empathize with the story. The descriptive language includes words such as "scrunched," "smushed," and the therapeutic "I'm going to Australia." Many adults love this book as much as children do.

Point of View. No matter what the style, all good literary narratives still include all of the components of good fiction or nonfiction. Besides such technical aspects as plot and setting, they include point of view as well.

The point of view from which the story is told has changed over the years. Today, stories are frequently told from the child's perspective, rather than from the perspective of an adult. Think of how a child might describe a kitchen. In the past, it might have sounded like, "My kitchen has four big chairs with shiny red seats. The cookie jar looks like a big fat doll and it's always full of yummy things to eat." Contemporary literature, using a more realistic child's point of view, might describe the same kitchen as, "The kitchen has lots of legs and a blue floor with crumbs and a sticky Kool-Aid patch that the cat licked almost clean." The latter description was by a three and one-half year old girl who described the kitchen not as an adult might think a child would see the kitchen, but as she actually did see it. The difference is important. The perceptive writer of children's books has the ability to see life or events from the child's perspective. It is this special ability that creates a child-loved classic. These are often the books children want to read again and again.

A good narrative style has several ingredients. First, the flow of language should be appropriate to the story. The use of words should enhance the story and the understandings it is attempting to convey. The narrative style should hold the reader's interest and contain a bit of intrigue, mystery, or surprise. The conflicts and conflict resolutions should make sense and feel right to the reader. They should draw the reader into the story enough to care about them both. Finally, the print choices should mesh with the author's purposes.

Topics and themes in children's literature have greatly expanded over the past several years, but the artistry of a good storyteller is still the cornerstone of a memorable book. The narrative style is a major part of the story that will be remembered, repeated, and enjoyed even when the book has long been misplaced or lost. A good narrative is real, touching the child as well as the child still hiding in every adult.

Good children's literature is good literature. It is difficult to resist its beauty, simplicity, and comedy. A good children's story gives adults the chance to remember, to dream again, and to find joy in the sense of wonder that was once theirs as children.

Illustrations and Photographs

The illustrations and photographs used in children's literature are as important for young children as the narrative. Children should be provided with high quality artwork as they begin their lives because exposure to fine artwork and photography builds an appreciation and love for art. Children have an openness of mind and imagination to appreciate a wide variety of art. They are not handicapped by opinion and bias about one type of art or another.

The criteria that should be used for making judgements about the illustrations and photographs in children's books include integration with the story, attention to detail, texture, and color.

Artistic Modes. The criteria used for judging the quality of illustrations can be applied to a variety of artistic modes. In using color, artists may choose crayon, oil pastels, chalk, water crayon, and so forth. Shading, detailing, and smudging are techniques that are used as part of this medium. Each gives a different expression to an illustration. These tools are used to create a soft feeling, a bold expression, or other emotion. Feodor Rojankovsky, Raymond Briggs, and Nancy Ekhorn Burkert are artists who display exceptional talent with the use of color.

Pen and ink is a traditional medium used quite often in children's books. It may be used as an outline or with various sketchings to enhance detail. Shel Silverstein, Nonny Hogrogian, E. H. Shepard, Robert Lawson, and Leonard Weisgard are masters of this technique.

Woodcuts and linocuts are used by several illustrators to create a broad range of finished products. They can yield very detailed results or bold and dramatic images. The colors can be brown, black, or other darker colors and may be used with or without a lighter wash. Each color can also be painted separately onto the woodcut and printed by hand. Superb examples of the technique can be seen in the works of Wanda Gag, Evaline Ness, Marcia Brown, Don Freeman, Antonio Frasconi, Ed Emberly, and Marie Hall Ets.

Colored pencils or charcoal yield a different texture and feel than crayon or paint. This is a very painstaking process to use for an entire book, but it can create an effect that other techniques cannot duplicate. Artists Susan Jeffers, Taro Yashima, and Chris Van Allsburg (conte pen) have produced outstanding examples of this process.

Photographers for children's literature are special people. They must be able to visualize as a child and also possess the technical skill to capture the picture that precisely meets the needs of the narrative. Tana Hoban, Roger Bester, and Thomas Mattieson provide dazzling examples of this type of photography.

Artists who choose collage must have a bit of the collector within themselves. Ezra Jack Keats pinned his fabric bits on his wall to keep them visible. The textures and feel that collage can offer are limitless. Materials can come from anywhere and anything. Tissue paper, as used by Eric Carle, and fabric and wallpaper, as used by Keats, are the more common materials. In addition to Carle and Keats, Leo Lionni, Marcia Brown, and Blair Lent (overlays) provide other fine examples of collage.

Painted Illustrations. Paint is by far the most common medium for art work in children's books. It is often used with other media to give a contrasting texture and color. Paint can be the thin, soft wash of tempera or watercolor, the bold, brash

Ezra Jack Keats. Courtesy Beverly Hall.

reds and purples of oil, or the thick, textured look of acrylics. This diversity and richness of color and texture makes it a popular medium. Maurice Sendak, Mitsamasa Anno, Gyo Fujikawa, Brian Wildsmith, David McPhail, Dick Bruna, Margot Zemach, Tasha Tudor, Tomie dePaola, Steven Kellogg, Arnold Lobel, Anita Lobel, and Donald Carrick are but a few of the fine painters whose illustrations appear in children's literature.

The most difficult part of the painter's job is to create a series of illustrations that satisfy the painter as well as his/her audience. Some artists prefer to work in one medium and perfect their craft while others prefer to use several types of medium. Marcia Brown is a multi-talented illustrator who has successfully tried almost every medium. For example, *Dick Whittington and His Cat* uses woodcut in black and white. Brown's book, *Cinderella,* a Caldecott medal winner, is done in subtle pastels. Her illustrations in *Shadow* by Blaise Cendrars, which also won a Caldecott medal, are done with contrasting collage.

Several artists use historical, master, and contemporary styles in their work. Leo and Diane Dillon, in *Ashanti to Zulu* by Margaret Musgrove, use tribal motifs. They use native American art and styles in Natalia Belting's *Whirlwind Is a Ghost Dancing.* Paul Goble uses beautifully expansive native American symbols in *The Girl Who Loved Wild Horses.* Alice and Martin Provensen use old world techniques in Nancy Willard's *A Visit to William Blake's Inn.* Barbara Cooney uses an old master style in *Ox-Cart Man* by Donald Hall. This book is reminiscent of a visit to an art museum's Americana collection. These styles require much research and attention to detail.

Effective use of light and dark is another tool of the skilled artist. Chris Van Allsburg paints with dramatic use of light in *The Polar Express* and *Jumanji*. *Owl Moon* by Jane Yolen incorporates a powerful use of light as the storyline progresses through the owl hunt. John Schoenherr's expansive style makes readers feel like they are walking through the woods themselves.

Rosemary Wells humorously uses type and illustration in a style all her own. For example, when she uses the word "between" in the text, it is actually placed between two objects in the illustrations. When Morris, in *Morris's Disappearing Bag,* uses a bag to hide in, children identify with him. They see themselves hiding in the bag as well.

All of these artists, along with John Burminham, Uri Shulevitz, Richard Egielski, Trina Schart Hyman, Gail Haley, William Steig, Peter Spier, Stan and Jan Berenstain, Frank Asch, and others will keep children's literature exciting for years to come. They follow the path of Randolph Caldecott, William Mulready, Kate Greenaway, Sir John Tenniel, and Leslie Brooke of the nineteenth century. New artists, like new writers, are emerging each year to both continue tradition and explore new possibilities.

When selecting books, ask if the choices you are making will stand the test of time and love. Every book used with children should be a quality book in both narrative and illustration. Additional in-depth information on children's book illustration can be found in the works of Patricia Cianciolo,[4] Judith Saltman,[5] Clifton Fadiman,[6] John W. Griffith and Charles H. Frey,[7] Charles Panati,[8] Betsy Hearne and Marilyn Kaye,[9] and May Hill Arbuthnot and Zena Sutherland.[10]

Integration with Text. The integration of the illustrations and photographs with the text refers to whether or not they fit all aspects of the narrative. A tale about jungle life would be ill-served by illustrations of snowy slopes. One reason that Leo and Diane Dillon are so successful with their two Caldecott-winning African tales is their ability to transport the reader to Africa. They do so with the effective use and integration of color, design, and setting.

Illustrations must be integrated with each other. Leo Lionni is a master of illustration-to-illustration unity. In *Swimmy,* he creates the feeling of enormity by allowing the reader to see the fish swimming in the entire ocean. The detail even includes a fish flowing off the page as if it is continuing to swim there. Donald Crews also shares this talent for integration. In *Freight Train,* the reader sees the train move from page to page at increasing speed.

Exemplary literature also integrates text and illustrations. In Tana Hoban's, *A Children's Zoo,* the white block lettering contrasts crisply with the bold, full-page photographs of the animals. The black background reinforces the boldness and

[4] Patricia Cianciolo, *Illustration in Children's Books* (Boston: Little Brown, 1970).
[5] Judith Saltman, *The Riverside Anthology of Children's Literature* (Boston: Houghton Mifflin, 1985).
[6] Clifton Fadiman, *The World Treasury of* Children's *Literature, Volume 1* (Boston: Little Brown, 1970).
[7] John W. Griffith and Charles H. Frey (Eds.), *Classics of Children's Literature* (New York: Macmillan, 1987).
[8] Charles Panati, *Extraordinary Origins of Everyday Things* (New York: Harper & Row, 1987).
[9] Betsy Hearne and Marilyn Kaye (Eds.), *Celebrating Children's Books* (New York: Lothrop, Lee & Shepard, 1981).
[10] May Hill Arbuthnot and Zena Sutherland, *Children and Books* (Chicago: Scott Foresman, 1985).

clarity of each page. In Aliki's, *We Are Best Friends,* the print is similar to a primer print. It is located throughout the book at the page bottoms, apart from the illustrations. The dramatic sadness of the tale is increased tenfold when the text shifts to the heartwrenching letter that is part of the story. The letter, written in a child's beginning handwriting, is expertly integrated into the narrative. Dr. Seuss is also most adept at effective and creative integration of text and illustration. In *The Shape of Me and Other Stuff,* he successfully integrates bright colors, large bold print, and shadow shapes. The words are clearly and enjoyably emphasized without distracting from the game of guessing the shadows.

Works of lesser quality do not include this thoughtful integration. They often use gimmicks that attempt to be clever. In actuality, such gimmicks detract from and disrupt the story flow. In previewing children's books, one should look at the type of print used to see if it is appropriate for the type of book and age level of the children. It should be checked to see if the words are clear and easy to find, rather than hidden throughout the page. The type should not be crowded, allowing the child's eye to pick up on the spacing between the words.

Attention to Detail. Quality illustrations and photographs stand out from mediocre art because of attention to detail. Illustrations need to accurately reflect the narrative. For example, if a story calls for a monkey to wear a red hat, it must be the same shade of red and the same hat throughout the story. Poor quality books may vary these details.

Children demand truth from their stories. They will count every object on a page to be certain that the twenty cats are there, just as the story said they would be.

The 1988 Caldecott winner, *Owl Moon* by Jane Yolen, illustrated by John Schoenherr, demonstrates a keen attention to detail. The owl seems to lift off the page and stand eye-to-eye with the reader. The illustrations in this book provide a breathless moment and are unencumbered by text except for a few words on the following page. Good illustration such as this draws the reader into the page. It offers something to be discovered. As is the case with good paintings, more is found each time one looks at the pictures.

The exemplary photographer does not merely provide a picture of a boat. Rather, a moment or a time of day is captured so that the photograph of the boat is something special. The backdrop of the shot is carefully chosen. The type of film and the speed of the film are considered. Perhaps hundreds of shots are taken in order to achieve the one best photograph. These details show in the final outcome and account for the quality difference found in better pictures.

Texture. Distinctive illustration possesses a feel and texture that is three-dimensional. Some artists use paint, some use collage, and some use woodcuts. The best work of each has a feeling to it that joins the picture, the text, and the reader. The skillful use of space and art should expand the text. An artist may outline figures in black to clarify shape, or use colors to define boundaries or special words. Whatever techniques are used, they should carefully tie together the text and the purpose of the story.

Illustration by John Schoenherr. Reprinted by permission of Philomel Books from *Owl Moon* by Jan Yolen, illustrations © 1987 by John Schoenherr.

Color. Color can lend a dramatic effect that adds beauty to an already acknowledged art work. However, it is important to realize that color alone is not an indicator of a book's quality. There are many excellent books without color, or with limited use of color, that are truly memorable. Just as some movies are meant to be seen in black and white, some books are meant to use color sparingly.

Harold and the Purple Crayon by Crockett Johnson is illustrated entirely with a purple crayon line drawing. The book is a favorite of young children and inspires them to create their own purple drawings. They readily respond to the humor and novelty of the book. *Little Bear's Friend* by Else Holmelund Minarik, illustrated by Maurice Sendak, is another superb example. It is wistfully and delicately illustrated in black line sketching with a soft wash of browns and greens. The effect visually enhances the text narration and is appealing to children. Alvin Tresselt's book, *I Saw the Sea Come In,* is deftly illustrated by Roger Duvoisin. The pages of black ink sketches, washed with blues and touched with black shading, emphasize the lonely beach scenes. When he uses full color as a contrast, the effect is riveting. These illustrations are also visually dramatic in terms of the story narrative.

The bold use of color in the woodcut version of *The House that Jack Built* by Antonio Frasconi accentuates the angular designs in the woodcuts. Bright yellow, lime green, hot pink, and orange, though not typical color combinations for a child's book, provide a feeling of integration here. In contrast, consider *Make Way for Ducklings* by Robert McCloskey. It is still one of the most popular books for youngsters, yet it has no color. The entire book is etched in soft brown sepia. The realism in the details within the illustrations make the pages come alive without the use of color.

Eric Carle and Ezra Jack Keats are illustrators who often choose to work with collage. The textures and colors in their work effectively invite children to touch the pages to see if the pictures are real. Indeed, some of Carle's books have a three-dimensional component that can be touched. The illustrations and text blend so well that they seem to be one.

The illustrations and photographs used in children's literature should not only be integrated, but they should possess a quality of design, color usage, and incorporation of texture. The reader should find the illustrations interesting and involving. These criteria are demanding, which is one of the reasons one must search for quality works among the large number of books published each year.

There are many talented artists who are worthy of being known as children's book artists. Young people everywhere, and adults as well, applaud their efforts. If the artist awakens in the developing child an awareness and love of art, this love will remain long after the child has become an adult. The artist will have opened a world of aesthetic joy forever. Children often attempt to recreate images from the story in a variety of ways. Figure 1 illustrates the range of possible images children may create after listening to a story about cats.

Anti-bias Factors

Respectable companies publishing children's books today do not accept works with open bias toward race, sex, religion, age, or disability. However, there are still many books from years gone by in libraries and school collections that do contain both subtle and overt negative bias. Anyone planning to use literature with children should preview the books for signs of bias.

Figure 1.   *Cat pictures.* Courtesy Diana Comer.

Many young adults do not remember the Dick and Jane type of books. In these stories, Jane wore a dress and passively watched as Dick did all of the exciting childhood activities. One might wish to share books of this type to appreciate the changes that have occurred in both our society and in children's literature. This activity can help to raise the consciousness of all against such bias.

Another less obvious prejudice is the lack of any characters other than white ones within stories. This is bias by omission, and is still prevalent in some classroom collections that have few multicultural books.

Sensitivity to bias by those who care for children ensures that collections of books reflect a realistic picture of society. Multicultural books should be included whether or not the student group includes minority children.

Identifying Bias. It is not difficult to determine if a book collection is biased by omission. First, count the number of books in the collection. Next, determine how many of the books contain animal characters, white children as characters, Hispanic children as characters, black children as characters, and other minority children as characters. Finally, look at the numbers and make your own decision. There is no magic number or percentage, but if the size of the numbers and percentages surprise you, action probably needs to be taken.

A good collection need not have all minority-based or multicultural books, but it should have a representative number of such books. The stories should appeal to all children, and not just be there because they include characters of certain race, sex, age or with a disability. Characters must fit into the story without artificial dynamics. The story should be the main element and the inclusion of the

Collage
Cloth, wallpaper, tissue paper, wrappers, foil

pointilism
pencil tip, brush, Bingo markers, crayons, q-tips

crayon
scribbles - straight - designs

prints
wood carving, sponges, styrofoam

Figure 1.   continued

minority group characters should mesh with the story. The fit should be so good that the children are left with the feeling that it is a great story, rather than the feeling that it is a great black story or great Hispanic story. Many themes of tales from Africa or the inner city touch all children. Many ethnic fairy tales or farm stories make all children share a common response and feeling. These are the

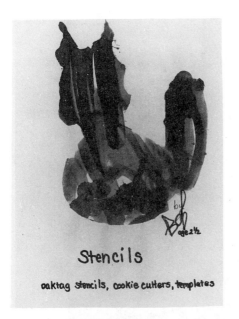

Stencils

oaktag stencils, cookie cutters, templates

marker/inks

straight - patterns -designs

printing

object, sponge, rubber stamps, little car wheels

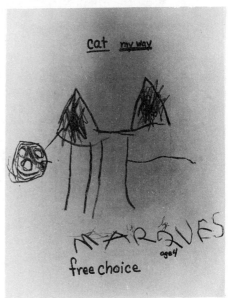

free choice

Figure 1. continued

books to add to a collection: the books that broaden the sensitivity and understanding of all children.

This same basic idea holds true for sexism in books. Characters such as Ramona Quimby in Beverly Cleary's books and Emily Arrow in Patricia Reilly Giff's stories are strong female models. They are not perfect children but they share a

Little friends in jungle deep

There are many excellent books that can help children understand both the differences among people and the things joining all people. Illustration by Gyo Fujikawa, reprinted by permission of Grosset and Dunlap from *Faraway Friends*, © 1981 by Gyo Fujikawa.

common humanity that is appreciated by all children. One can bring sexism out into the open and discuss it with children by using books such as *Nice Little Girls* by Elizabeth Levy. In this warm and supportive story, the problem of girl jobs versus boy jobs is addressed. Divisions, such as depicted in the book, are still found in some of today's classrooms. Subtle sexism is prejudice that often dissipates when teachers and parents are aware of its existence.

Other biases exist against handicapped individuals and those with religious or regional class differences. Inclusion of books such as Harriet Sobol's *My Brother Steven Is Retarded* and Carol Carrick's *Stay Away from Simon* can help teachers and students become sensitive to such realities of our world. If approached in the same manner as with the others, these biases by omission can also be remedied.

SUMMARY

Choosing the best books available for use with young children is critically important. Since children are forming their thoughts and opinions about almost everything, one must help and encourage them with useful, sensitive, and thought-provoking ideas. Exposure to the best possible stories and illustrations will help them in this area while giving them an appreciation for quality literature as well. The criteria for choosing literature may seem involved. However, once a teacher or parent gains these critical skills, it becomes second nature to apply them.

The criteria combine judging aspects of literature and assessing how stories are presented. Good literature will motivate children to want to hear stories and to learn to read. Teacher sensitivity allows children to learn to be careful, thoughtful readers who have already started to develop critical thinking skills about facts and information.

QUESTIONS FOR THOUGHT AND DISCUSSION

1. How can a teacher go about choosing good literature?
2. Why can an understanding of the aspects of literature and a knowledge of presentation be helpful in choosing quality literature?
3. How can a list of Caldecott Medal winners be helpful in selecting books?
4. What are the limitations of using only books that have won Caldecott Medals?
5. How can one determine if the illustrations in a book are appropriate?
6. What are some general goals for using literature with children?
7. Why is it important to consider plot, character, setting, and theme when selecting books?
8. Why is it important to look for bias in children's books?
9. What are some of the different media used in book illustration?

CHILDREN'S BOOKS CITED

Verna Aardema, *Why Mosquitoes Buzz in People's Ears* (New York: Scholastic, 1985).

Aliki (Brandenberg), *We Are Best Friends* (New York: Greenwillow, 1982).

Harry Allard, *The Stupids Die* (Boston: Houghton Mifflin, 1981).

Harry Allard, *The Stupids Have a Ball* (Boston: Houghton Mifflin, 1978).

Harry Allard, *The Stupids Step Out* (Boston: Houghton Mifflin, 1974).

Judith Barrett, *Old MacDonald Had an Apartment House* (New York: Atheneum, 1979).

Natalia Belting, *Whirlwind Is a Ghost Dancing* (New York: Dutton, 1974).

Ludwig Bemelmans, *Madeline* (New York: Viking, 1939).

Marcia Brown, *Cinderella* (New York: Scribner, 1939).

Marcia Brown, *Dick Whittington and His Cat* (New York: Scribner, 1950).

Margaret Wise Brown, *Goodnight Moon* (New York: Harper & Row, 1947).

Virginia Lee Burton, *Choo Choo: The Story of a Little Engine Who Ran Away* (Boston: Houghton Mifflin, 1937).

Virginia Lee Burton, *The Little House* (Boston: Houghton Mifflin, 1937).

Eric Carle, *The Grouchy Ladybug* (New York: Crowell, 1977).

Nancy Carlson, *Arnie and the Stolen Markers* (New York: Viking Penguin, 1987).

Nancy Carlson, *Witch Lady* (New York: Viking Penguin, 1985).

Carol Carrick, *Stay Away from Simon* (New York: Clarion, 1985).

Lewis Carroll, *Alice's Adventures in Wonderland* (New York: Knopf, 1983).

Blaise Cendrars, *Shadow* (New York: Scribner, 1982).

Barbara Cooney, *Miss Rumphius* (New York: Viking Penguin, 1982).

Nancy Evans Cooney, *The Blanket that Had to Go* (New York: Putnam, 1981).

Donald Crews, *Freight Train* (New York: Greenwillow, 1978).

Eileen Curran, *Life in the Forest* (Mahwah, NJ: Troll, 1985)

Jean de Brunhoff, *Babar and the King* (New York: Random House, 1963).

Tomie dePaola, *The Art Lesson* (New York: Putnam, 1989).

Tomie dePaola, *Nana Upstairs and Nana Downstairs* (New York: Putnam, 1973).

Roger Duvoisin, *Veronica* (New York: Knopf, 1969).

Marie Hall Ets, *Play with Me* (New York: Viking Penguin, 1955).

Antonio Frasconi, *The House that Jack Built* (New York: Harcourt, 1958).

Wanda Gag, *Millions of Cats* (New York: Coward McCann, 1928).

Patricia Reilly Giff, *Happy Birthday, Ronald Morgan* (New York: Viking Kestral, 1986).

Patricia Reilly Giff, *Today Was a Terrible Day* (New York: Viking Penguin, 1980).

Patricia Reilly Giff, *Watch Out, Ronald Morgan* (New York: Viking Penguin, 1985).

Paul Goble, *The Girl Who Loved Wild Horses* (New York: Macmillan, 1978).

Donald Hall, *Ox-Cart Man* (New York: Viking Penguin, 1979).

Barbara Shook Hazen, *Tight Times* (New York: Viking, 1979).

Tana Hoban, *A Children's Zoo* (New York: Mulberry, 1985).

Susan Jeschke, *Perfect the Pig* (New York: Scholastic, 1980)

Crockett Johnson, *Harold and the Purple Crayon* (New York: Harper & Row, 1955).

William Joyce, *George Shrinks* (New York: Harper & Row, 1985).

Holly Keller, *Goodbye, Max* (New York: Greenwillow, 1987).

Holly Keller, *Lizzy's Invitation* (New York: Greenwillow, 1987).

Steven Kellogg, *Much Bigger than Martin* (New York: Dutton, 1976).

Dorothy Kunhardt, *Pat the Bunny* (Racine, WI: Western, 1962).

Munro Leaf, *The Story of Ferdinand* (New York: Viking, 1936).

Elizabeth Levy, *Nice Little Girls* (New York: Delacorte, 1974).

Leo Lionni, *Swimmy* (New York: Pantheon, 1963).

James Marshall, *George and Martha* (Boston: Houghton Mifflin, 1972).

Robert McCloskey, *Make Way for Ducklings* (New York: Viking, 1941).

David McPhail, *Great Cat* (New York: Dutton, 1982).

David McPhail, *Snow Lion* (New York: Pantheon, 1983).

Susan Meddaugh, *Beast* (Boston: Houghton Mifflin, 1981).

Else Holmelund Minarik, *Little Bear's Friend* (New York: Harper & Row, 1960).

Robert Munsch, *I Have to Go* (Toronto, Ontario, Canada: Annick, 1987).

Robert Munsch, *Love You Forever* (Scarborough, Ontario, Canada: Firefly, 1986).

Margaret Musgrove, *Ashanti to Zulu: African Traditions* (New York: Dial, 1977).

H. A. and Margaret Rey, *Curious George* (New York: Houghton Mifflin, 1941).

Cynthia Rylant, *When I Was Young in the Mountains* (New York: Dutton, 1982).

Maurice Sendak, *Where the Wild Things Are* (New York: Harper & Row, 1963).

Dr. Seuss (pseud. for Theodor Geisel), *Hop on Pop* (New York: Random House, 1963).

Dr. Seuss, *Horton Hatches the Egg* (New York: Random House, 1940).

Dr. Seuss, *The Lorax* (New York: Random House, 1971).

Dr. Seuss, *The Shape of Me and Other Stuff* (New York: Random House, 1973).

Marlene Fanta Shyer, *Here I Am, an Only Child* (New York: Macmillan, 1985).

Shel Silverstein, *The Giving Tree* (New York: Harper & Row, 1964).

Harriet Sobol, *My Brother Steven Is Retarded* (New York: Macmillan, 1977).

John Steptoe, *Mufaro's Beautiful Daughters* (New York: Lothrop, Lee & Shepard, 1987).

Alvin Tresselt, *Hide and Seek Fog* (New York: Mulberry, 1965).

Alvin Tresselt, *I Saw the Sea Come In* (New York: Lothrop, Lee & Shepard, 1954).

Brinton Turkle, *Thy Friend, Obadiah* (New York: Viking Penguin, 1965).

Chris Van Allsburg, *Jumanji* (Boston: Houghton Mifflin, 1982).

Chris Van Allsburg, *The Polar Express* (Boston: Houghton Mifflin, 1985).

Judith Viorst, *Alexander and the Terrible, Horrible, No Good, Very Bad Day* (New York: Atheneum, 1972).

Bernard Waber, *Ira Sleeps Over* (Boston: Houghton Mifflin, 1972).

Lynd Ward, *The Biggest Bear* (Boston: Houghton Mifflin, 1982).

Rosemary Wells, *Morris's Disappearing Bag* (New York: Dutton, 1975).

Nancy Willard, *A Visit to William Blake's Inn* (New York: Harcourt, Brace Jovanovich, 1981).

Jane Yolen, *Owl Moon* (New York: Philomel, 1987).

Arthur Yorinks, *Louis the Fish* (New York: Farrar, Straus, Giroux, 1980).

Charlotte Zolotow, *Big Sister and Little Sister* (New York: Harper & Row, 1966).

Charlotte Zolotow, *William's Doll* (New York: Harper and Row, 1982).

SELECTED REFERENCES

Daniel N. Fader and E. B. McNeil, *Hooked on Books: Program and Proof* (New York: Berkeley, 1968).

Linda Leonard Lamme, *Learning to Love Literature: Preschool through Grade Three* (Urbana, Illinois: National Council of Teachers of English, 1981).

Greta Barclay Lipson and Jane A. Romatowski, *Ethnic Pride—Explorations into Your Ethnic Heritage, Cultural Information—Activities and Student Research* (Chicago: Good Apple, 1983).

John Warren Stewig, *Children and Literature* (Boston: Houghton Mifflin, 1988).

Jim Trelease, *The New Read-Aloud Handbook* (New York: Viking Penguin, 1989).

Using Various Types of Literature

hile it is important to have books on the children's level, it is also a good idea to surround children with a variety of books at several levels to help motivate and inspire them to want to read "all by themselves."

Books used in beginning elementary school reading programs are known as basal readers. A basal reader is a book that is a part of an integrated set of textbooks, workbooks, teacher's manuals, and related materials used to provide developmental reading instruction. Basal readers usually contain a selection of short pieces written for that particular text. The vocabulary of the selections is usually carefully controlled to use only certain words at different levels. Basals might be included in programs for young children, but they are not necessary. They tend to neither contain sufficient quality literature nor take advantage of a child's natural curiosity and language.

Because of all that must be considered, much time is needed to make the right choices. Since time is not what most early childhood educators possess in large quantities, it is imperative that the teacher use time effectively. If good matches are to be made between children and books, one must have a deep understanding of the children, a solid knowledge of how to select appropriate books, and a broad knowledge of the children's books available. The purpose of this chapter is to help the reader develop this knowledge of traditional and current children's literature. This is done by summarizing a wide range of literature for young people.

The categories used to classify kinds of books may vary. The categories used here represent a broad approach of discussing types of books and methods for using them. One can increase the depth of knowledge in any one category through additional research into specific categories. This can be done by studying book reviews or, better yet, through reading and discussing the actual books.

FINGERPLAYS/CHANTS/RHYMES

Young children benefit from the acquisition of the rhythm and sounds of language. Through adult modeling of fingerplays, chants, and rhymes, children can learn these rhythms and sounds. Perhaps this is why such literary forms are found in almost every culture, country, and language. The song-like quality of these language forms makes them easy to listen to, respond to, and learn. Since these forms are often short, they allow children to retain the words when they are repeated several times. This repetition can help children learn to speak words as they are needed. In addition, fingerplays allow children to coordinate hand motions with words in a manner that facilitates small muscle development and eye-hand coordination.

Adults should always support children's development of self-esteem. The fact that these literary forms enable children to experience success is an important reason to use them. The successful acquisition of fingerplays and rhymes makes children feel competent about their learning ability while providing a language skill achievement that will enhance their literacy development.

Fingerplays and Chants

A fingerplay is a short poem put to rhyme or beat. A fingerplay has hand motions; a chant does not. Any fingerplay can be chanted in a sing-song fashion and many chants can be made into fingerplays. A teacher can make up and sing a chant such as, "It's clean up time, it's clean up time. Let's all cooperate," to help children with the transition from free play to circle time. Chants and fingerplays are positive ways to help children learn about social expectations and concept development in an informal manner. An example of a rectangle concept fingerplay is, "Long–short, long–short. The rectangle is long–short, long–short." As the fingerplay is sung, children trace the rectangle shape in the air. As the word "rectangle" is reached, the children might be encouraged to shout it out. This fingerplay can be used when tracing the shape or drawing it and can be used to help differentiate between the square and the rectangle.

Fingerplays and chants can be invented by adapting favorite short poems and can include motion or action. The teacher can invent fingerplays or have children help to invent some. For example, after sighting a helicopter, this easy, concrete fingerplay was invented:

WORDS	ACTIONS
Up and down,	Children move up and down
Up and down.	with the words, arms out to the
Round and round,	sides, then spin
Round and round.	in a circle.
The helicopter . . .	Children run off
Goes off to town.	to a corner of the room.

Every teacher of young children has a varied repertoire of fingerplays and chants. They may be recorded on file cards that are easy to use and store. Fingerplays for transititions, about basic concepts, about holidays, and even about commonplace concepts such as naptime can simplify the daily routine and enhance a program.

One source of fingerplays is the book *Finger Frolics* by Liz Cromwell and Dixie Hibner.[1] It provides a wide range of easy-to-learn fingerplays.

Rhymes

Rhymes can be simple poems or chants. They can be used as one would use the fingerplay or chant. Silly rhymes are particularly enjoyable even for young toddlers and are easily created. Children love rhymes that use their names or the names of friends and family members.

Rhymes have been passed down from generation to generation. There are rhymes for jumping rope, learning colors, and just about anything else children find important, frightening, or silly.

"One, two, buckle my shoe"; "Blue, blue, God loves you"; "One potato, two potato, three potato, four"; "Lizzy Borden took an axe . . . " are all rhymes that most remember from childhood. Horrendous rhymes were often created as a way of helping children express and cope with fear. "Ring around the Rosie" was originally an expression of children's fears about death and the terrible processing of bodies during the plague in England. "Ashes to ashes, we all fall down" was play-acting the deaths that the children feared. Ridicule is one way that children diminish and process fears. New rhymes are forever adding to the heritage that one group of children passes to the next as a ritual part of childhood.

MOTHER GOOSE TALES/NURSERY RHYMES

Who was Mother Goose? There are various versions of the origin of Mother Goose. Some credit the term to the French author Charles Perrault who in 1697 referred to the rhymes as those told by an old woman tending geese. Others attribute Mother Goose to the English author, John Newbury, who first used the term in a book he published in 1765. Still others claim that Mother Goose was a Boston woman by the name of Elizabeth Goose. She was the mother-in-law of a publisher of a slim volume titled *Mother Goose Melodies for Children* published in Boston in 1719. Though the proof is lost in the archives of the Antiquarian Society Collection in Worcester, Massachusetts, it is unimportant who first used the term. Mother Goose is known by children all over the world as a symbol of rhymes and the enjoyment gained from their use.

Mother Goose Activities

Mother Goose stories are easily used to stimulate language acquisition and to develop social behavior rules. They can be used for their humor as simple flannel board stories or as dramatic productions with props and costumes. They can be adapted for art activities as well.

Many of the Mother Goose tales are found in collections. A large collection will offer many rhymes that the teacher may never have seen or heard. They can be used at story time, circle time, or even for transitions. "Jack be nimble, Jack be

[1] Liz Cromwell and Dixie Hibner, *Finger Frolics* (New York: Gryphon Press, 1976).

quick . . . '' can be a transition rhyme for leaving the room. Children can say the rhyme as they jump over a paper candlestick while leaving the room one by one. Several Mother Goose tales have been made into picture books with beautiful illustrations. *Old Mother Hubbard and Her Dog* by Sarah Catherine Martin is a good example.

In addition to Mother Goose, rhymes from other countries or collections such as *Gregory Griggs and Other Nursery Rhyme People* by Arnold Lobel are also useful. For example, "The Farmer of Leeds" is a wonderful spring rhyme about the grass growing. It can lead into a grass growing activity using sponges. The sponges can be cut into the shape of a person and grass seeds may be added. If placed upright in a dish of water, grass hair will sprout. Such an activity adds much to the enjoyment of the rhymes.

Nursery Rhymes

Collections of Mother Goose and other nursery rhymes have always been passed around, added to, changed, and revised. Some were originally written as political satires poking fun at the king or government from the safety of street songs and children's rhymes. These changes explain why rhymes vary from country to country and from region to region within a country.

"Mary Had a Little Lamb" is an example of a Mother Goose rhyme that was added to the collection well after many of the original rhymes were written. The tale was originally written by Sarah Josepha Hale and was first published in 1830. Contemporary writers such as Ruth I. Dowell are continuing to add to the Mother Goose collection with such tantalizing titles as "I'm rather short Larry Bird," "Pennsylvania Pete," "Mama's Poppin' Popcorn," and "Myrtle Was a Turtle."

The traditions and wording of rhymes are important to children. The tongue twisters and secret words found in so many rhymes are like echoes of ancient fireside rituals. They provide children with reassurance and control over the mysteries of the adult world. Such carefully followed advice as "Step on a crack, break your mother's back" or "See a pin and pick it up, all the day you'll have good luck" are part of our treasured childhood memories.

FABLES/FOLK TALES/FAIRY TALES

For young children, the use of fables, folk tales, and fairy tales is a treat that teaches and inspires. These tales are often the vehicle for teaching a society's value system, but many are now enjoyed for the stories themselves. Handed down through oral tradition, they were told to each new generation by storytellers, people revered by earlier cultures.

Fables

A fable is a story used to teach a moral to people. While most fables use animals as the characters, this is not always the case. Fables with animal characters are called beast fables. Other fables may use people or inanimate objects as charac-

Mother Goose stories can be a good foundation to build on. Illustration by Richard Walz, reprinted by permission of Grosset and Dunlap from *The Pudgy Book of Mother Goose*, illustrations © 1984 by Richard Walz.

ters. Fables are found in every culture throughout the world. In the West, people are most familiar with the fables credited to Aesop. Many other fables have also become part of the English speaking tradition. These include Uncle Remus stories by Joel Chandler Harris, as well as Rudyard Kipling's *Jungle Books.* Phrases from the fables often find their way into common language: ''That's just sour grapes,'' or ''No use crying over spilt milk.''

Fables can be used for both enjoyment and discussion of the morals of the stories. Classroom activities related to fables include creating fables about school rules or table manners, illustrating the fables, and acting out the fables.

Folk Tales

Folk tales are the common man's fairy tale. They are unadorned stories. As with fairy tales and legends, folk tales share common plots where good overcomes evil and justice is served. Every culture possesses these tales. They serve to explain society, history, and natural phenomena and offer a sense of security while sometimes poking fun at things people wish to change.

Fairy Tales

Fairy tales are folk stories or legends in which an author incorporates additional aspects of literature. They tend to be more involved and more polished than folk tales and legends.

Concern has been expressed by some about the impact of these tales on young children. They can be frightening and sometimes include violence. The justice served in the tales can be swift and bloody and some of the tales are grim and graphic. The best judge of whether these stories should be used is someone who knows the children. However, one should consider the fact that childhood is full of frightening monsters and unknown fears. Adults sometimes fail to realize that children will invent these fearsome characters as part of their way of developing coping skills. Using the tales may help children by providing positive role models. Listening to stories about the devotion of the good characters and the destruction of evil forces can reassure children that their own inner conflicts and fears will likewise be settled and resolved positively.

Fairy tales provide heroes who at times use their might. Unlike television characters, however, the hero of a fairy tale will more often use wit, cleverness, and intelligence to defeat a foe. These are admirable traits for a child to aspire to.

There are some tales that one should take care in using due to their excessive violence. There are some versions that include less violence and might be suitable for young listeners. Children do find the tales both enjoyable and reassuring. The endings always seem to reaffirm that the world is right again and that order has been restored.

Different Versions

Contrasting different versions of the same story is a way to explore the content and to help children respond to the stories. Children can be encouraged to discuss how they feel about the stories and the varied resolutions of the plot. Take, for example, the story of Hansel and Gretel. It is a scary story which can reaffirm the importance of parental care, the danger of going off alone, and the resolution of a child's fear of being alone. The story addresses the themes of stepmother and stranger. In one version, retold by Linda Hayward, the wicked stepmother leaves and the children find their way home by their own devices. In another version, retold by Barbara Shook Hazen, the children cleverly escape from the witch, leave with a bag of jewels, and return home to find a reformed and repentant stepmother with whom they live happily ever after. After reading the two versions, one might discuss with the children which version they liked best and their reasons for choosing that version.

A class discussion allows children to bring up hidden fears and issues. Verbalizing can help children understand that others also share and understand their feelings. It is important to validate children's rights to their feelings. One should not allow ridicule or negative attitudes to impede these discussions.

Fairy tales are a part of childhood. Illustration by Karen Milone, reprinted by permission of Troll Associates from *The Wild Swans* by Hans Christian Anderson, © 1981 by Troll Associates.

Legends

Ethnic tales, myths, and legends lend themselves to the preschool program. For example, when teaching about the earth traveling around the sun, the Greek myth about Apollo and his chariot can be included. When teaching about safety and the need to avoid yelling in the pool or yard, the story of "The Boy Who Cried Wolf" clearly illustrates the dangers in pretending to need help. When learning about sharing, "The Fisherman and His Wife" can illustrate what happens when greed gets out of control.

Folk tales and legends can encourage language acquisition with their effective use of repetition of words and word sounds such as "Fee, fie, foe, fum"; "All the better to see you with my dear"; and "Who is the fairest of them all?" Children naturally join in with the words of the story. Local tales, ethnic legends and ethnic tales can also be helpful in integrating minority children into the mainstream within the classroom. Sharing one's cultural heritage is a strengthening and unifying way to build understanding among children while helping each child's ego development. Parents, churches, and libraries can often supply tapes or stories that would meet the needs of the class. Cultural storytellers can also be invited to come into the class to tell tales to the children.

PICTURE BOOKS/WORDLESS PICTURE BOOKS

A picture book is a special kind of book for a special audience. Unlike the child who can read many words, younger children gain much of their understanding of a story from the illustrations and through listening to the story. A picture book must possess a well developed plot, theme, setting, and characterization. It should also use an appropriate style, print dimension, and page size. In addition, a picture book must have a special unity between text and illustration. The two must provide an understandable telling of the story for those who are not yet fluent readers. Picture books take this one step further by providing a story through effective illustrations. The words printed on the page are not usually necessary to comprehend the action, flow, and intent of the story. The author, illustrator, and reader enjoy a communal experience that transcends the written language.

One Frog Too Many by Mercer and Marianna Mayer is an illustrated wordless picture book done in brown pen. In this book, the reader empathizes with the little frog who must adjust to a new smaller frog as his little boy's new pet. His anger, fear, jealousy, vengeance, sorrow, and happiness draws readers into the story. With exceptional clarity, the emotions are shared with the reader as the plot unfolds to its happy ending. All of this interaction and sharing takes place without one word of text; the pictures alone tell the story.

The picture book isn't really a type of book as are the other categories, but emphasis needs to be given due to its unique place in children's literature. Although the rest of the books discussed are nearly all picture books, they focus on different concepts or types of stories.

CONCEPT BOOKS

Concept books, which include counting and ABC books, are an area of children's literature that has seen tremendous growth and some interesting developments over the past few years. They may be pop-up books, pop-out books, poke-through-the-hole books, puppet books, books cut into shapes, books cut into puzzles, big books, mini books, and textured books. With such talented artists as Peter Seymour, Tana Hoban, Eric Carle, Richard Scarry, and Dr. Seuss involved, it is not a problem finding a concept book. Rather, the problem is making a decision as to which is most appropriate for a particular purpose. Concept books are fun to use and they help motivate children to want to learn about spatial concepts, numbers, and colors.

In selecting concept books, some general guidelines might be kept in mind. First, the concept should be clearly described and illustrated in the book. The facts included should have validity. If the book is about magnetism, the illustrations shouldn't show a magnet picking up pennies because magnets are not attracted to copper. The illustrations should possess numerical accuracy as well. If a counting book indicates that there are five objects on a page, there should be five objects on the page. The presentation of the concept should be interesting. If the teacher has to struggle to keep the children focused on the book, the book is probably boring. A good concept book motivates children to use it. They will want to listen to the story and look at the pictures. All books should be constructed sturdily so that children can use them after the teacher has presented them. Finally, the book should have a sustaining factor. The children should be drawn back to the book after the initial reading by an adult. If this does not occur, perhaps it wasn't appropriate in the first place. These guidelines, of course, assume that other criteria including age-appropriateness were followed as well.

Counting Books

Many teachers will use several different books for each concept they teach. If the concept is counting, for example, it could be introduced with Eric Carle's *I, 2, 3 to the Zoo.* This could be followed with Tana Hoban's *Count and See* in the block corner. The book could be left there so children could use it with the blocks later. At storytime, the teacher could read aloud Amy Ehrlich's *The Everyday Train,* followed by an art activity using a train and numbers. The day could end with a reading of Ezra Jack Keats's *Over in the Meadow* and a homework mission for children to check their own yards for things read about in the story. The books can always be left out for the children to use independently in the classroom. They will often discover that it is more fun to share counting with a friend using books and blocks than to use a workbook page or a ditto to learn the same concept. The social skills used are also developmentally beneficial for children. Additional activities that can be coordinated with concept books include creating concept books with real objects and magazine pictures, creating concept posters centered around a book, and acting out a concept with blocks, pillows, or other props.

Alphabet (ABC) Books

The alphabet comprises most of the symbols used in our written language. The more comfortable children become with the letters and their sounds, the less confusing written language will be for them. Since it should not be expected that children will learn the letters and sounds until the elementary school grades, there should be no pressure on them to repeat, write, or memorize the letters. If children learn the letters on their own that is fine, but it should not be an expectation. The goal is familiarity and confidence with language and meaning.

Books such as this can reinforce the understanding of many basic concepts.
Courtesy Delmar Publishers Inc.

Alphabet books have a long history. Many illustrators of both children's and adult books have designed ABC books in their careers. In fact, there are literally hundreds of alphabet books from which to choose. They are found in every imaginable illustration technique from wood carving to etching to photography.

Selecting Alphabet Books

In selecting ABC books, certain general criteria may be helpful. The objects depicting the letters should be an appropriate size and readily identifiable. A limited number of objects should be used, perhaps one or two per letter. The lettering choice should be particularly legible. Ordinarily, the letter is best placed on the page with the illustrations. The objects should be clearly representative of the sound of the letter. The design of the book should be colorful and attractive.

It is important that these criteria be considered. It is especially important that the page is not so overwhelming that the child is unable to successfully find the letter and objects. Another key aspect is that the letter sounds should be heard clearly in the name of the objects used. For example, the letter "T" should use objects such as a tiger, top, or teacup for its illustration, rather than objects in which the "T" sound is blended, such as three, tree, or throat. Other letters one might examine in ABC books include "S," "W," and "D." The letters "C" and "G" should be illustrated with objects representing the hard sound of the letter (e.g., cat for "C"; girl for "G"). The concept of hard and soft sounds for the same letter is often confusing to young children.

Humor is often found in successful ABC books. The humor may emerge in the method of presentation as in *The Alphabet Tale* by Jan Garten where the tails precede the letters and animals by one page. It can also appear in the choice of verse as found in Edward Lear's *An Edward Lear Alphabet.*

There is a variety of ABC books that are particularly striking. *Cindy Szekere's ABC* by the author of the same name features excellent definitions, sturdy construction, and brilliant colors. Sandra Boynton's *A Is for Angry* includes large letters, each assigned an emotion. *Brian Wildsmith's ABC,* possesses stunning colors and striking contrasts. The same is true for *Bruno Munari's ABC.* City scenes with a superb multicultural appeal are featured in Rachel Isadora's *City Seen from A to Z.*

Alphabet Activities

As with numbers, a set of coordinated activities to go along with alphabet books may be developed. After reading an animal alphabet book, children can draw or paint an animal for a particular letter. After reading an object ABC book, a letter hunt can be organized to search the room for objects beginning with the same letter. Cooking something beginning with a certain letter can be combined with other concepts. If the letter is "S," one could make strawberry sundaes. The letter "N" could be reinforced by having each child cook nine noodles. The group could construct its own tactile alphabet book, alphabet sock puppets, or language-experience story. A language-experience story is a story dictated by the children and recorded by the teacher on the chalkboard or a poster book. The story is ordinarily about an experience all the children understand or have shared. If a language experience story is used, perhaps using words beginning with a particular letter, the focus should be on meaning rather than on memorizing a letter. It should always be remembered that the main function of learning about letters is to arrive at the meaning of the printed words.

FICTION: REALISTIC FICTION/FANTASY FICTION

The main purpose of fiction is to entertain the reader. However, its purpose is often to inform and persuade as well. Fiction is a narrative that comes from the imagination of the author rather than from history or factual information. Fiction gives the reader the author's vision of reality in concrete terms.

Realistic Fiction

Realistic fiction is a story that could have happened, and some parts of it may be from the author's own experiences. The author of realistic fiction is often trying to help children deal with a situation or problem. The world is presented as the author perceives it. The reader is not asked to believe in purple cows or singing dogs. Yet this is still fiction because the scenes, characters, and dialogues spring from the author's imagination. Robert Cormier, in explaining his purpose in writing realistic fiction, stated, " . . . I was trying to write realistically even though I knew it would upset some people. The fact is the good guys don't always win in real life . . . I also wanted to indict those who don't try to help, who remain indifferent in the face of evil or wrongdoing. They are as bad or probably worse than the villains themselves."[2]

Realistic fiction helps children confront the good and bad human feelings within all of us. It allows readers to recognize that all people share these same human emotions and thoughts. Readers are able to explore their own feelings from a safe distance through the characters. An example of realistic fiction is *Lost in the Storm* by Carol Carrick. The story deals with a dog lost in an island storm and the anguished search of his owner to find him. *The Tenth Good Thing about Barney* by Judith Viorst helps children learn to cope with death, in this case, the death of a pet cat. Other topics that realistic fiction may help young children understand include separation, school social situation, divorce, old age, illness, and sibling rivalry.

Historical Fiction

Realistic fiction also includes historical fiction, which provides an imaginary story based on a historical event or person. The author goes beyond the facts to create a fictional piece. An increasing number of books are becoming available in this area. Brinton Turkle's books about Obadiah are a series of historical but fictional accounts of Nantucket Island in colonial times. Jean Fritz has written a series of historical fiction works including *And Then What Happened, Paul Revere?, What's the Big Idea, Ben Franklin?* and *George Washington's Breakfast.* Each story presents a lively account of history and includes notes containing additional facts at the end of each book. Ann McGovern's, *Wanted: Dead or Alive* is the story of Harriet Tubman. In *Wagon Wheels,* Barbara Brenner explores the westward expansion of the nineteenth century. Eleanor Coerr details the life of Carlotta Myers, the nineteenth century balloonist, in *The Big Balloon Race.* Many of these books pro-

---

[2] Betsy Hearne and Marilyn Kaye (Eds.), *Celebrating Children's Books* (New York: Lothrop, Lee & Shepard, 1981), 48.

vide an added bonus by including women and minorities in nontraditional roles. Historical fiction written at a higher reading level can also be read aloud.

Fantasy Fiction

Many of the stories written for children are fantasy stories. An author of a fantasy asks the reader to suspend the rules of reality. A fantasy takes place in a non-existent world and may include unreal characters. The use of physical or scientific principles unknown to the reader's experience is also found in fantasies. Mirra Ginsburg's retelling of the Armenian tale, *Where Does the Sun Go at Night?* is an example of fantasy. Through Ariane Dewey's and Jose Aruego's illustrations, readers visualize the sun being tucked in at night, animals sleeping or traveling on clouds, and other delightfully outrageous sights.

In fantasy, imagination is stretched and brought into an art form. The author, illustrator, and reader all share the new experience. Fantasy is accepted readily by children because their imaginations allow the belief that anything is possible. Magic, imaginary worlds, and marvelous creatures are all real to children. What they can imagine, can exist. Paula Fox explains, "imagination is random and elusive. We deduce its presence by its effects, just as we deduce that a breeze has sprung up, a breeze we can't see, because we hear and see the rustling of the leaves in a tree. It is the guardian spirit that we sense in all great stories; we feel its rustling."[3]

A sense of humor is a powerful and positive coping mechanism not only for children, but for adults as well. It helps one to deal with the stress of modern life. The humor often found in fantasy fiction is contagious and healing. Few children can resist the silliness in Judi Barrett's *Animals Should Definitely Wear Clothes.* It hits preschoolers right in the funnybone. *Cloudy with a Chance of Meatballs,* also by Judi Barrett, creates a crazy world with pancakes and maple syrup covering the streets. A world is constructed that is quite different from the child's reality. The antics of the city-dwelling Lyle the crocodile, a character in several of Bernard Waber's books, amuse and delight young readers. Susan Ramsey Hoguet has a winner in the book, *I Unpacked My Grandmother's Trunk.* In this story, both the main character and the reader enjoy the items found in the trunk. Since the trunk contains everything from igloos to a live bear, it is just the kind of book toddlers and preschoolers love to have read again and again.

Fantasy fiction may have absurd characters, imaginary characters, or animals who behave as people. Fantasy fiction can be based on real world settings, or call for reality to be totally suspended and substitute almost anything in its place. Yet all fiction must still provide the basic components of a clearly defined plot, believable characters, an appropriate setting, and relevant themes. Without these skillfully woven into the story, the book fails to move the reader. *Sarah's Unicorn* by Bruce Coville is a superb example of fantasy fiction with each of these elements combined in a way that makes the reader truly care about the outcome.

[3] Hearne and Kaye, *Celebrating Children's Books,* 24. (New York: Harper & Row, 1987).

Children are willing to suspend their beliefs in order to enjoy a story about a frog driving a motorcycle. Illustration from *Fun on Wheels*, Delmar Publishers Inc.

NONFICTION/INFORMATIONAL BOOKS

Nonfiction books are written for the purpose of providing factual information. Such books for young readers use either a text or a narrative format. The latter is often used because of its familiarity to children. The author of such books has an obligation to impart only accurate information to children. Misinformation, misleading information, and outdated information should be clarified for the children. It doesn't matter if there is no fault attached to the cause of the misinformation. Such inaccuracies may occur because a book is outdated or because new information has been discovered.

Presenting Information

Antiquated books can be useful for showing children how people used to think about a topic, but the teacher should ensure that children understand the correct information. Children should become aware of the fact that information is not absolute, especially in the area of science. The teacher should always preface science information presentations with such phrases as, "At this time, this is the information that we believe to be true about . . . " Children will gain from the understanding that information changes with more research. For example, a book about animals that states that giraffes make no sound need not be discarded. The photographs of the giraffe and perhaps much of the text can still be used. The teacher can simply add the correct information. Although it was once thought that giraffes made no sound, it is now known that they do make throaty sounds and do communicate.

Learning that information changes fosters the beginnings of critical thinking. A child with a specific interest may also have more current information than either the book or the teacher. Children should be encouraged to question information they feel is wrong. Also, resource books and telephone calls to verify information teach children, through example, an important lesson: a primary reason for learning to read is to find answers to questions.

Subtle misconceptions can trickle into a curriculum through a lack of knowledge. The same teacher who would never knowingly bring prejudice into the classroom by reading offensive material might perpetuate misconceptions about Indians and pilgrims at Thanksgiving. Will the children learn that Indians no longer live the way they did during colonial times? Will the teacher update the class on current Indian lifestyles? If not, then an inaccurate portrayal of an entire cultural group is being given to every child in the class. The sensitive teacher will provide the whole truth whenever factual information is being provided.

In choosing factual books, certain guidelines may be helpful to consider:

1. The book should be checked for accuracy of information;
2. Note the copyright date to ensure that the material is as up-to-date as possible;
3. When charts or pictures are used, they should be simple, clear, and easy to read;
4. The readability of the material should be appropriate for the children's age level.

POETRY

Poetry is not stuffy! It is not boring! It is not just for greeting cards! A poem is a song without notes. It is the form used for the most intense and imaginative writing about our world and ourselves. Poetry is lyrical, succinct, heart-touching, and also great fun. The poet selects each word carefully so the impact of what is said and meant is startling to the reader or listener. No matter what the rhyme patterns, the rhythm and the cadence attract children in much the same way as a song or a jingle. The descriptive use of language conjures up visions in the head of the reader, much like watching a movie or actually witnessing the subject of the poem. Winnie-the-Pooh is a favorite poetic character, yet few children are consciously aware that the story of Christopher Robin is written in poetry. They just know that the story is a favorite.

Poetic Devices

Formal poetry has metered verse. It uses syllables, line length, and special structures to create the differences in haiku, tanka, cinquain, sonnet, limerick, and two-word poetry. There are several frequently used word devices in poetry that has been written specifically for children. Onomatopoeia is the use of specific words because their sound suggests what is happening in the poem (e.g., pop, sizzle, hiss, bang). Personification occurs when human characteristics or emotions are given to inanimate objects or animals (e.g., Pop, pop, pop! I'm inside out and warm and hot! Do not fail to put butter and salt on my top!). A simile is used to compare two things that are different, using words such as "like" and "as" (e.g., the puddle was as wet as a puppy's nose or her hair was as soft as a fire's glow). A metaphor is an analogy that gives some of the characteristics of one object to a second object (e.g., my crumb of bread is the giant feasty for all the little ants and buglike beasties). Alliteration is the repetition of the initial consonant of a word several times in a line (e.g., Little Lyle laughed loudly).

Using Poetry

With young children, poetry written beyond their reading level can be used. It should be read with expression and tied to the children's level of understanding. Corrine Bostic's lovely poem, "Earth's Melody," is enjoyable for both young and old:

> I like to feel the sunshine on my face
> While lying in some isolated place.
> I like to hear the pelting of the rain
> And watch unchartered rivers in the lane.
> I like to hear the roaring of the surf,
> To hear birds sing in harmony with earth.
> I like the coolness offered by a tree
> And listening to the wind's soothing melody.
> And when I sit and ponder o'er the plan,
> Then it seems as if the world and I walk hand in hand.

> *Permission courtesy of Walter Bostic*

Settling down for naptime on a rainy day or lying on the playground lawn are wonderful times to read this poem.

Dorothy Aldis and Leland B. Jacobs also write simple, self-explanatory poems. They write about everyday things like curbstones and the circus. "Hush-a-bye Baby" is a simple poem inspired by the native American custom of hanging cradles from birch trees. It was written by a pilgrim who was impressed by the custom.[4] It has been called the first poem of rhyme written in the new world, a lullabye rhyme:

---

[4] Charles Panati, *Extraordinary Origins of Everyday Things* (New York: Harper & Row, 1987).

Hush-a-bye baby, on the treetop,
When the wind blows, the cradle will rock.
When the bough breaks, the cradle will fall,
And down will come baby, cradle and all.

This Boston area version of the lullabye first appeared in print in 1765 in *Mother Goose's Melody.* Children have no problem understanding the meaning of the piece, but adding this other information makes it more interesting.

Shel Silverstein is one of the best known children's poets. He captures children's imaginations with topics from spaghetti to trees. His black and white line illustrations add much to his fine words.

Robert Louis Stevenson and Henry Wadsworth Longfellow are two traditional favorites. Many little girls, especially on off days, feel a kindred spirit with Longfellow's daughter who inspired the poem that begins, "There was a little girl, who had a little curl right in the middle of her forehead . . . " If a child is sick in bed, Stevenson's "The Land of Counterpane" is MUST reading. It is especially comforting when the child can use toy soldiers to act out the sheet battles. Stevenson's language is always vivid. From the poem "My Shadow," note the expressive lines:

For he sometimes shoots up taller
 like an India rubber ball,
And he sometimes gets so little
 that there's none of him at all.

Stevenson's lines show how timeless and universal good poetry can be for children. Many fine poets have written verses for children: Walter de la Mare, Langston Hughes, Edward Lear, Lewis Carroll, John Ciardi, Ogden Nash, Carl Sandburg, William Blake, and Eve Merriam.

Fostering Creativity with Poetry

Poetry lends itself to visual creativity as well. Robert Froman puts the poem into the form of the theme. For example, in his book *Seeing Things: A Book of Poems,* a poem about a guitar might be shaped like a guitar. This concrete format is especially appropriate for early childhood as it can be both seen and heard.

Edward Lear is considered the father of nonsense poetry. His *Book of Nonsense,* published in 1846, began the collection of limericks, poems, and rhymes known as nonsense poems.

Two-word poetry is an easy way to involve young children in creating nonsense verse. The two words, one a noun and one an adjective, can rhyme or not. They can be silly or not. They can be added to other two-word verses to create larger nonsense poems. Illustrations are always a pleasant follow-up to a poem such as:

Sleeping farmer rubbed his purple eyes.
A polka-dot pig with a talking dog.
Wow cow and golly gee, what a sight to see.

It may not be memorable poetry, but it is fun and demonstrates the sense of creativity and excitement that surrounds poetry.

Finally, no discussion of poetry for children would be complete without considering the work of Jack Prelutsky. A prolific writer, his books address most of the major holidays with such titles as *It's Valentine's Day, It's Thanksgiving,* and *It's Christmas.* Other titles such as *Rainy, Rainy Saturday, Rolling Harvey down the Hill* and *The New Kid on the Block* address themes from loneliness, to friendship, to family relationships.

Selecting Poetry

Criteria for selecting poetry to use with children should focus on content rather than the technical aspects of meter and rhyme scheme. The poetry should be melodic with the rhythm and beat alive and clear. It should have vivid language. While poetry can be about any thought-provoking topic, it should be interesting and relevant to the audience. A variety of classic, contemporary, nonsense, and one's own poetry should be included to give children a broad exposure. This will allow children to appreciate all types of poetry and to develop individual preferences. One should always remember that poetry is meant to be read aloud. Decide how the poem ought to be read before reading it to an audience. Then, read it with feeling.

When introducing a poem, it is important to set the mood for what is to come. Care should be taken not to over-explain the poem prior to the reading. Since poetry touches us in different ways, children should be allowed to experience the poem with their own imaginations. Never make children memorize a poem. Reread it often if the children enjoy it, but don't require memorization. Use an abundance of humorous poetry. Start writing poetry for the children as soon as the reading of poetry is introduced. The two are partners in developing a full appreciation and enjoyment of poetry.

AWARDS AND PRIZES IN CHILDREN'S LITERATURE

Outstanding works by children's authors and illustrators are recognized through a variety of awards and honors. These include formal awards and medals, magazine awards, and library awards. The most famous award for picture books is the Caldecott Medal. This American award is given each year to an illustrator by the Association for Library Services to Children. The Caldecott Medal is named for the British illustrator of children's books, Randolph Caldecott (1846–1886). It was first given in 1937 when Frederic G. Melcher established it, as he had the Newbury Award in 1922. The Caldecott Medal is limited to a resident or citizen of the United States. It is ironic that this "Americans only" award is named after a British subject. While not every well-known children's book illustrator has received this award, many have received either the medal itself or the honor medals given to runners-up. A Caldecott Medal-winning book has a gold seal with the award on the cover. Caldecott Honor Award-winning books have a silver seal on their covers.

A list of winning books provides a good starting point for a search for quality books. (Winners of the Caldecott Medal are listed in Appendix B.) However, it is important to remember that an award does not necessarily mean that a book is appropriate for class use or for a teacher's purpose. One should keep in mind that it is adults who give the award based on criteria developed by adults. The genuine award for a quality book is the enthusiastic response of generations of children to a particular work.

Other awards for excellence in children's poetry, illustrations, and writing are given in the United States and in other countries. The Kate Greenaway Medal is given by the British Library Association for distinguished work in the illustration of children's books. The Amelia Frances Howard-Gibbon Medal is a similar award given to a Canadian citizen by the Canada Library Association. The Laura Ingalls Wilder Award is given every three years by the Association for Library Services to Children to an author or illustrator whose books, published in the United States, have made a substantial contribution to children's literature. The Newbury Medal is given annually by the same organization to a United States author for the most distinguished contribution to children's literature during the past year. Other awards for children's literature are listed in *Children's Books: Awards and Prizes.*[5] Any time authors, poets, or illustrators win one of these prestigious awards, their work has been chosen from over 2,400 books printed annually.

To learn about new works by favorite illustrators or authors one can refer to *Books in Print,* published annually by R. R. Bowker. There are three volumes in the set: an index by author's name, an index by title, and a volume with publishers' updated information. If one is interested in specific subject matter, the four volume annual *Subject Guide to Books in Print* may be useful. It too is published by R. R. Bowker. All of these resources are found in the library.

SUMMARY

It is important to expose children to a wide variety of quality literature. The focus of exposing children to literature is, first and foremost, to gain meaning. This is an important step on the road to literacy. There is a tremendous range of literature available to young children. Even if children are not yet reading, they can benefit from listening to stories written several years above their reading level. The literature can be used to reinforce other activities or it can serve as a starting point for an activity. Basic to all of this is the fact that literature should help create meaning. It should serve as a means of enjoying our lives. It should help us to make sense of our world.

QUESTIONS FOR THOUGHT AND DISCUSSION

1. What is a fingerplay?
2. What is a chant?
3. What is a rhyme?

[5] Author, *Children's Books: Awards and Prizes* (New York: Children's Book Council, 1989).

4. What is the difference between fantasy and realistic fiction? Why should a teacher use each type?
5. Why should a teacher use Mother Goose tales?
6. How can fingerplays be used in the classroom?
7. What are the differences between fable, folk tale, and fairy tale?
8. What are the dangers of using fairy tales with young children? How can these dangers be avoided?
9. How should one select nonfiction books?
10. Why are picture books important in an early childhood classroom?
11. Why is it permissible to use poems that are written above a child's reading level?
12. How should one select poetry?
13. How should one use poetry with children?

CHILDREN'S BOOKS CITED

Judith Barrett, *Animals Should Definitely Wear Clothes* (New York: Atheneum, 1980).

Judith Barrett, *Cloudy with a Chance of Meatballs* (New York: Atheneum, 1978).

Sandra Boynton, *A Is for Angry* (New York: Workman, 1983).

Barbara Brenner, *Wagon Wheels* (New York: Harper & Row, 1978).

Eric Carle, *1, 2, 3 to the Zoo* (New York: Collins World, 1969).

Carol Carrick, *Lost in the Storm* (New York: Clarion, 1974).

Eleanor Coerr, *The Big Balloon Race* (New York: Harper & Row, 1981).

Bruce Coville, *Sarah's Unicorn* (New York: Harper & Row, 1979).

Amy Ehrlich, *The Everyday Train* (New York: Greenwillow, 1983).

Jean Fritz, *And Then What Happened, Paul Revere?* (New York: Coward-McCann, 1973).

Jean Fritz, *George Washington's Breakfast* (New York: Coward-McCann, 1969).

Jean Fritz, *What's the Big Idea, Ben Franklin?* (New York: Coward-McCann, 1976).

Robert Froman, *Seeing Things: A Book of Poems* (New York: Crowell, 1974).

Jan Garten, *The Alphabet Tale* (New York: Random House, 1964).

Mirra Ginsburg, *Where Does the Sun Go at Night?* (New York: Greenwillow, 1980).

Tana Hoban, *Count and See* (New York: Macmillan, 1972).

Susan Ramsey Hoguet, *I Unpacked My Grandmother's Trunk* (New York: Dutton, 1983).

Rachel Isadora, *City Seen from A to Z* (New York: Greenwillow, 1983).

Ezra Jack Keats, *Over in the Meadow* (New York: Four Winds, 1972).

Edward Lear, *An Edward Lear Alphabet* (New York: Lothrop, Lee & Shepard, 1983).

Edward Lear, *Book of Nonsense* (New York: Garland, 1976).

Arnold Lobel, *Gregory Griggs and Other Nursery Rhyme People* (New York: Greenwillow, 1978).

Sarah Catherine Martin, *Old Mother Hubbard and Her Dog* (New York: McGraw Hill, 1960).

Mercer and Marianna Mayer, *One Frog Too Many* (New York, Dial, 1975).

Ann McGovern, *Wanted: Dead or Alive* (New York: Scholastic, 1965).

Bruno Munari, *Bruno Munari's ABC* (New York: Collins-World, 1960).

Jack Prelutsky, *It's Christmas* (New York: Greenwillow, 1980).

Jack Prelutsky, *It's Thanksgiving* (New York: Greenwillow, 1982).

Jack Prelutsky, *It's Valentine's Day* (New York: Greenwillow, 1983).

Jack Prelutsky, *The New Kid on the Block* (New York: Greenwillow, 1984).

Jack Prelutsky, *Rainy, Rainy Saturday* (New York: Greenwillow, 1980).

Jack Prelutsky, *Rolling Harvey down the Hill* (New York: Greenwillow, 1980).

Cindy Szekere, *Cindy Szekere's ABC* (Racine, WI: Western, 1983).

Judith Viorst, *Alexander and the Terrible, Horrible, No Good, Very Bad Day* (New York: Atheneum, 1972).

Judith Viorst, *The Tenth Good Thing about Barney* (New York: Atheneum, 1971).

Brian Wildsmith, *Brian Wildsmith's ABC* (New York: Watts Franklin, 1962).

SELECTED REFERENCES

Kathleen M. Bayless and Marjorie Ramsay, *Music: A Way of Life* (Chicago: Scott Foresman, 1985).

Bruno Bettelheim, *The Uses of Enchantment* (New York: Knopf, 1976).

Andrea Cascardi, *Children's Books: Awards and Prizes* (New York: Children's Book Council, 1987).

J. H. Dileo, *Young Children and Their Drawings* (New York: Bruner-Mazel, 1970).

Daniel N. Fader and E. B. McNeil, *Hooked on Books: Program and Proof* (New York: Berkeley, 1968).

Michele Landsberg, *Reading for the Love of It: Best Books for Young Readers* (New York: Prentice Hall, 1987).

V. Lowenfeld and N. L. Brittain, *Creative and Mental Growth* (New York: Macmillan, 1982).

E. Pitcher and L. Schultz, *Boys and Girls at Play: The Development of Sex Roles* (South Hadley, MA: Bergin & Garvey, 1983).

John Warren Stewig, *Children and Literature* (Boston: Houghton Mifflin, 1988).

Jim Trelease, *The New Read-Aloud Handbook* (New York: Viking Penquin, 1989).

Jean Warren, *More Piggyback Songs* (Everett, WA: Warren, 1984).

5 Magic Motivations

"ou gotta shake, shake, shake your sillies out" is the start of a wonderful song by Raffi, the popular singer of children's music. Raffi knows, as does every teacher, that young children need to wriggle. Even when they try to be still they seem to shake, shimmy, and move about. The individual movements of each child combine with those of others in a subtle wrestling ballet. This interaction can progress, if left unattended, into a brawl.

Every teacher has experienced the following situation: Child one taps child two . . . child two reacts with a subtle kick of child one . . . child one counters with a leg pinch . . . child two holds in a yell while stretching a leg into child one's back . . . child one escalates the action with a solid shove . . . and so on. When it becomes visible, adults intervene and one or both children are likely to be reprimanded. The fact of the matter, however, is that much has occurred before the adult saw what was happening. Therefore, the reprimand may be directed toward the wrong child and toward an activity that was merely a reaction to something else. It is critical for the teacher to understand how to help children listen, focus on appropriate behaviors, and benefit from the learning situation.

CAPTURING THE ATTENTION OF CHILDREN

Totally eliminating unacceptable peer behaviors may not be possible. However, much can be done to decrease them. Children often engage in inappropriate behaviors when they do not perceive any acceptable behaviors that are of interest to them. Many poor behaviors can be avoided or minimized by using a combination of planning, common sense, and creativity in the presentation of stories. Nevertheless, the teacher who attempts to have perfectly still and quiet children during any activity, including a story reading, is destined to fail. This does not mean that children cannot sit reasonably still or that they should not be expected to listen. Rather, much of the success will depend on realistic expectations of children's behavior as well as the teacher's ability to interest, motivate, and plan for the children. Planning to work with the normal wriggles and giggles makes more sense than trying to totally eliminate them.

Transitions are important for all young children. One should not expect children to leave free play or an outdoor activity and immediately sit still for a story.

Without some type of a transition, a smooth change from one activity to another is nearly impossible for many children. Once settled with a transition song or fingerplay, the children must want to listen to the story. For this to happen, the teacher must set the stage for the story. By doing this effectively, the teacher will motivate the children to want to listen.

Listening is a crucial language skill as well as an important socialization life skill. Telling and reading stories to children can help them increase their listening attention span in a natural and enjoyable manner. Assuming that the book choice is appropriate and that the setting for telling the story is comfortable, one can consider other factors that affect the story reading.

Planning the Sharing of a Story

Planning a lesson is an interesting and challenging activity for anyone who understands how the teacher, child, and story must interact. Too often, reading a story appears to be so simple a process that a plan is forgotten or not developed. A good lesson plan stretches the teacher's thinking to include planning for disaster. Planning for potential problems within a story sharing session can help eliminate them. The teacher must plan for wriggles, giggles, and other possible disruptions. This can be done by analyzing not only the choice of books, but the method of presentation as well. A lesson plan is an organized way to look at the components of a lesson. It allows one to see how the various pieces fit together, what is missing, and what can be changed. It can also provide a record of the title, author, and publisher of the book as well as the children's response to the story. This record will assist the teacher in revising the plan for the next time the book is shared with children. A lesson plan form makes the recording and planning easier. Figure 1 contains a sample lesson plan form.

Objectives. After listing the specific book to be used, the four major parts of the plan are objectives, motivation, sharing procedures, and evaluation. Objectives refer to the changes you would like to see in the child as a result of interacting with the story. With literature, many of the changes would be related to feelings, attitudes, discovery of self, and new understandings of the world. Objectives focused primarily on remembering factual information from a story are misguided when using literature with young children. Literature should help the individual grow as a person. Take, for example, the reading of a story in which one of the characters is blind. It is far better for a child to learn about the common humanity of all people regardless of their disability than for the child to learn a definition for the word "blind." In most cases, recalling something such as the specific disability isn't nearly as important as the message for understanding and accepting human differences. Therefore, it is important to think carefully about what a book should accomplish. The teacher must consider the curriculum, the book's purpose, and the development of the children in deciding upon the objectives of the lesson.

Motivation. Motivation is a critical key to successful story times. Simply stated, motivation is the process of leading children into a desire to listen to and interact

Literature Lesson Plan

Subject _____   Date _____

Title _____   Author _____

Publisher _____   Year of Publ. _____

Source (if applicable) _____

Materials Needed _____

Concepts included: _____

Objectives: At the end of the lesson, the students will . . .

1. _____

2. _____

Motivation: To involve the children, I will . . .

_____

_____

_____

Sharing: To achieve the lesson objectives, I will . . .

_____

_____

_____

_____

Evaluation: At the conclusion, the children will be able to . . .

_____

_____

_____

Attach file card with any poem or fingerplay used by teacher.

Figure 1.   Literature lesson plan. Courtesy Walter Sawyer.

with the story. It is the way children come to see the story as having interest and meaning for themselves. Story motivations can include the use of objects, sounds, fingerplays, games, and personal recollections. Objects such as mystery boxes, silk scarves, and large feathers can bring fun to the activity. Motivations are usually brief, but can be more lengthy if necessary. A good motivation is best judged by how well it works.

Consider the possibilities for sharing *The Berenstain Bears and the Spooky Old Tree* by Stan and Jan Berenstain. Before the lesson, one might place a stick, a piece of rope, and a flashlight into a box or bag. The teacher could then ask the children to feel the objects and guess what they are. By suggesting how these relate to the story, the children now have a personal interest and involvement. Approaching the same story from a different direction, one might display a large picture of a bear. The teacher would ask the children how they might feel if they met such a bear. With just a bit of acting, the teacher might fearfully shake all over while explaining fears. With a frightened voice, the teacher could ask the children what kinds of things scare them. This particular story is just a bit scary, but great fun for even older infants and toddlers. The excitement mounts as readers follow the bear children through the spooky old tree. All ends well. The teacher should remember to wink at the children from time to time while pretending to be scared. This subtle clue will assure children that it is all in fun while still maintaining the feeling of being scared.

Consider the book *Peter Pan* by James M. Barrie as another example. The teacher might begin by gazing around the room and calling softly to TinkerBell. By sprinkling a bit of glitter in the air, the children would see the "fairy dust" and know that Tink is near. The teacher could also brandish a pirate sword while growling a few of Captain Hook's lines about catching Peter Pan. The teacher might also begin by holding a stuffed dog while making barking sounds. Looking around the room, the teacher might ask the children what they think the dog is barking at. After a few guesses, it can be explained that Nanna the dog is the only one who saw something strange in the night sky. Following this, the teacher could invite the children to find out what Nanna saw on that special night.

If the book used is *The Snowman* by Raymond Briggs, one could motivate the children by hiding a real miniature snowman behind one's back. After guessing what is being hidden, the children could be shown the snowman. This might be followed by asking them if they would like to have a real live snowman to play with. An alternative activity might include a pantomime of the making of a snowman. Still another idea might involve the placing of a scarf, hat, and pieces of coal in a box or bag. After identifying the items, children could be asked to think of something that could be made using these items.

The ideas and objects used to motivate children are only limited by the teacher's imagination. Some motivational objects can be held by the children during the story. If a particular child has difficulty attending to a story, that child might be asked to hold the stuffed animal or to wear the fireman's hat. Some teachers use a rotating list of students for sharing the story motivation objects. A clever teacher keeps an eye open at yard sales and flea markets for stuffed toys and props to be used as future motivation tools. Post-holiday sales are good sources for materials related to holiday stories.

Sharing. The plan for sharing a story should include ideas for making the story interesting and meaningful to children. Jim Trelease's *The Read-Aloud Handbook* contains an excellent chapter on the "do's" and "don'ts" of reading a book to children.[1] From Jim Trelease's summary, one can form a number of questions to

---

[1] Jim Trelease, *The Read-Aloud Handbook* (Newark, Delaware: International Reading Association, 1989).

Teacher with cotton ''snow'' prepares the children to focus on an upcoming story about winter. Courtesy Diana Comer.

consider when developing the plan for the actual reading of picture books: How will I make sure that everyone can see the pictures? Will I read every word, or will I summarize some parts? What pace or speed of reading will I use? What can I tell the children about the author? Will I have the children draw a picture of the story as I read, in order to keep their hands busy? Where are the suspenseful parts where I can pause for questions and discussion?

In addition to these questions, one should keep in mind some additional factors. First, make sure there is enough time to finish the book. Secondly, try to use a variety of unfamiliar books. It is more difficult to create interest in a book when children already know what is going to happen. Finally, be prepared for the involvement of children. Allow them to ask questions at appropriate times. Let them know when such times arrive. Discuss the story with them. Accept interpretations of the story that differ from one's own.

The end of the sharing should include a closure. Closure refers to a procedure for recalling all of the important points of the story. At this level, however, enjoyment and language growth will be the most common objectives. These are best assessed by observing the children's attention to the story and by listening to their discussion about the story.

Evaluation. The evaluation is the final part of the plan. At this point one needs to see if the objectives were met. This is when the teacher attempts to honestly determine what worked, what did not, and what could be changed to improve the story presentation the next time it is used. The sharing of the story can lead into the evaluation, which could include a list of questions or ideas to discuss. One might also replay or reread the story while the children place the appropriate flannel board characters on the board at the correct time. It might be an activity that relates to the story. For example, the children could make bunnies out of pieces of paper after listening to *Let's Make Rabbits* by Leo Lionni. This would be appropriate if the unit objective was for the children to learn the physical characteristics of rabbits.

More Motivation Ideas

The best and most successful motivation ideas are those developed by individual teachers with a specific story and group of children in mind. Given this, it should be clear that there are many possibilities for motivating children for any one story. For example, consider *The Tale of Peter Rabbit* by Beatrix Potter. One might use stuffed toys or puppets to introduce the book. The teacher might also hold up a small jacket with a rip in it and ask the children how they thought it could have been torn. Still another approach might be to show the children a small watering can. After explaining how it might be a good hiding place for a small animal, the teacher could pull a small stuffed rabbit out of the can.

Peek-A-Boo: I See You by Joan Phillips is a fun book for toddlers. The story motivation might begin by placing a blanket over the teacher's head. The teacher would say nothing until one of the curious toddlers pulled the blanket off. This would lead right into the story. A similar procedure can be used for Pauline Watson's *The Walking Coat,* in which a boy inherits a huge old coat. For this story, the teacher might enter the reading area totally wrapped up in a gigantic old coat. When a child is curious enough to investigate who is inside, the interest will be high enough for the story to begin.

There are a variety of ways to motivate children for *Peter Spier's Little Animal Books*. One might motivate for each animal story by making the sound of the animal or by pantomiming the animal's movements. A bag mask or stick puppet may be useful for a book such as this. Also, the teacher could hide a stuffed or real animal in a box or cage. The children can be asked to find or guess what each animal is.

Emmy Payne's *Katy No-Pocket* can provide the teacher with the opportunity for a comedy routine motivation activity. The teacher would come into the reading area with hands full of things, some of them dropping on the floor. While wearing clothes without pockets for the day, the teacher can use this humorous scene to began talking to the children about the need for pockets. An alternative to this is to motivate using a picture of a sad, tearful, pocketless kangaroo named Katy. As the story progresses, the group can take off the tears, replace the frown with a smile, and add a sandwich baggie pocket to Katy.

Another humorous motivational routine can be created by the teacher for Esphyr Slobodkina's *Caps for Sale.* Here, the teacher could walk slowly and carefully to the reading area while wearing a huge stack of hats. An alternative to

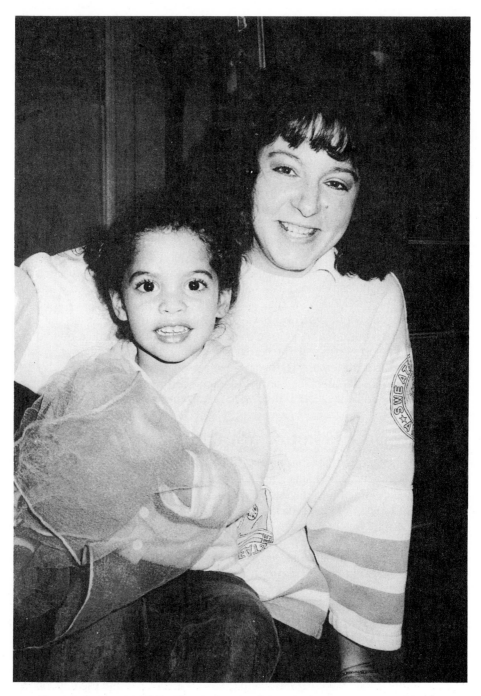

The teacher and child will use the scarf for music, movement, and story activities. Courtesy Diana Comer.

this might include the use of a stuffed or puppet monkey. The toy monkey whispers only to the teacher, who then translates the message to the class. The monkey begins by whispering that it has a great story about other monkeys and hats. A hat or hats can be placed on the monkey as the story is told.

Hey, Al by Arthur Yoricks can be introduced by having the teacher rush into the reading area. Wearing a baseball cap and pushing a broom, the teacher rapidly pantomimes the activities of a janitor at work. Using the broom and a dust rag to clean under and around the children will create much fun and interest. A quieter approach to the same story would entail the teacher placing a janitor's cap, a fern, and a small broom into a box or bag. The children can be asked to identify what each one is and what they have in common.

Children are usually quite aware of their own health, and familiar with doctors and nurses. Helen Oxenbury's *The Check-Up* is a book to which they will usually be able to relate. The teacher might begin by entering the reading area wearing medical garb, either real or homemade. Using medical tools from a box, the teacher would pantomime a medical exam with a doll or puppet. An alternative to this might be to use a doll, animal, or puppet in place of the teacher. Having an alligator doctor do a medical exam on an elephant would surely create interest.

One can even create interest and excitement for a story about objects such as a rock. William Stieg's *Sylvester and the Magic Pebble* is a good example. The teacher might begin by having the children guess what is concealed in a hand. After revealing a brightly colored pebble, the children could be told that the pebble contains magic just like the one in today's story. Another way of gaining each child's involvement is to give each child a magic pebble to hold for the story reading. The pebbles can help the children think of a picture of their own wishes. They could then draw their wishes and take their special pebbles home.

IDENTIFYING POSSIBLE PROBLEMS

It is important for the teacher to be familiar with the story being presented so that problems can be anticipated. Even if a book is age-appropriate, it may be uninteresting or confusing for the children. One should be ready to add some excitement to the reading by involving the children in the story. There are a variety of ways to do this. One may pause to ask the children what they think will happen next. Other aspects of the presentation may be changed as well.

The effective use of voice will often help children focus on what is being said. One can keep younger children involved in the rather lengthy book *Green Eggs and Ham* by Dr. Seuss by periodically asking them, ''Will he eat the green eggs and ham this time?'' When the children respond with a ''No,'' the teacher should quickly read the ever growing list of negative responses from the character in the book. Older children thoroughly enjoy this story and have little trouble staying with it. Even though the book is written as an early reader, younger children can follow it and enjoy its fun. Follow up the reading by cooking scrambled eggs and use green food color to color them green. This will recreate the experience. In conjunction with this story, one might also read Mitchell Sharmat's *Gregory, the Terrible Eater* in which a goat also refuses to eat his food.

When conducting a lesson involving science or social studies, it is quite valid to use books geared for older children when the subject cannot be found in age-appropriate books. If the pictures are clear and large, the book can be used by deleting the text that is too difficult. The information contained in those sections can be paraphrased for the children. It is recommended, however, that age-appropriate books are used whenever possible. They are easier for both the teacher and the children to use.

The Importance of Prereading

Prereading the story allows the teacher to know where emotional support may be needed, especially with young children. Tomie dePaola's *Nana Upstairs and Nana Downstairs* has a very sad part in the middle of the story. Knowing this ahead of time, the teacher can anticipate the need for support if or when the children seem upset. This depends on the class. During the story, one might ask such questions as "How do you think Tommy feels? . . . Would you feel this way? . . . There are more pages in the book; would you like to see what happens?" Feelings are important to children. It is a healthy sign when a book such as this can arouse such empathy for Tommy.

Many books involve children's emotions and one must be sensitive to this. The teacher needs to anticipate reactions when using books that deal with death, divorce, new babies, and so forth. A reading can be a wonderful support for children coping with a similar situation in real life. It can also cause a disruption as children deal with the surfacing of these feelings. When planning to use such books to help a child, have that child sit next to the teacher or another adult in the room. Be ready to provide support to the child. Allow time at the end of such stories to discuss the children's feelings. Let them know at the beginning of a book that there will be time to talk after the story. This minimizes disruptions, allowing children to respond to the story in their own personal way.

Children's Interests

One possible problem with a story choice is the concept of interest. An age-appropriate book that holds little interest for children is of little value to the class. This sometimes occurs when adults "remember" great books from their own childhoods. It may have been a great book, but childhood memory is not always the best guide for choosing books. The story may be meaningful to the adult because of a person or event surrounding the story rather than the story itself. The story may have been fine in the 1950s or the 1960s, but it may be outdated today. Our society has changed a great deal since then. The Dick and Jane books of that time are no longer wise choices for children of today. Besides being rather dull, they are filled with subtle sexism and elitism. In addition, there is an absence of minority characters. The best way to assess remembered books is to reread them as an early childhood educator. Doing so clarifies the actual value of the book as a choice for children today.

The interests of adults may or may not be the interests of children. While it is fine to expose children to new interests, it is important to plan for the children's

Children's activities and the interests they imply can be used by adults as a guide to select books and maintain interest. Courtesy Diana Comer.

interests as well. If the children are fascinated with dinosaurs, be sure to include books that relate to prehistoric times. If they are interested in superheroes, share storybooks which include such heroes. Be wary of books that seem particularly "cute." Such books are often designed to attract adults by their appearance rather than their interest to children. Flowery language and ornate illustrations will probably not attract most infants, toddlers and preschoolers.

SMOOTH TRANSITIONS

Transitions are often difficult for both teachers and children. It is hard to abruptly leave an activity in which one is truly involved. Although stories are usually viewed as enjoyable by most children, some children react with acting out behavior when story time is mentioned. Some children equate story time with negative thoughts of having to sit perfectly still. They find it just too difficult. A good transition makes it easier for these children to shift gears with less anxiety.

Good teachers have found that songs, poems, and fingerplays are effective transitional activities for several reasons. Children naturally respond to the rhythms of this type of literature. There are many short forms of these rhymes that fit nicely into a transition time frame. Anyone who has ever heard a young child repeating a jingle knows that they are capable and willing to learn and respond to them. Children also pay attention to the songs and songlike quality of fingerplays and poetry. Part of the reason for a transition is to turn the child's attention to the teacher and to the next activity. Through being involved in the transition activity, the child already wants to participate in the new activity.

Transition Ideas

Teachers may choose to either make up their own transition activities or borrow them from books such as Jean Warren's *Piggyback Songs.* Chanting messages or singing the message to a familiar tune are other ways to establish a pattern for change. For example, moving from art time to story time may be done by using the following rhyme to the melody of "O Tannenbaum":

"Cooperate, cooperate . . . it's time to clean up now. "
"O Story, O story . . . it's time to listen now. "

Some other ways to facilitate transitions are to use unusual objects. For example, find a gaudy old rhinestone ring, the bigger and more colorful the better. Tell the children that this is a magic ring given to you by a sorcerer. Holding up the ring for all to see, make a special wish for the children to quietly listen to your story. Adding a couple of phrases like "Abracadabra" will help put a feeling of magic into the children's desire to hear the story.

Magic wands can be great aids to transitions. One can use a water and glitter filled wand, a tinsel filled wand, a glow-in-the-dark wand or a light-up wand. Children love to see the wand waved in the air over their heads while the teacher chants magical words and phrases. The children realize that the wand is not really magic, but they love the fun of pretending. A wand draws their attention and that makes it work.

It is comforting for children to know what will come next. Many teachers and storytellers use a transitional song or poem at the beginning of each story-telling or reading session. They use the same one each and every time. A second song or poem may be added, but the story time will always begin with the familiar one.

Wriggle songs, poems, and fingerplays are also useful before a story begins. They allow movement prior to the story that helps to keep the children from need-ing to wriggle so much during the story. The best wriggle activities proceed from active wriggling to nose twitching or eye blinking. This readies the children for a quieter time. Active participation of children is a key factor in any transition.

There are several good choices for de-wriggling children. In *Music: A Way of Life for the Young Child*[2] by Kathleen M. Bayless and Marjorie E. Ramsey, one can find a favorite song titled "Open, Shut Them." Written by Laura Pendleton MacCartney, this musical fingerplay has been around since the early part of the century. It is an excellent tool to guide children to an attentive listening attitude.

Although the form of transition the teacher plans to use is an individual decision, the use of a transition is a mandatory part of the planning. It eliminates many behavior problems by avoiding the conflicts caused by a change in routine. The child who tends to act out has more of an opportunity to choose acceptable behaviors when transition activities are provided.

KEEPING ORDER

There are many strategies used by experienced teachers to keep order in a class reading situation. Experience can be a valuable teacher, as it allows one to try different procedures over time. One can also learn from the experience that others have gained. One should bear in mind, however, that no procedure is effective every time with every child or group. Children and classes have distinct personali-ties. A procedure that works one time for one group may be ineffective at another time or with another group.

The fact that there is no blueprint or plan that one can always follow is part of the challenge of working with children over time. The teacher must always be willing to approach problems in new and creative ways. There are several potential problems that tend to occur more frequently than others. They include children sitting too close, disruptions during the reading, acting out children, and inappro-priate peer relationships. One also has to be aware of what behaviors must be accepted as normal, how to regain the attention of the group after a problem has been solved, and how to avoid using inappropriate procedures for dealing with problems. The teacher must consider a variety of factors within each of these areas.

[2] Kathleen M. Bayless and Marjorie E. Ramsey, *Music: A Way of Life for the Young Child* (Columbus, Ohio: Merrill, 1987).

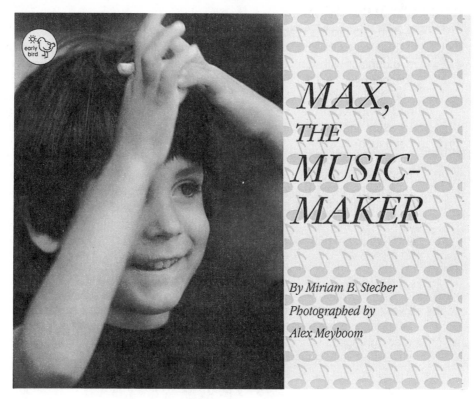

MAX,
THE
MUSIC-
MAKER

By Miriam B. Stecher
Photographed by
Alex Meyboom

Music is an excellent tool for making transitions. It can be combined with books about music for added effectiveness. Courtesy Delmar Publishers Inc.

Children Sitting Too Close

When children sit too close to each other, problems can easily occur. Youngsters need to have enough space to accommodate their normal movements. A most common solution to this is to place hearts, stars, stickers, or markers at the places where children are to sit. The seating arrangement may be in the form of a circle, semi-circle, or a random pattern. Each child might be assigned a permanent spot, or children could choose an available spot. If permanent spots are assigned to children, names can be added to reinforce name recognition.

Another approach might be to have the children stand up and hold hands in a circle. After stretching out to a full arm's length between each child, they could let go of each other's hands and sit in the spot they are standing. This yields a good space between each child. One might also tape a circle on the floor or carpet. A cross tape can be placed at each point where a child is expected to sit. Finally, using clear contact paper, tape each child's picture to the spot on the floor where that child is to sit. This works well for toddlers and younger children who can not yet read their own names.

Disruptions While Reading

A disruption to the reading can occur for a variety of reasons that may or may not be related to the story. The most obvious solution to this problem is to establish eye contact with the child and send a brief nonverbal message. For example, the teacher might nod to the child and mouth the word "after." If this is not effective, one might verbally acknowledge the child but ask that he or she wait until the end to speak. If the interruption is pursuant to the story, the teacher might wish to allow the child to briefly share the information. The reading could then be continued.

If the group is losing interest in the story, one can attempt to rekindle it with a more exciting tone of voice. If this fails, stop everything. Consider the possibility that the children need to stretch. Use a wriggle or giggle fingerplay and then continue the story. If this problem is anticipated, one can make the story a serial story by continuing it later in the day or the next day. Teachers must use their instinct, judgement, and knowledge of the group to decide which course of action to follow.

Acting Out Children

Every class seems to have one or two children who might be described as active or mischievous. These children can be asked to sit near the teacher before the reading begins. Children who are known to have difficulty sitting near each other should be seated apart.

Involving these children is often effective. Give them the motivational items to hold during the reading. If they are made to feel that they have an important role during the story time, they will have less need for attention. The teacher might also make a contract for stickers or a snack at the end of the reading period. For example, gingerbread cookies or stickers might be appropriate after the story of the "Gingerbread Man." One should take care using this procedure. Literature is its own reward. One doesn't grow to appreciate it by having one's silence "bought" for sitting through it.

A better approach would be to have the children create a special book to bring home with something drawn on the page that represents the story read that day. The book title and author can be written on the page as well. In this way, children can talk about the story later and parents can reinforce the story. By doing this, children learn that they are expected to attend to the reading so they can share it with their parents. Praise the whole group for doing a good job of listening and learning. This also shows all children that they are part of a social group with certain responsibilities.

Peer Relations

Children do bump and nudge each other. Sometimes it is not intended, while at other times it does appear to be conscious. When it appears that a safety problem exists or that a behavior is interfering with the reading, the teacher must take some type of action. The goal is to have the least amount of disruption. Therefore, the first course of action might be to simply motion for the child to come and sit next to the teacher or an aide. The story can be immediately continued. A reader who is standing can move near the child and involve the child in the story. Involving the child with the reader's presence and the story line can often eliminate the inappropriate behavior. Read some of the words: "He huffed and he puffed, Michael" directly to the child. It's difficult to ignore the story when brought back into it in this way.

Sometimes children ignore these signals. As a last resort, they should be removed from the group. It should be done as quietly as possible, without stating anything to them. They can be moved to sit at a table. The teacher should return to the group and continue the story for the others. The less attention given to the situation, the less it disturbs the flow of the story. If there are a couple of stories being read, or if there are appropriate points to pause in the story, the child can be asked to return to the group if ready to participate properly.

Ignoring Normal Behaviors

Children stretch and wriggle. Children react verbally to various parts of a story. Children twist their hair around their fingers. Many times, these are unconscious behaviors that harm no one and actually show that children are listening. Adults can mistakenly try to eliminate all motion from the listening child. Since it is normal for children to act in these ways, they should not be penalized for these behaviors.

If a child exhibits a behavior that the teacher feels needs to be addressed, it should be done quietly. "No problem" situations can become real problems for both the teacher and the child if one attempts to eliminate all of them.

Regaining Attention

It can be difficult to regain a group's attention after a distraction. A dog walking into a room or a call on the intercom can disrupt the momentum of a story. It is best to handle the situation by using intuition and common sense. If it appears to be too late to continue the story, it is best not to attempt it. The children can be told that the story will be concluded later or during the next day. Rushing through the end of a book can be most unsatisfactory for all. It can cause the story to lose its charm. If there is enough time to continue, the children can be regrouped with a quiet fingerplay or song. The teacher should repeat some of the past action and resume the story. Better yet, one can involve the children in the retelling of what has happened in the story prior to continuing the reading.

How Not to Handle Disruptions

At some time in life, everyone has seen the wrong way to handle a situation. The "wrong way" refers to a procedure that ultimately may do more harm than good. Humiliating youngsters in front of their peers may quiet them down, but is also likely to bring years of mistrust, resentment, and lowered self-esteem. There are a variety of negative, yet common, methods for handling problems at story time. Since they often do more harm than good, they should be avoided.

Several of the methods to be avoided merely reveal the adult's frustration.

Rolling one's eyes while saying, "Oh, no, not you again," is a good example. Yelling, accusing, a child of ruining the reading group, and removing a child with a great deal of visible annoyance all fall into this category.

Threatening, particularly with actions that will not be taken, is not appropriate. For example, threatening children with comments such as, "If you don't settle down, there will be no more stories," is a mistake. It may work for the moment, but it has a better chance of backfiring. In making such a statement, the teacher has surrendered control to the disruptive children who may enjoy their newly discovered attention. Children know that there will always be more stories. It is also a grave mistake to link literature and punishment together in such a way. Threatening to tell a child's parents about a behavior is also ineffective. This admits to a child that the teacher cannot handle the problem and is likely to cause more serious problems in the future.

Negative comments, in general, are usually ineffective. It is far better to use positive comments to praise those students who are acting appropriately. Negative comments are merely an attempt to decrease an inappropriate behavior in a child. They don't offer the child an alternate activity. Positive comments provide children with an alternative to inappropriate behavior. They provide attention, build self-esteem and are effective in managing behavior. Let children hear phrases such as "I like the way Juan is listening," "I see Beth and Isaac are ready," "I just love the way you look at me with that smile when it is time to read a story."

SUMMARY

Much of the success of reading a story depends on the motivation provided by the teacher. Armed with a good sense of humor, common sense, and a knowledge of child development, teachers can successfully bring magic into story times. Creative and whimsical methods of motivation enhance the enjoyment of literature for both the teacher and the children. When teachers are motivated to make books an integral and enjoyable part of life, children will respond with delight and a sense of wonder at the world of literature opening before them.

The teacher's choice of books and their presentation is critical in enhancing children's interest in books. The atmosphere the teacher creates in the classroom is important to listening and learning. To create an effective atmosphere, teachers need to be responsive to children and their needs. Magic boxes, stuffed animals, puppets, and interesting objects do more than just motivate children for a particular book. The special ways that teachers use them help children develop an interest in literature.

Helping children learn how to adjust to change, interact with literature, and develop listening skills is an important part of the teacher's role. When these skills are learned, the children will more likely become productive and responsive social beings. This does not occur simply by reading a book to children. The teacher needs to carefully plan the readings, taking into account both how literature can be exciting and how problems can occur. Careful planning will prevent many problems from occurring in the first place. When students do exhibit inappropriate behaviors during story time, a set of sensitive and effective strategies for dealing with them is indispensible to the teacher.

QUESTIONS FOR THOUGHT AND DISCUSSION

1. What are some of the things a teacher can do to avoid or minimize disruptive interactions between children?
2. How can a teacher help children increase their listening time spans?
3. Why should teachers develop lesson plans?
4. Why is a motivational procedure important in a lesson plan?
5. Choose a story and give some examples of motivations that might be used.
6. Children should never be read books that are above their age-appropriate level. Defend or refute this statement.
7. Why is it beneficial, for children, if the teacher prereads a book?
8. Why should the children's interests be part of planning the choice of books?
9. Describe a transitional activity a teacher might use in a classroom.
10. What is meant by the term "wriggle song"?
11. How might a teacher deal with the problem of children sitting too close together during story time?
12. What steps could one take with a child who disrupts the reading time?
13. What can the teacher do with children who act out during story time?
14. The aggressive child who starts fighting with another child during story time should never be removed from the group as it makes him/her feel left out. Defend or refute this statement.

CHILDREN'S BOOKS CITED

James M. Barrie, *Peter Pan* (New York: Random House, 1957).

Stan and Jan Berenstain, *The Berenstain Bears and the Spooky Old Tree* (New York: Random House, 1978).

Raymond Briggs, *The Snowman* (New York: Random House, 1986).

Tomie dePaola, *Nana Upstairs and Nana Downstairs* (New York: Dutton, 1973).

Leo Lionni, *Let's Make Rabbits* (New York: Pantheon, 1982).

Helen Oxenbury, *The Check-Up* (New York: Dutton, 1983).

Emmy Payne, *Katy No-Pocket* (New York: Holiday House, 1983).

Joan Phillips, *Peek-A-Boo: I See You* (New York: Grosset and Dunlap, 1983).

Beatrix Potter, *The Tale of Peter Rabbit* (New York: Warne, 1902).

Dr. Seuss (pseud. for Theodor Geisel), *Green Eggs and Ham* (New York: Random House, 1960).

Mitchell Sharmat, *Gregory, the Terrible Eater* (New York: Scholastic, 1980).

Esphyr Slobodkina, *Caps for Sale* (New York: Addison Wesley, 1940).

Peter Spier, *Peter Spier's Little Animal Books* (New York: Doubleday, 1984).

William Stieg, *Sylvester and the Magic Pebble* (New York: Simon and Schuster, 1970).

Jean Warren, *Piggyback Songs* (Everett, Washington: Warren, 1983).

Pauline Watson, *The Walking Coat* (Englewood Cliffs, New Jersey: Prentice-Hall, 1980).

Arthur Yoricks, *Hey, Al* (New York: Farrar, Straus and Giroux, 1986).

SELECTED REFERENCES

Eva L. Esse, *A Practical Guide to Solving Preschool Behavior Problems,* 2d ed. (Albany, New York: Delmar, 1990).

Tom Glazer, *Music for One's and Two's: Songs and Games for the Very Young Child* (Garden City, New York: Doubleday, 1983).

Jane Hart, *Singing Bee!* (New York: Lothrop, Lee and Shepard, 1982).

Clyde Watson, *Father Fox's Feast of Songs* (New York: Philomel, 1983).

How Many Ways Can a Story Be Told?

daily structure provides an important security and reassurance to children. Yet, variations in routine can provide interest and excitement to the day. No matter how enjoyable a routine might be, the sameness can create boredom over time. Good literature, as well, can be enhanced with a variety of presentation methods.

Some may be intimidated by the idea of changing the way a story is shared. Others welcome the opportunity to experiment with a variety of presentations. Those who do try a variety of approaches often find the changes refreshing for both the children and themselves. The changes made can range from subtle shifts within a familiar presentation style to experimenting with totally new sharing methods. By starting with less obvious changes and proceeding to totally different styles, adults develop a confidence in their ability to use different styles.

This chapter explores the possibilities of using such diverse methods as oral storytelling, reading aloud, flannel board stories, theatrical story presentations, and children as authors. Each of these methods has a number of possibilities within it. One may also choose to combine the various presentation methods. In doing this, the possible ways of sharing stories are endless.

READING ALOUD

Reading aloud to children should begin when they are infants. The sounds of a caring voice and the rhythms of the language provide reassurance. The child who is read to grows up with the idea that reading is a normal part of life. As the language becomes meaningful, children see new worlds constantly opening up before them. Reading stimulates their imaginations and provides a foundation upon which to build new knowledge.

The terms ''reading readiness'' and ''reading readiness skills'' give a false impression of what is entailed in learning to read. There really is no clearly defined set of skills that children must master before they are ready to learn to read. Learning to read is a long, ongoing process beginning with being read to as an infant. It culminates in an ability and desire to engage in reading as an enjoyable part of life.

All of the reading aloud done with children is a part of learning to read. According to Jim Trelease, author of *The New Read-Aloud Handbook,* the child who follows the reader's finger across the page will make a natural connection between the sounds of the words and the letters on the page.[1] It is important that this learning not be pushed upon the child. Children will make this connection at their own individual rates and adults must be willing to let the connection occur naturally. By doing so, reading will be seen as something that possesses joy, mystery, and excitement.

Jim Trelease compares the planting of a desire to read in a child with the kind of advertising done by McDonald's Restaurants. McDonald's achieved success by advertising so frequently that people become familiar with both the commercials and the characters within the commercials. Trelease is concerned that the "commercials" for reading—frequently reading aloud to children—do not continue during the school years. Reading aloud should be a part of the everyday routine of children throughout their school lives. Yet, the frequency of reading books aloud to children decreases dramatically as children move up through the grades. By the time children graduate from high school, reading aloud has usually ceased to exist as a regular part of the school day.

Using Read-Aloud Books

Besides planning the read-aloud experience for children, it is helpful to consider the ways one can make the reading a fascinating and exciting experience. It is easiest to do this by using voice, pace, and a flexible approach. One does not need to be a professional storyteller to read aloud more effectively. This skill can be achieved by attention and practice.

To begin, one can practice using different voice inflections, pitches, and volume levels. Knowing the story helps to determine when one should vary these elements. For example, one can lower the voice to a whisper at an exciting part of the action. One might even stop reading completely to allow the children to think about what is happening for a moment. Reading slowly helps the children use their imaginations to keep up with the story. Speeding up during certain parts where the action picks up can have them sitting on the edge of their seats.

When the reader is excited and enthusiastic about the story, the feeling is usually contagious. This provides a good role model for experiencing the fun of literature. Such enthusiasm can be achieved by carefully choosing the books to be read aloud. There is no substitute for selecting books that both the reader and the children like. Humorous books are good beginning choices, as the humor provides a built-in motivation. As reading aloud becomes a practice, varying story themes and plots will provide children with the opportunity to experience all types of literature, possibly including riddle books, poetry, and more serious stories.

Use the language of the read-aloud book to promote good language and language growth. Talk about some of the phrases and sentences the author uses.

[1] Jim Trelease, *The New Read-Aloud Handbook* (New York: Viking Penguin, 1989).

This encourages children to use language provided by good models. While good books can usually be read in their entirety, one should not be afraid to summarize or paraphrase some parts of the story. This might be done to adjust a more difficult book to the audience, to recapture the children's interest, or to better assist the children in understanding the story.

Good Choices for Read-Alouds

Most children's picture books were meant to be read aloud. This does not mean, of course, that every picture book can be read aloud successfully. While there are criteria one can apply to selecting books for children, some additional elements might be included when considering books to be read aloud.

A good read-aloud book will depend somewhat on the age of the children. Infants benefit from books with clear, colorful illustrations with little text. They also enjoy short, simple rhymes and poems. Large pictures and pictures of familiar scenes are enjoyed after the reading is done. Books that encourage the naming of objects, letters, and numbers are also good selections because they often contain familiar sights and sounds.

Toddlers are ready for more sophisticated rhymes and stories. They especially like books with predictable repeated lines. They enjoy the feeling of mastery in joining in and saying the lines after the first couple of repetitions. For example, consider the story of ''The Farmer in the Dell.'' As both a story and a song, its familiar lines are quickly mastered by the young child.

Toddlers also like books that describe mischievous antics of characters to whom they can relate. Lynd Ward's *The Biggest Bear* relates the problems encountered in trying to tame something that was meant to be left in the wilderness. A sense of the absurd is found in many Dr. Seuss books. This type of humor is often an effective device for involving the independent two year old. Lois Lenski and Mercer Mayer have written several small books that toddlers feel are just their size. Many of their books are about toddlers' favorite big people such as cowboys and firemen.

Preschoolers and kindergarteners are ready for more involved plots and a wider range of themes. Humor is still a good choice. Arnold Lobel's *Frog and Toad Are Friends* and Jane Yolen's *No Bath Tonight* create a world where the humor is more subtle and where human nature shines through. Adventure stories become an area of interest at this age. Good choices might include *Five Chinese Brothers* by Kurt Wiese and Claire Huchet Bishop, *Tikki Tikki Tembo* retold by Arlene Mosel, *One Monday Morning* by Uri Schulevitz and *Little Tim and the Brave Sea Captain* by Edward Ardizzone. An excellent choice for a read-aloud book at bedtime might be Doris Schwerin's *The Tomorrow Book* which explores the meaning of tomorrow.

Identifying good read-aloud books is not a difficult task. Knowing the children is an important first step. Using the criteria for good literature, one can select appropriate books for the class. A third element is identifying which of these books will best lend themselves to an exciting and enjoyable read-aloud experience. When this has been done, the reader must review the book and know just how the story will be read. If this is not done, the reading will not be as effective as it could be and a good deal of potential will be wasted.

Becoming familiar with a large number of books is an efficient way to help plan read-aloud experiences. Having this knowledge of books will enable the reader to be more spontaneous when using read-aloud activities. The reader will always have a set of well-planned read-aloud books to use when the need arises. The special sharing that will occur will be a more effective "commercial" for reading. Read-alouds that do not possess this air of excitement will pose the risk of losing children to some other activity that may seem more interesting. Once lost, it may be difficult to bring these children back.

STORYTELLING

In most cultures throughout time, the storyteller was a valuable member of the community. In the preliterary world, storytellers were the keepers of the culture. They were both the newspaper of the present and the link to the people's past. They were often the honored guests of kings and queens. As literacy increased, storytellers lost some of their importance. Yet, in regions of the world with high illiteracy rates, storytellers continue to hold a position of esteem.

Good storytellers will always hold the power to enchant. They help us to reflect upon our lives, make us laugh, and make us cry. They are honored by most as artists in the literary field. A storyteller is both a performing artist and a careful student of literature. Some storytellers specialize in a type of presentation, using a dialect from a particular region, songs, or costumes. Others will focus on certain subject matter such as African tales, humor, or stories of the sea. They may also combine some of these elements to create a new style unique to themselves.

How to Be a Storyteller

The skill and talent of a professional storyteller is wonderful to see and hear. It should be a welcome event for any group of children. However, such an event cannot usually be scheduled very frequently. Since almost anyone can become at least an amateur storyteller, it makes sense to learn some of the methods used by storytellers. The oral sharing of stories is an old tradition. If done with care and thought, it will provide another effective way of sharing stories with children.

One of the best ways to learn the craft of the storyteller is to listen to practicing storytellers explain how they go about their work. Aili Paal Singer, a New England storyteller, has a background in teaching, writing, and performing. Along with storytelling, she also works in theater and television. Her presentations include the use of puppetry, mime, and acting. She provides activities and materials designed to involve the children in the stories. Figures 1–4 provide a glimpse into the mind of Ms. Singer as she describes how she approaches her work. Also included are two of her short pieces for sharing.

Another New England storyteller is Doug Lipman. He too shares a background in teaching, writing, and performing. In addition, he has also been

Figure 1.   Aili Paal Singer demonstrates how to be a tree in a story by using the entire body to play the role. Courtesy Diana Comer.

involved in music and working with handicapped children. His presentations include a good deal of active participation and singing. The stories he presents often deal with the themes of African tales, Hasidism, equality of the sexes, and superheroes. He believes that stories should have real content and say something to us as human beings. In Figure 5, Doug Lipman shares his ideas for sharing children's stories by using a participatory approach.

Good Choices for Oral Storytelling

Almost any good story that meets the criteria for good literature is a good possibility for oral storytelling. It is important to be aware of the fact that this method of sharing is more difficult than reading aloud. In reading aloud, the readers can rely on the book to provide the language. In oral storytelling, readers must put some of themselves and their language into the presentation. The story must be a part of the storyteller's imagination. It would not be effective for one to forget the story at midpoint and to begin reading from the book. The spell of the storyteller would be broken.

It is best to select stories with clear, strong characters. This is especially true if one wishes the children to participate. The setting should be fairly simple in order for children to picture it in their imaginations. Stories with interesting narratives and lines for choral responses by the children are effective. When children are involved,

Figure 2.   Aili Paal Singer sets the scene for her African story with props such as a drum. Courtesy Diana Comer.

Figure 3. Aili Paal Singer uses children with masks as an integral part of her stories. This participation can help the shy child take a more active role in a class. Courtesy Diana Comer.

they are more likely to continue following the story. Finally, the story should be fascinating to the storyteller. Without this, it will lack the natural enthusiasm demanded by a good storytelling.

Most storytellers interpret a work before using it. This means that they make some decisions about what the story means, what it is useful for, and how this can be brought out in the telling. They make decisions concerning the character, such as the costumes, voice, and actions to be used. Decisions are made about the actual story. This may include the length of time needed, portions of the story to be summarized or lengthened, and ways to increase the interest and value of the story. Decisions are made about the audience. This might include determining the appropriateness of the story for the expected audience, the degree of audience participation planned, and the needs of the audience.

FLANNEL BOARD STORIES

A variation of storytelling is the flannel board story. A flannel board is a piece of wood or other rigid material covered with felt or flannel. Characters and objects cut from felt are placed on the flannel board to portray the visual action of the story as

I like to tell stories which allow students to join me in acting out the characters and events. Children have often asked me to tell a story in which everyone in the class can participate.

It isn't easy to find a ready made story that could offer parts for 53 people (2 classes of 25 children, 2 teachers, and a storyteller). That is what I was looking for. Fortunately, I found one when I read the African folktale ''The King's Drum'' in *A Treasury of African Folklore* by Harold Courlander (Crown Publishers, 1975). Though I would retell it and adapt It, I knew it would work well with younger children.

I proceeded to design and construct 53 masks out of various weight colored construction paper: a lion, a monkey, a spider, leopards, giraffes, porcupines, elephants, antelopes. I wanted the children to be able to watch everything without obstruction, so I chose to make the mask surround an opening for the face.

These designs were then adapted to more practical sized masks, for 8½" by 11" paper, which I could give out as a follow-up art activity for students.

''What good is it to make a mask if you can't use it?'' I asked myself. So, I sat down to write some little stories that could be read and acted out. They contained only the animal characters for which I had masks. These stories were included in my Program Guide for teachers as follow-up material.

Reprinted with permission from NOTES: THE KING'S DRUM © 1988, Aili Paal Singer.

Characters: LIONS LEOPARDS PORCUPINES ANTELOPES GIRAFFES

The neighborhood was quiet and all the animals were asleep.
But the Lions began snoring with sounds loud and deep.

The Leopards woke up and began to complain.
The Porcupines called out, "You sound like a train!"

The Antelopes screamed, "Quiet down, please!"
The Giraffes jumped up startled, and ran to the trees.

They galloped with hooves pounding hard on the ground.
The Lions slept on without hearing a sound.

In the morning, they yawned, smiled and said,
"How nice it is to get a good night's sleep in one's bed."

When the families of Leopard, Porcupine, Antelope and Giraffe
Heard what the Lions said, they had a good laugh.

Reprinted with permission from THE QUIET NIGHT © 1988, Aili Paal Singer.

Characters: ANTELOPE FAMILY   GIRAFFE

The Antelope family was taking a walk.

Giraffe was standing tall, eating the top leaves of a tree.
Antelope's children pointed to Giraffe.
They giggled and said,
             "What a funny long neck and such skinny legs!"

Giraffe looked down and said,
             "I see Lion coming down the path behind the tree."
He then ran away as fast as the wind.
Antelope's famly leaped all the way home.

The next day, the Antelope family again took a walk.

Giraffe was eating the top leaves of a tree.
Antelope's children pointed to Giraffe.
They said, "What a fine long neck, and a great pair of legs!"

Reprinted with permission from ANTELOPE'S CHILDREN, © 1988, Aili Paal Singer.

Figure 4. In Aili Paal Singer's, "The King's Drum," poetry, drama, and storytelling combine to provide children with a powerful experience. Children with masks can easily be included in the story. The masks can be reused or taken home. Making the masks can be both an art project and a follow-up activity. Photo courtesy Diana Comer.

Figure 5.   Making stories participatory. Courtesy Doug Lipman. *To present a story effectively, one must use voice, movement, body language, and facial expressions.* Photos courtesy Diana Comer.

Any story can be made into a participation story. In general, the audience may participate by joining in with their voices or with their bodies, or by making suggestions.

Join in with the Voice

In the riddle story "In Summer I Die," the audience joins in verbally by repeating rhythmic, chant-like speech: e.g., *"Mama, mama, wake up, we're bored."* This is the easiest way to join in with the voice, because rhythmic speech has simpler, more predictable rhythms than normal speech.

One step beyond rhythmic speech is singing; the only difference between rhythmic speech and song is the presence of melody. If teller and audience can be induced to sing, it adds to the fun and the mood. If one or the other is too shy, though, or the words are too minor to warrant melody, we may be better to chant than to give up on all rhythm.

Once the audience has heard a story or a phrase several times, they can join in by filling in missing words. To cue an audience for this, we can start a sentence they have heard before, but stop before the end. Our gestures and face indicate that they are to continue. For example, the storyteller begins:

In summer I . . .

and stops, mouth open, gesture stopped mid-air, with an expression of expectancy; and the audience chimes in:

. . . die.

A special case of filling in words is filling in sound effects. For example, "we rang the doorbell, and it went . . ."

Figure 5.   continued

All these forms of verbal participation can be varied or intensified by saying them in different tones of voice, repeating them, or repeating them with additions, as in a cumulative story.

Join in with the Body

Younger children often find it less threatening to join in with movements than with words; older children and adults often find movements *more* threatening. Depending on the age of our audience, therefore, movements may become a tool for winning our audience, or a sign that we have already succeeded in gaining their attention and trust.

Rhythmic movements, such as those to accompany the refrain *"Mama, mama, wake up, I'm bored,"* or the rhyme *"In summer I die . . . ,"* are a natural accompaniment to rhythmic speech. Simple miming of a motion, such as knocking on a door or shaking a sleeping person, can be added almost anywhere to snag the wandering attention of preschoolers. These actions become central to the story if they are repeated at different points with different feeling or with a sense of growing urgency or silliness.

Body participation can also include postures. For example, we could ask our audience to "show me how you'd sit if you were bored." Or: "How would you stand if you had just figured out the answer to Grandmother's riddle?" When we say things in a particular posture, by the way, it often affects our tone of voice.

The furthest extreme of body participation is to actually enact a part of the story. Enactment can be done by a whole group at once, all acting out one part after another—or by small groups or individuals taking on separate roles.

Figure 5. continued

Make Suggestions

Up until now, we, the teller, have made all the choices, and the audience has been invited only to follow along. We can also, however, invite the audience to participate by adding their own point of view, and giving suggestions.

From the teller's perspective, the easiest form of suggestions to manage are "advisory only": suggestions that are not incorporated into the story. For example, we could ask, "What would you do if you were bored and no one else was awake?" After listening to a few answers, our story continues as planned all along. This allows audience members to express their thoughts, and involves them internally in the situation the character faces. It encourages spontaneity from the audience. And yet it allows the teller to preserve the carefully learned and rehearsed sequence of the story.

At the opposite extreme, we can throw open the gate of the story for the audience to find its own way through. A round-robin story is the result. The teller, of course, can still retain the role of shepherd:

"And what do you suppose we did, since we were so bored?"

Audience: watched TV.

"So we turned on the TV. What was on?"

Audience: Batman!

"Seeing Batman made us think of something in our back yard. What was it?"

Audience: our toy Batmobile.

"So we went outside to play in our toy Batmobile. But suddenly we saw something very unusual. What do you think it was? . . . "

Between the extreme of no audience control and complete audience control, of course, there are still more middle positions. To give the audience some influence over the story, we can incorporate their suggestions into minor details of the story. For example, we can ask what kind of a house we lived in. Were there steps leading up to the front door? What did we have to cross to get to our friend's house? These details can then be incorporated into the story immediately: "So we climbed down the steps, across the playground, waited for a green light, looked both ways, then crossed the street." But we have to remember these details if they are relevant later: "Then we ran back with the icicles, waited for the green light, looked both ways, crossed the street, ran across the playground, and climbed back up the steps of our house."

The audience suggestions in "In Summer I Die" influence more of the plot than simple details would, but are still contained in a predictable framework. The choice of whom to wake up next stimulates a whole new cycle of waking, chanting, and reacting, but it loops us right back to the same point in the plot: "So we went to find someone else . . . ." The teller decides when to break out of that loop and go on to Grandmother.

A similar loop is repeated later, when the audience suggests what we saw next, and the teller helps compare it to the riddle: "A carrot! What a great idea. So we opened the refrigerator, pulled open the bottom drawer, and took out a carrot. Maybe this is it! Does it die in the summer? . . . " Again, the teller decides when to break out of that loop by taking us outdoors to play with the snow—and when to enter it again to guess outdoor things or the icicle itself.

A Balance of Participation.

Any story can be made participatory, by just including some of the techniques described above. The teller's biggest job, though, is to find the right balance: too little participation, and a younger audience loses attention, or we lose an opportunity for fun and feedback; too much, or the wrong kind of participation, and the story itself suffers. A story with too much participation feels "gimicky", and its central triumph becomes obscured. As adapters or creators of stories, we strive to choose the techniques of participation—and the places to use them—that will clarify a story's structure and events, and heighten its emotional impact.

To choose well, we need to be aware of all of our options. Voice, body, suggestions: these three words can remind us of the many choices we have.

Reprinted with permission from General Hints for Making Stories Participatory, © 1985, Doug Lipman

Figure 5. continued

it is being told. While the story may be read from a book, the additional task of manipulating pieces on the flannel board suggests that an oral presentation would be easier.

Flannel board stories can be easy and fun to make. A small group of adults can cut the necessary pieces for several stories in a short work session. Once made, they are available for years for sharing with other groups of students. The story can be adopted to different age groups by simplifying the plot. New plot twists can be added by adding new pieces and events to the story.

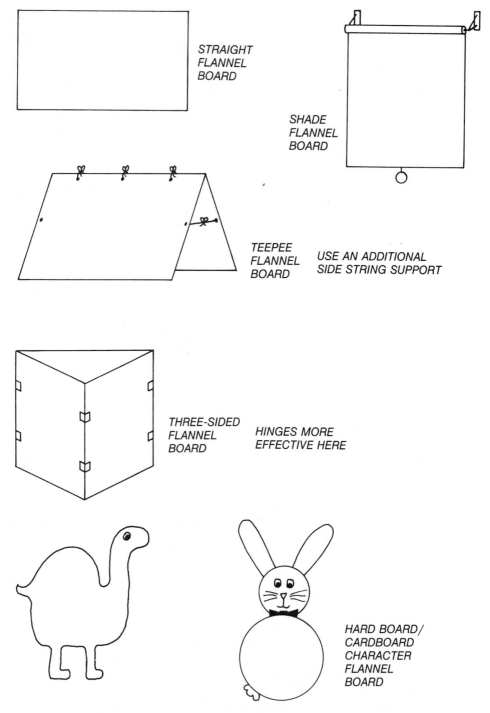

STRAIGHT
FLANNEL
BOARD

SHADE
FLANNEL
BOARD

TEEPEE
FLANNEL
BOARD

USE AN ADDITIONAL
SIDE STRING SUPPORT

THREE-SIDED
FLANNEL
BOARD

HINGES MORE
EFFECTIVE HERE

HARD BOARD/
CARDBOARD
CHARACTER
FLANNEL
BOARD

Figure 6.   *Flannel board designs can be simple or complex. Either way, they belong in every early childhood classroom. Courtesy Diana Comer.*

Making Flannel Board Materials

The basic components for flannel board stories are the flannel board itself, the characters, and the other objects needed to tell the story.

Flannel Board. While they can be purchased commercially, flannel boards are relatively easy to make. Constructing one's own allows the board to be made in a variety of sizes and shapes. First, the backing is cut from thick cardboard, plywood, masonite, acrylic plastic, or any other flat, rigid material. It is then covered with either flannel or felt. There are a variety of styles that can be used or adopted. Several styles are shown in Figure 6.

Besides a basic straight design, one might consider a teepee or tent design. Either two separate boards can be joined at the top, or a single board can be folded over. This design provides two flannel board surfaces, allowing a story scene to remain in place over time if desired. A three-sided design provides even more flexibility. If space is limited, one might wish to consider a window shade flannel board. To make this one, the shade is covered with the flannel and mounted with brackets on a wall. The wall provides the rigid surface. Animal shape flannel boards lend a whimsical touch to the flannel board method. They might be used for units using a variety of animal books.

Characters and Objects. As with flannel boards, the objects used with the flannel board can come from a variety of sources. Sets of flannel board objects, characters, letters, and numbers can be purchased commercially. Acquiring such a set may be a good basis upon which to build a collection of additional characters and objects. The most common material from which to make the pieces is felt. It is thicker and more sturdy than flannel, though the latter is often used. Other materials such as clothes dryer softener sheets, sandpaper, velcro, and double-faced carpet tape are also used. Pictures, hand colored or cut from magazines, can be glued to flannel pieces as well. The felt pieces can also be painted.

A flannel board story library will eventually emerge. The pieces required for a particular book and a copy of the book can be stored together in a plastic storage bag or a heavy envelope. In this way, flannel board stories can be used without the need to collect or make the necessary pieces each time the story is shared.

How to Share Flannel Board Stories

As with any story sharing procedure, planning is a key element. The story should be carefully selected and known to the teacher. The story should be reviewed before it is used. Even if the story is familiar, one can momentarily forget the next part of the action. Such a pause can cause a disruption to the flow of the story.

The pieces needed to tell the story should be lined up in the order they are to be used. This will eliminate the need to search for a missing piece half way through the story. With a flannel board story, remembering to maintain eye contact with the audience is important. It is easy to forget to do this after adding a piece to the board. Eye contact is helpful in maintaining the attention of the children. It also ensures that the children will hear the teacher's voice.

Telling a flannel board story a bit slower keeps the story suspenseful and fun. If things occur too quickly the presentation can become confusing. Children are expected to both listen and look to experience a flannel board story. By taking one's time, adding sly expressions and poignant pauses, the story will have a powerful effect. This does not mean the story should drag. Lively verbal expression and movements are beneficial only when they are appropriate to the story.

Encouraging interaction will draw the children into the story. Follow the first telling with a retelling of the story by the children. Distribute character and object pieces to children for the retelling. Allow the children to add the correct pieces as the story requires them. A second retelling may be done if the group is larger. Leave the flannel board up and the pieces out for a time. Allow the children to retell or create new stories after reading time. When children engage in this kind of activity, they are recreating their learning and dealing with their language.

Good Choices for Flannel Board Stories

The best stories for flannel boards are those in which there is a clear progression of events or characters. This allows the teller to add characters and objects as the tale is told. A good example is *The Napping House* by Audrey Wood. The story begins with a sleeping grandmother during a bad storm. As the action progresses, she is joined in the cozy bed by an assortment of other characters. The beautifully illustrated book contains a wonderful surprise ending. One might wish to follow up the reading of the book with an oral retelling using a flannel board. Children delight in the hands-on fun of adding characters to the bed.

Too Much Noise by Ann McGovern is another book that is appropriate for a flannel board retelling after an initial reading. Peter, the main character in the story, finds that his house is too noisy. The animals in the house contribute much to that situation. As each animal is turned loose, the house becomes quieter until it returns to normal. Children enjoy the opportunity to contribute to a flannel board retelling.

Strega Nona by Tomie dePaola can make a hilarious flannel board story. In this book, Big Anthony attempts to use Strega Nona's magic pasta pot. Not knowing how to control the magic, things quickly get out of hand for Big Anthony. Pasta is everywhere. White felt pieces with white yarn ''spaghetti'' glued on should provide a good picture of the problem on a flanel board.

Usually one can tell on a first reading whether or not a book will make a good flannel board story. The best stories are those where characters and objects are added gradually. Their addition should be closely related to the problem the plot is exploring. If nothing is added or removed as the story goes along, the flannel board is little more than a still picture.

THEATRICAL STORY TELLING

Everyone likes to see a show performed on stage. The excitement surrounding a performance creates a magic of its own. Even if done on a very small scale it is a special event. Using a theatrical performance also provides an opportunity to teach children the schema or procedure for going to the theater. Before a performance begins, the children can practice the roles of ticket sellers, ushers, announcers, concession stand clerks, and audience.

There are several possible avenues for telling a story using a theatrical framework. The two explored here are puppetry and creative dramatics. Each has strengths and drawbacks. Each works best with a different type of story.

Puppetry

Most children love puppets. Therefore, they are an enjoyable and easy way to enhance or interpret a story for children. Infants, of course, may not quite know what to make of a puppet the first time they see one. If presented with slow, deliberate movements and a soft voice, however, puppets are usually welcome additions to a young child's surroundings.

Puppets can be safe imaginary friends. They are found everywhere. Most adults as well as children seem to respond instinctively to them. Shy children will often speak to a puppet before they will speak to an unknown person. Children know that the puppet is not real. They know that it is the person holding the puppet who is actually speaking. Yet, the puppet has a reality of its own. Children speak to the puppet without reservation. They don't have to talk as though they are talking to the adult holding the puppet.

Puppets are allowed to be all of the things that people might like to be at times. They can be naughty, silly, brave, and mean. Perhaps that is why children feel they can speak to the puppet so freely; puppets will accept them because they understand about not being perfect.

Since puppets make such good friends, it makes sense to use them in a variety of story sharing activities. Purple monster puppets can help teach the color purple. A monkey puppet can motivate, comment, and ask questions when H. A. and Margaret Rey's books about Curious George the monkey are used. If it seems appropriate, stories can even be told by puppets. This is especially true for fables since they usually only have two or three characters.

How to Use Puppets. Effectively using puppets requires a knowledge of things one should not do with puppets. Do not try to be a ventriloquist. When not done expertly, it is distracting. Do not use too much body movement. Enthusiasm is important, but too much hand waving detracts from the words of the puppet. Do not distribute puppets to children without planning and guidance. The puppets will simply become toys to fight over. Do not expect puppets to do it all. Many stories can be told with a combination of puppets and a narrator. Do not be afraid to take risks. Try new and different kinds of puppets. The children will not be harsh when a puppet doesn't work out as well as expected. The audience loves the show before it even begins.

There are no specific rules for using puppets. They can tell the story or take part in the story. It is mostly a matter of the teacher trying a variety of procedures and learning what is comfortable. One of the best ways to continue enthusiasm for puppets is to use a variety of puppet types. While puppets can always be

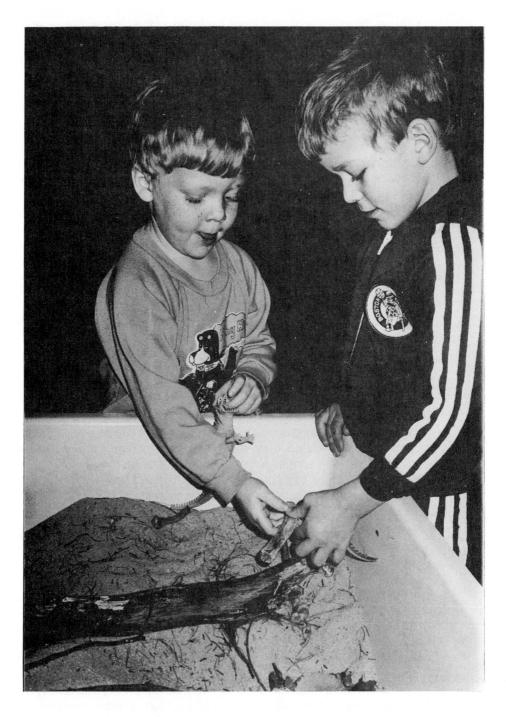

Children can use toys, such as these dinosaurs, to serve the role of puppets when recreating a story. Courtesy Diana Comer.

Homemade puppets can be inexpensive and fun to make. These older girls made these puppets with simple materials. Courtesy Diana Comer.

purchased commercially, some of the most interesting ones are homemade. Figure 7 illustrates some of the possibilities for making puppets.

Finger puppets are easily constructed from the cut-off fingers of a glove. Facial features can be painted or glued on. Stick puppets are simple and easy to make as well. The puppet can be a photograph or drawing of a character glued onto a stick. Even a story with several characters can be converted to puppets by using a coloring book format of the story or pictures made with a photocopier. The sticks used can be tongue depressors, craft sticks, straws, rulers, or sticks found in the yard.

String puppets are usually made with older children, but even younger ones enjoy making simple versions of these puppets. They are two or three dimensional puppets connected with two or more strings to a cross stick or sticks. Depending on the sophistication of the design, the sticks are held above the puppet. The sticks and strings control the puppet's body parts. Other puppet types are also available commercially or can be made.

Beginning Puppetry. Trying anything new can make one anxious. Getting accustomed to using puppets is no exception. Start small, build confidence in your ability, and then expand. Rather than starting with stories, explore the range of possibilities for just using the puppets with the children.

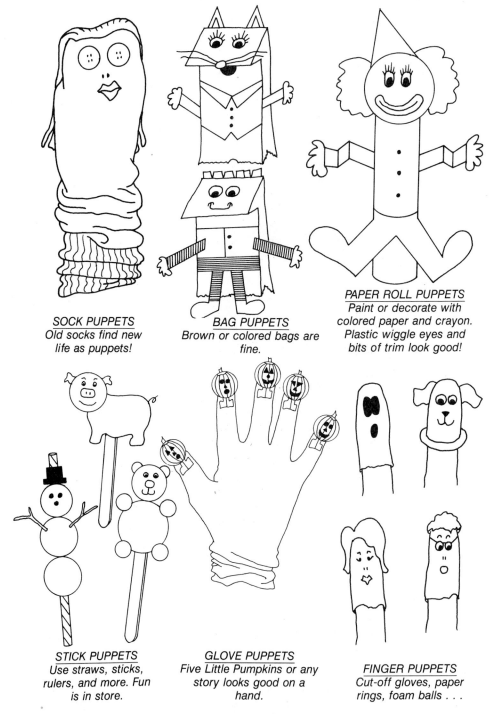

SOCK PUPPETS
Old socks find new
life as puppets!

BAG PUPPETS
Brown or colored bags are
fine.

PAPER ROLL PUPPETS
Paint or decorate with
colored paper and crayon.
Plastic wiggle eyes and
bits of trim look good!

STICK PUPPETS
Use straws, sticks,
rulers, and more. Fun
is in store.

GLOVE PUPPETS
Five Little Pumpkins or any
story looks good on a
hand.

FINGER PUPPETS
Cut-off gloves, paper
rings, foam balls . . .

Figure 7.   Puppet designs don't have to be too complicated. A simple puppet
can still make a story memorable. Courtesy Diana Comer.

Begin by seating the children in front of a mirror so that they can see both the puppet and themselves. Practice emotions by having the puppet look sad while saying, "I lost my favorite teddy bear." Make the puppet look angry while saying, "I'll NEVER go to bed until I'm two hundred years old!" Include other ideas from the children.

Get used to the idea of puppets handling dialogue by using two play telephones. Give one to the puppet and have the children take turns using the other. Allow the script to emerge spontaneously. Expand this by having the teacher and a puppet on one phone with a child and a puppet on the other. Another way to become comfortable with puppet dialogue is to have the teacher and puppet engage in a game such as Simon Says. Use motions at first and then follow up with lines such as "Simon says, 'Say meatball' . . . Simon says, 'Say curly caterpillar.' "

Involve the children to expand the possibilities. For example, have several children each hold a puppet at snack time. Explain that each puppet has to take a turn commenting on the snack and answering questions asked by the other puppets. Other scenarios can be used as well for this activity. They include discussions about playground behaviors, getting in line, and so on. When teacher and children are comfortable with their skills, it is time to use puppets to tell and recreate stories.

Good Choices for Puppetry. The best kinds of stories for puppet presentations are those with a simple plot and only a few main characters. Since stage settings can be difficult, a few simple props must make the story a reality for the children. *The Carrot Seed* by Ruth Krauss makes a good puppet show. The boy, the sun, the rain, and the ever growing carrot are all that are needed. Any boy puppet would do. A paper plate sun, a hand drawn rain cloud and a real carrot would complete the primary roles. The real carrot can be pushed up from behind the stage as the story unfolds. The sun and the cloud, with mouths and eyes drawn on, can become starring characters.

Tomie dePaola's *Charlie Needs a Cloak* is a superb story for a puppet presentation. It is the story of a shepherd who finds that his old faithful cloak is too tattered and worn to keep him warm in the winter anymore. He spends the following spring and summer shearing, spinning, weaving, dyeing and sewing wool into a new cloak. By the following autumn he is ready to face the winter in a new warm red cloak. The story can be told with a boy puppet, one or two sheep puppets and a few scraps of yarn and fabric.

Diane Paterson's book, *Smile for Auntie,* will delight children as a puppet story. In the book a baby with a tremendous frown refuses to smile for his aunt. The aunt tries everything to get the baby to smile, all to no avail. The surprise ending is done without a word being spoken. Only two puppets are needed to make this story come alive.

Harriet Ziefert's *Mike and Tony: Best Friends* is a book that explores the meaning of true friendship and forgiveness. It can be told using just two boy puppets and a few common objects such as a ball and a play telephone. *Beast,* by Susan Meddaugh, can be retold using a girl puppet, a monster puppet, and a

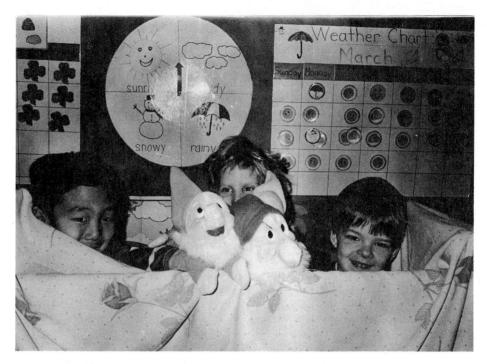

Puppet shows put on by children give them both language experiences and opportunities to share their feelings. Courtesy Diana Comer.

snack. Other characters in the story can all be handled by a narrator holding the puppets. The story explores the themes of bravery and of thinking for one's self. This type of story allows the teacher to more fully explore the possibilities of literature with young children.

Creative Dramatics

Drama is only a bit more formal than puppetry. Creative dramatics is a type of drama that is not designed for the production of a play for an audience. Rather, it is a more spontaneous process aimed at communicating some message, emotion, or story using dramatic techniques. In conjunction with the sharing of the message, it seeks to increase sensitivity of the feelings of others, build positive self-concepts, increase confidence and concentration, provide new relationships, and build an appreciation of the arts.[2] Creative dramatics includes the use of pantomime, mime, and acting to create and recreate ideas and stories.

Why is drama such a powerful tool? Why is it so effective for helping children develop language and an understanding of themselves? Drama is a natural activity for most children. Their play is often a suspension of reality which allows them to

[2] Walter Sawyer and Arlene Leff, "Elementary School Creative Dramatics: Coming to Your Senses" pp. 29–32, in Nancy Brizendine and James Thomas (Editors) *Learning through Dramatics: Ideas for Teachers and Librarians* (Phoenix, Arizona: Oryx, 1982).

explore the possibilities of their environments. When children delve into dramatic play, they cross the line between reality and fantasy. Yet, they are still aware of reality. This allows children to become astronauts, dinosaur hunters, parents, and buildings. Because it is play, children can easily move among the roles of cowboy, fireman, and medical doctor. They possess a total belief in their roles at the moment they are in those roles. Such an emotional commitment is only achieved through the child's careful attention and focus.

How to Use Creative Dramatics. The guiding rule for using creative dramatics is to keep things simple. This applies to dialogue, characters, setting, and plot. In contrast to puppetry, this format can and should include everyone. Each child is not a main character, but each can be included as a fourth little pig, another stepsister, or as one of the sheep in a story. The staging, costumes, and settings can be created by the group. Everyone can help move furniture props, paint a chimney for a Santa Claus story, and bring in old clothes for costumes. All should be involved in the choosing of what will be done. If everyone is emotionally involved, the effort and enthusiasm will be contagious.

Carefully consider the dialogue. If a chorus line is to be repeated several times, have a group of children do it rather than just a single child. The group will provide security for each of its members. Use a narrator on difficult parts of the story to help the dialogue flow more smoothly.

Costumes can give a feeling of importance to children taking part in the drama. Costumes can be real clothing, old Halloween outfits, yard sale leftovers, and old uniforms. They are relatively easy to collect and any classroom can quickly accumulate an adequate variety. Help children use their imaginations in using costumes. They do not have to find the entire outfit to play the role. An old army hat and a dark jacket make an airline pilot. A hat with ears attached, brown mittens, and a piece of rope can make a cat. A white shirt and a headband with a round silver foil disc create a doctor's outfit. With just these bits and pieces of costumes available, imagination will do the rest.

Settings should be simple. If scenery is absolutely essential, a single sheet can be painted or drawn on with markers for a backdrop. Figure 8 illustrates two ways to create a scene in this way. Small setting pieces can be cut out of cardboard and painted. They may be free standing or simply leaned against a chair or a wall.

Props are objects needed to make the scene look more realistic or to help in the telling of the story. They may include such things as pails, brooms, chairs, crowns, and food items. Props should be minimal and need not be real objects. Play telephones or bananas cut from yellow construction paper work just as well as the real thing.

Good Choices for Creative Dramatics. Mother Goose stories and nursery rhymes make a great introduction to creative dramatics. They can be portrayed quite easily with a minimum of costumes and props. Poems and songs can be dramatized with a minimum amount of preparation as well.

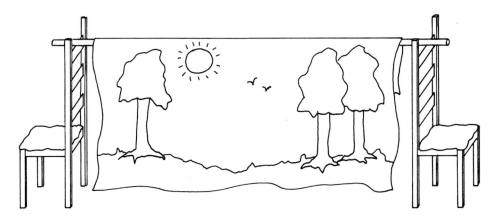

A sheet can be placed over a pole that is attached to two chairs.

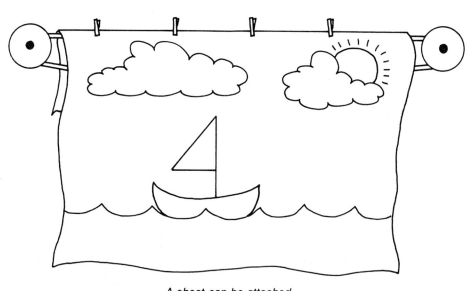

A sheet can be attached with clothespins to a rope.

Figure 8.   Quick and easy stage settings. Courtesy Diana Comer.

Good possibilities for dramatization include stories with many parts or with groups of characters. This enables varying numbers of children to have an involvement in the experience. Humorous stories and stories with action and suspense make good choices. *Corduroy* by Don Freeman is a wonderful story about a bear searching for a friend. The book has roles that are expandable since the setting is a department store. It has a great ending and makes a good play.

Cloudy with a Chance of Meatballs by Judi Barrett is a very funny book that could become a very funny play. The story takes place in a land where it rains various kinds of food. Naturally, something goes wrong and a solution to the problem must be found. In one part, it rains meatballs as big as basketballs. Meatballs, dropping out of a net from the ceiling, could be made from balloons covered with brown paper. The story would not soon be forgotten.

Legends, fairy tales, and folk tales make good plays because they combine magic, mystery, and action. *Babushka,* retold by Charles Mikolaycak is an old Russian Christmas legend. After reading the story to the children, it would not be difficult to recreate the story as a play. With some Russian folk music and some costuming, the ethnic flavor of the country would come alive. Julie Lane's *The Life and Adventures of Santa Claus* is a book with a number of dramatic possibilities. Set in the Baltic Sea region of Europe, it recounts the early life of Santa Claus. It captures the old world flavor of early Christmas celebrations. Children are fascinated with knowing more about the life of one of their favorite characters.

Current children's literature has much to offer as well. Many stories meet the requirements for creative dramatics: appropriate numbers of characters, simple plots, memorable dialogue, and few prop requirements. Lore Segal's *All the Way Home* has great action, a variety of animal characters, and a simple humorous situation. Robert Kraus's *Another Mouse to Feed* can be made into a drama with any number of characters. The situation of the harried mouse parents trying to raise all of their mouse children will strike a sympathetic chord with most youngsters. *Ten Little Babies* by Robert Priest is a story told through a poem. The repeating line will have children joining in by the second or third page. It can be done with even young children since they will be able to participate with only a narrator reading the book.

Creative dramatics takes some planning, but can be done more spontaneously than putting on a play. The positive results of a dramatic experience are well worth the effort. This type of drama is supportive of children's efforts and is a memorable experience for children. They learn much about life from the pretend situations found in books made real through creative dramatics. They get to act out their feelings and can experiment with their reactions to situations. Creative dramatics gives a shy child the opportunity to safely take some risks, while allowing the aggressive child to take on the role of a shy character. By seeing themselves in new roles, children ultimately learn more about themselves.

CHILDREN AS AUTHORS AND STORYTELLERS

Children are beginning to write as soon as they begin to draw. They are attempting to make sense through some type of visual process. Some children seem to have more to say than others. Some children seem to be more creative than others. All children, however, do have something to say and have a variety of ways of saying it. This is to be encouraged. Adults must be accepting of children's attempts at writing. If willingness to take risks is destroyed, growth as authors and storytellers will be damaged as well.

In traditional elementary school programs, much of children's creativity is overlooked. The goal has long seemed to be to have children spell, punctuate, and print correctly. Unfortunately, focusing on the mechanics of writing has had quite the opposite effect of what was intended. Children whose papers are returned full of red correction marks are most likely to write shorter, less interesting pieces in the future. Focusing on mechanics also obscures the more important aspects of writing such as clarity, organization, and a freshness of thinking. Some of this is changing as the whole language movement makes its way into the country's education systems.

Stimulating experiences and experiences that involve them are beneficial to children as authors and storytellers. Exposure to quality illustrations, either through books or in museums and galleries, provides new ideas to think about and talk about. As these opportunities are increased, the potential for intellectual growth is increased as well. Writing and storytelling are thinking activities. The ability to engage in them depends upon one's ability to analyze, question, organize, generate, and reorganize facts and reality. Yet, no two people see things in exactly the same way. Figure 9 illustrates how different children can take a single topic and come up with several different stories about it.

JUNGLE STORY by Marissa and Megan (Becker Day Care Center)

One day there was an alligator and he was getting a suntan. He got a purple suntan and he put apples on it. His mother got a crab and pinched him. He put a bandaid on it. He laid in bed for a nap. The end.

JUNGLE STORY by Dania and Mellissa (Becker Day Care Center)

One day we went to the jungle. We saw an elephant. He was eating grass. His mommy said to eat snacks and juice and junk. We also saw a hippo and a lion and they were fighting each other. They scratched and they were licking each other. The end.

JUNGLE STORY by Elizabeth and Bryan (Becker Day Care Center)

One day we saw a leopard and a snake. They were eating grass. The leopard was jumping and he saw something and he started to roar. It was a bumblebee who stung him and he bit the bumblebee and he ate the bumblebee up. The snake did go in the water to get a drink of water. The end.

Figure 9. Child-dictated jungle stories. Courtesy Diana Comer.

How to Encourage Children as Authors

Children usually have something to say that they feel is important. Sometimes they are reluctant to say it, but everyone has a story to tell. Providing rich experiences will help keep children's minds active and will help them to construct new meanings and new stories. Since many young children will be able to use much more language than they can write, an adult must serve as a transcriber and facilitator for their stories. These stories can take a variety of forms.

Classroom Books. A classroom book is a good beginning activity. It is particularly appropriate after the class has shared a common experience. The experience could be a walk to the firehouse, a visit from a pet rabbit, or a simple science demonstration. Each child draws a picture depicting the experience. After the picture is completed, the child tells the teacher about the picture. The teacher writes, at the bottom of the picture, a brief sentence or key phrase that the child has stated. All of the illustrations and the writing are bound, glued, or stapled together to form a book. The book can be shared with the class several times over the next few days. This reinforces the idea that children have an understanding of their world, have something important to say, and are authors who write books.

An approach which is related to this is the language experience approach or LEA. The LEA uses the child's own language to teach beginning reading and writing. The basis for the story might be an experience the class has shared, a story they have heard, or their imaginations. The children generate a story that the teacher writes. It usually has a time frame and possesses many of the characteristics of literature.

Frequently LEA stories are written on large sheets of poster paper so that they can be made into "Big Books." Children draw the illustrations for the various pages. They may also illustrate it by pasting pictures on the pages. The story is then shared several times with the group. The teacher points to each word as it is read. Often the story has a repeated line. When this occurs, children begin to recognize or anticipate the line and join in the reading.

The mechanics of constructing these classroom books are important. The books should be sturdy, so that children will be able to handle them repeatedly. Oaktag or cardboard covers can be used to protect the pages. Clear contact paper on each of the pages protects them over a long period of time. The pages are best bound with yarn or cord to keep them together. Finally, the printing should be done in large manuscript lettering. Typing the words will make them too small for a shared reading with children. Photo albums with clear magnetic pages are a good commercial alternative that could also be used for this purpose.

Good Choices for Child-Created Stories

Making books builds self-confidence and a sense of mastery over language. It may be done with large classroom types of books using the LEA. It may also be done on an individual or small group basis. While children often have many things to tell about, various themes may be helpful ideas. For example, ABC books, counting books and concept books can be created by individual youngsters or groups of children. Figure 10 contains stories created by small groups of children on the concept of spring.

THEME: WHAT HAPPENS IN SPRING?

Charles, David, Jackie, and Marci: "Daffodils grow. It starts to rain. The bees come out and sting you. An elephant at the zoo jumps on you. The Easter Bunny brings eggs and toys. He brings you rabbit candy and chocolate eggs."

Eli, Justin, Erica, and Elizabeth: "In spring, wear spring jackets. Or wear an eagle shirt that says something about a motorcycle. Or wear a Minnie Mouse shirt. Bunnies are funny. I like birds. My favorite is a blue bird. There are blue and white flowers by some trees. I had a dream last night about some yellow flowers that are supposed to grow in spring."

Ryan, Danielle, Ben, and Stacie: "Birds eat worms. They love worms. Bunnies and chickies come out. Easter bunnies hide baskets on tables and behind couches. Sometimes you write on paper when it's spring. Yellow flowers grow in sunshine. Sometimes flowers talk. Sometimes birds take care of worms. Trees begin to get food because they're hungry. Leaves grow."

Reprinted with permission by Judy Brown-DuPaul's class.

Figure 10.   Group-invented stories: Spring. Courtesy Diana Comer.

Creating books that involve the senses can be very successful. For example, a Christmas holiday book might use the senses of sight, smell, and touch. If an activity for the day is baking cookies, cinnamon and other spices can be sprinkled on a spot of glue in the book. When decorating with pine boughs, a twig can be pressed and glued into the book. Sawdust can be added to the page that pictures the tree being cut down. The pictures and stories about the holiday will be greatly enhanced by these additions.

The creation of books can be basic and simple. The key is not how professional the books look. Rather, the most important part of this activity is the validation of the children's thoughts. If adults are accepting of children's literary attempts, children will begin to see themselves as authors. The correct use of mechanics often comes as children become more familiar with language and books. At this early stage, making sense of language is the most important part of the process.

SUMMARY

There are literally hundreds of fascinating ways to share stories. Taking a new look at some common sense approaches is helpful. Reading aloud is a most effective way to share stories. Yet, it is not simply a matter of opening a book and reading it to children. It requires some planning and a little bit of acting. Oral storytelling has a long tradition, but is practiced less today. While it may be more difficult than

Creating rebus stories by stamping with picture stamps is one way to help children enjoy the experience of authorship. Courtesy Diana Comer.

reading aloud, people of all ages are mesmerized by the spell a good storyteller can cast over an audience. With practice, amateur storytellers can capture some of that magic.

Various materials can be added to the sharing of stories to create diversity and artistic effects. Flannel boards are effective tools for sharing stories. They provide an avenue for both oral and hands-on involvement by children in the telling of the story. Theatrical storytelling takes this one step further. By using puppetry and creative dramatics, children are given the power to suspend reality and enter a magical world created exclusively for them.

The more involved the children are in the storytelling process, the greater their creative and intellectual growth can be. The ultimate goal is, of course, helping children to attain literacy. Involving them early as authors is a critical step in this journey. For this reason, allowing children to create class books is strongly encouraged. The positive self-concepts they gain by creating stories for sensitive and caring audiences will provide them with confidence to continue on the road to literacy.

QUESTIONS FOR THOUGHT AND DISCUSSION

1. Why should a variety of approaches for sharing stories be used?
2. Which method of sharing stories is easiest to begin with?

3. What can one do to prepare to read a story aloud?
4. Why should a teacher read a story aloud to the children every day?
5. What should one consider when choosing a book to read aloud?
6. Why is child involvement important in oral storytelling?
7. What are the characteristics of a good story for oral telling?
8. What materials are needed for a flannel board story?
9. What are some things a teacher telling a flannel board story should be aware of?
10. What are the characteristics of a good flannel board story?
11. Why should one use flannel board stories with children?
12. Why are puppets effective as storytelling tools?
13. Defend or refute this statement: A teacher who uses puppets must learn to be a ventriloquist.
14. What kinds of stories are best to use with puppets?
15. Why is drama a useful tool for telling stories to young children?
16. What should be considered when planning a creative dramatics experience with children?
17. Why should young children use costumes and props when involved in dramatics?
18. Defend or refute this statement: Young children are unable to write stories.
19. What is a classroom book?
20. Is the Language Experience Approach useful for preschool children? Why?

CHILDREN'S BOOKS CITED

Edward Ardizzone, *Little Tim and the Brave Sea Captain* (New York: Puffin, 1977).

Judi Barrett, *Cloudy with a Chance of Meatballs* (New York: Atheneum, 1978).

Tomie dePaola, *Charlie Needs a Cloak* (Englewood Cliffs, New Jersey: Prentice Hall, 1973).

Tomie dePaola, *Strega Nona* (Englewood Cliffs, New Jersey: Prentice Hall, 1975).

Don Freeman, *Corduroy* (New York: Puffin, 1976).

Robert Krauss, *Another Mouse to Feed* (New York: Prentice Hall, 1980).

Ruth Krauss, *The Carrot Seed* (New York: Harper & Row, 1945).

Julie Lane, *The Life and Adventures of Santa Claus* (Orford, New Hampshire: Equity, 1979).

Arnold Lobel, *Frog and Toad Are Friends* (New York: Harper & Row, 1979).

Ann McGovern, *Too Much Noise* (Boston: Houghton Mifflin, 1967).

Susan Meddaugh, *Beast* (Boston: Houghton Mifflin, 1981).

Charles Mikolaycak (Retold by), *Babushka* (New York: Holiday House, 1984).

Arlene Mosel, *Tikki Tikki Tembo* (New York: Holt, Rinehart and Winston, 1968).

Diane Paterson, *Smile for Auntie* (New York: Dial, 1976).

Robert Priest, *Ten Little Babies* (Windsor, Ontario, Canada: Black Moss, 1989).

Uri Schulevitz, *One Monday Morning* (New York: Scribner's, 1967).

Doris Schwerin, *The Tomorrow Book* (New York: Pantheon, 1984).

Lore Segal, *All the Way Home* (New York: Farrar, Straus and Giroux, 1973).

Lynd Ward, *The Biggest Bear* (Boston: Houghton Mifflin, 1952).

Kurt Wiese and Claire Huchet Bishop, *Five Chinese Brothers* (New York: Coward McCann, 1938).

Audrey Wood, *The Napping House* (New York: Harcourt, 1984).

Jane Yolen, *No Bath Tonight* (New York: Crowell, 1978).

Harriet Ziefert, *Mike and Tony: Best Friends* (New York: Viking Penguin, 1987).

SELECTED REFERENCES

Nancy Brizendine and James Thomas (Editors), *Learning through Dramatics: Ideas for Teachers and Librarians* (Phoenix, Arizona: Oryx, 1982).

Mary Lewis, *Acting for Children* (New York: John Day, 1969).

Nellie McCaslin, *Creative Dramatics in the Classroom* (New York: David McKay, 1968).

Jim Trelease, *The New Read-Aloud Handbook* (New York: Viking Penguin, 1989).

Jean Warren, *More Piggyback Songs* (Everett, Washington: Totline, 1984).

Integrating Literature into the Curriculum

arly childhood classrooms must include a wide range of topics and activities. This variety is needed to address the total development of each child. Literature is sometimes seen as only one of the things that must be provided to children in their formative years. Age-appropriate academics, art, music, free play, nutrition, and other parts of the program must all be addressed as well. One might easily feel overwhelmed by the number of topics and activities that should be provided.

How can all of these parts be provided? Should some be dropped from the program? How can one decide how to include everything? Can anything be combined with something else? These questions can be puzzling. Obviously, one will need to plan carefully in order to avoid leaving out parts of a program that have a truly legitimate purpose. This chapter discusses an innovative strategy for including each of the important aspects of the program. The strategy is the use of a web as an aid to planning the early childhood program unit.

WEBS AS ORGANIZATIONAL TOOLS

Much time has been spent over the past two decades studying how the human brain works. Scientists have examined this field by trying to make computers behave in the same way as a human brain. Since the computer is a machine and a human being possesses natural intelligence, this concept is known as artificial intelligence. From these experiments, several conclusions have been reached. One conclusion refers to how people understand new ideas, new concepts, and new problems. It is believed that people comprehend things by relating the new to the known.[1] This means that the way to best understand a new idea or concept is to see how it best fits with what one already comprehends.

This idea can be applied to planning the various components of an early childhood program. In doing this, one is simply attempting to understand how the parts are related. That is, rather than looking at each part of the program as an

---

[1] P. David Pearson and Dale D. Johnson, *Teaching Reading Comprehension* (New York: Holt, Rinehart and Winston, 1978).

isolated activity, the separate parts are seen as pieces of a whole. In order to do this, one has to visualize and come to an understanding of how each part fits in with other parts. As new parts of the program are considered, they can be related to the program as it is understood by the teacher. This technique is much like the understanding that scientists attempt to duplicate in studies of artificial intelligence. That is, they try to get the computer to understand something new by having it place the new information within what it already knows about that topic.

A Web for Understanding

Perhaps the best way to understand how a web might work is to visualize how a young child might come to an understanding of how something new fits with what the child already knows. Consider a young child who sees a man walking a dog on a leash down the street. The child might never have seen the dog, or even that particular breed of dog prior to this time. Yet, the child points at the animal and proudly exclaims, "Doggy!" How the child knew what the animal was is explained by understanding how the child took the new information (i.e., the dog being walked) and fit it in with the known (i.e., what the child already knew about dogs).

Although the child might not have been able to explain everything about dogs, the child already knew some things about dogs. Such things as barking, Lassie, a wagging tail, and chasing cats are things the child could probably associate with dogs. It is reasonable to believe that a young child would possess most of the information contained in Figure 1 which depicts a knowledge web for dogs. The web organizes the information under four subheadings. By possessing the information in the web and by viewing the new dog, the child is able to identify several things that fit in with what is already known about dogs. This might have included the leash, collar, four legs, a tail, walking, and perhaps a bark. These characteristics fit with the child's knowledge about what constitutes a dog. The child concludes that it is a dog even though it does not look like any previous dog the child has seen. Of course, this doesn't always work out so neatly, which is why children are often heard making errors. The child might just as easily have seen a horse and called it a dog. This false conclusion might be reached because the child didn't have enough information about horses to clearly identify one.

In any case, it is seen in Figure 1 that the information is organized. It is believed that the human mind organizes knowledge in a similar way. That is why one doesn't constantly mistake cats for dogs and vice versa. Upon meeting the new dog, the child could learn its name and add that new name to examples of dogs that are known to the child. The process the child has gone through is an example of relating the new to the known. It is done by all human beings throughout life.

The lines that make up Figure 1 are similar to the lines that form the web constructed by a spider. Therefore, the term web is used to describe the designs used to depict these figures. The web is helpful in understanding how children comprehend information. It is also helpful in assisting the teacher in understanding how the various components of a program can be related and integrated with others.

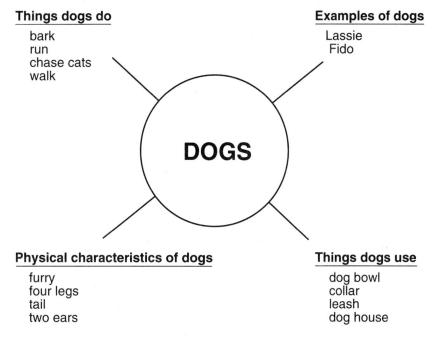

Things dogs do
- bark
- run
- chase cats
- walk

Examples of dogs
- Lassie
- Fido

DOGS

Physical characteristics of dogs
- furry
- four legs
- tail
- two ears

Things dogs use
- dog bowl
- collar
- leash
- dog house

Figure 1.   A knowledge web for dogs or for any other concept follows the same basic procedure. Courtesy Walter Sawyer.

Planning with a Web

A web is a useful tool in a variety of planning situations. It may be used to visualize or organize a total program or just certain aspects of a program.

To construct a web, one must begin with a central theme. Using a free-flowing brainstorming approach, one lists a variety of aspects related to that central theme. The next step might be to select relevant items from the list and organize them under subheadings. The final step is to create a web that visually represents the total picture. Figure 2 illustrates the steps one might follow when considering a topic such as toys. Notice that some items appear under more than one subheading. Dotted lines are used to point out this relationship in the actual web. As new ideas or new knowledge is gained, the web grows outward and the lines showing relationship may increase.

This same process may be used to plan a unit for a classroom. The central idea might be art, music, literature, science, social studies, nutrition, or math. The teacher might then generate related ideas such as activities or books to use with the theme. The ideas could be organized under subheadings and a web could be created.

Literature Web

A web might be constructed for a literature theme. That is, when a topic has been identified, the teacher might wish to focus mainly on the literature concerning the topic. In this case, the subheadings might include poems, fingerplays, and stories

Step 1: Brainstorm a list of related terms:

blocks	cars	trucks	stuffed animals
rattles	pots	pans	teddy bears
clay	crayons	paints	board games
balls	bats	markers	rubber duck

Step 2: Select items and organize under subheadings:

Soft Toys	**Bed Toys**	**Group Toys**	**Art Toys**
stuffed animals	stuffed animals	balls	crayons
teddy bears	teddy bears	board games	clay
clay	rubber duck		paint
balls			markers

Step 3: Create a web and show relationships:

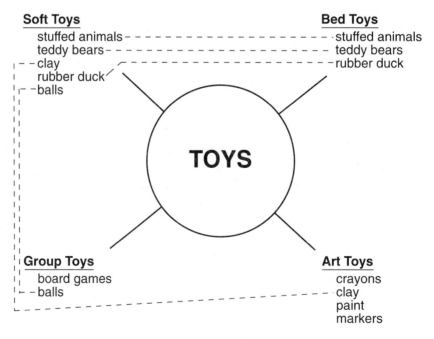

Figure 2.   Creating a web for toys. Courtesy Walter Sawyer.

related to a particular literature theme. Under each subheading would be a listing
of examples that might be used in the unit.

Figure 3 depicts a literature web for the theme of owls. Notice that the web is drawn in a slightly different way than those depicted in Figures 1 and 2. There is no specific method for designing a web. The design should be one that makes sense to the individual using the web. Using the web in Figure 3, the teacher might designate certain pieces of literature to be used at specific times of a day or week. The teacher has an overall understanding of each piece of literature to be used throughout the unit. Because of this, reference can easily be made to what might be coming in the future or what the class did that morning.

If the teacher doesn't know where the class is heading, chances are the program is lost. Used as a roadmap for the day or week, the web can be a tremendous help in preventing such a situation. Webs can be revised each year. They can be added to or have sections deleted as needed. Keeping the web on file helps reduce planning time in subsequent years.

THEMES FOR DEVELOPING WEBS

Teachers do not need to think of each theme or book around which to develop a curriculum or literature web. Borrowing and learning from others is a teaching tradition that can and should be relied on. Doris Bullock has written a book containing a wealth of ideas for expanding many of the books commonly used in early childhood education.[2]

Webs can be used to plan around one book or a theme using several books. They may be used to plan for a single day or a longer period of time such as a one week unit. There are several themes that might be considered due to their importance to early childhood education.

Subject Area Themes

Themes may be developed around a specific subject area. However, one should also consider combining subject areas through related elements or books that combine the different subject areas. Several subject areas will be considered including science, social studies, mathematics, arts, basic concepts, language, movement, and celebrations.

Science. The most common topic within this area is the study of ourselves. Children are very curious about their bodies. Topics for themes might include the body, teeth, foods we eat, illness, good health, and accident prevention. The study of other living things should also be considered. This would include pets and pet care, plants and animals, ocean/pond life, insects, sex differences, and babies. Natural phenomena are also of interest. This includes magnetism, bubbles, weather, how things grow, electricity, simple machines (e.g., pulleys, wheels), stars and planets.

Social Studies. In social studies, the focus is often on the community and neighborhood helpers. Safety issues can be investigated with themes on personal safety, emotions, and families. The focus can expand to other communities as well in units such as the farm, the city, the desert, the mountains, lifestyles, outer

[2] Doris Bullock, *Designed to Delight* (Belmont, CA: Fearon, 1986).

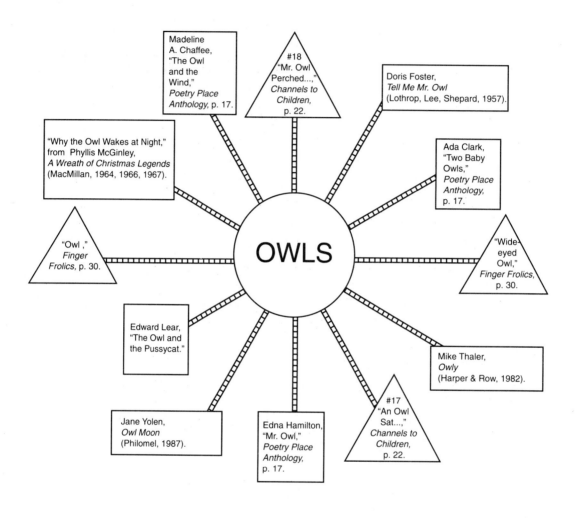

KEY: ☐ POEM   △ FINGERPLAY   ▭ STORY

Figure 3. Literature web. Courtesy Diana Comer.

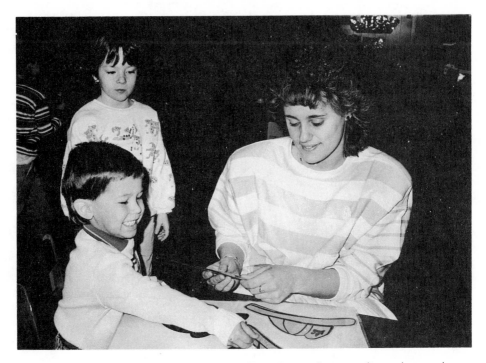

This student teacher created a game using colors and community workers and helps a child experience success. This enthusiasm can be transferred to a literature unit on community workers. Courtesy Diana Comer.

space, and climates. A sense of time can be developed in units on history, dinosaurs, and historical figures. The world community can come alive with themes on the differences and similarities of people, cultural heritage, holidays around the world, climates, ethnic celebrations, and geography.

Mathematics. Mathematics in early childhood education includes more than just learning numbers. Themes can be developed on building principles using shapes, blocks, and estimating. Early computation skills include the concepts of counting and adding and subtracting by using concrete objects. Other mathematics themes might include predicting, metrics, graphing, and charting.

The Arts. The arts include music, drama, and the visual arts. Music themes might include songs, fingerplays, instruments, and choral singing. Drama themes include plays, puppetry, fingerplays, costuming, skits, and role playing. Themes in the visual arts could include color, design, collage, painting, markers, clay, 3-D art, junk art, easel art, and ecology art.

Basic Concepts. The term "basic concepts" includes all of the taken-for-granted aspects of life that explain such things as size, proximity, and action. They include spatial concepts such as near, far, in front of, on top of, behind, and so on; actions

The arts and literature can be combined by helping children make models of story characters from clay. Courtesy Diana Comer.

such as push, pull, open, fast and close; size and weight concepts such as big, small, heavy, and light; sensory concepts such as color, sound, taste, feel, sweet, soft, and bright. Each can be studied as a separate concept. However, it makes much more sense to integrate their study. One seldom sees just ''red'' or experiences the concept of ''near'' in isolation. One sees red crayons, red fire engines, and red mittens. One is near a cat, or near a mommy, or near a friend. Each of these concepts is integrated in life. It makes sense to integrate them with other components of a program.

Language. Language, of course, can be easily integrated with any of the other theme areas. Language is used to describe and deal with each of them. When considering language, one is concerned with ABC's, color words, word patterns, sequencing, solving puzzles, rebus writing, labeling, name learning, literature, picture dictionaries, listening, etc. It is often helpful to see language as a device that can be used to link and integrate two or more of the other themes together.

Movement. During the early years, children acquire a great deal of control over their bodies. This aspect of a program can easily be integrated with other themes. Included in a movement theme are such concepts as growth and development, muscle control, body fluidity, coordination, challenging oneself, and group cooperation. After reading a book about colors, one can easily construct a game in which children are asked to take turns placing a number of objects of various colors at different locations around the room. This activity integrates colors and listening (language and art), spatial awareness (basic concepts), and muscle control (movement) with literature (reading of the book).

Nontraditional Celebrations. The category of nontraditional celebrations can cover virtually everything else one wants to do. Nontraditional refers to the idea of times other than holidays or the changing of seasons. In a classroom, the teacher and children are in charge of celebrations. There are many unique celebrations that can be created using professional resources such as Kathy Flagella's resource guide for celebrations.[3] One can give free rein to imagination and a sense of adventure. New celebrations can be created during weeks that do not contain a Thanksgiving, Valentine's Day, or Halloween. Common themes can be given a sense of excitement by creation of a week long celebration for them. A "Pets in Our World" week might include books on pets, a trip to a veterinarian or pet shop, making pet rocks, and a contest for drawings of favorite pets. A "Teddy Bear Celebration" might include books about teddy bears, a teddy bear picnic, a teddy dance, bring a teddy bear day, and snacks made with honey. These celebrations can easily be molded to include activities and content from each of the other theme areas.

The more that concepts are integrated into the curriculum, the better the learning. If children have had an enjoyable experience, the memories they recreate from that experience will reinforce the concepts learned. Children often benefit from a multi-sensory, hands-on approach to learning. Therefore, planning that includes this approach will result in more effective instruction. The use of literature provides interest, motivation, and language that can be used to integrate many parts of the curriculum.

Books that Don't Fit Themes

Sometimes one plans a unit for which there doesn't seem to be a good book. At other times, one discovers a particularly good book that doesn't seem to fit any of the units being planned. This doesn't mean that either the unit being planned or the wonderful book should not be used. A unit that provides stimulating learning should always be used even if literature cannot be integrated with it. A good book can always be read simply for the enjoyment of the story. In fact, many good books can and should be read solely for that reason.

In addition, one might discover a book such as Robert McCloskey's *Time of Wonder* and know that a unit on the sea is planned for May. It makes sense to hold the book aside until the unit is begun. On the other hand, one might be planning to use Douglas Florian's *Discovering Frogs* during the month of June, but a child brings in a jar of tadpoles at the beginning of May. The book should be used immediately while the interest is high. Saving it until the June unit on pond life

---

[3] Kathy Flagella, *Celebrate Every Day: Hundreds of Celebrations for Early Childhood Classrooms* (Bridgeport, CT: First Teacher Press, 1987).

would serve no purpose. Common sense and flexibility often go hand in hand in situations such as this.

Adjusting a book or poem to fit a particular purpose should also be considered when an exact match between a book and a theme cannot be found. In telling a story, one can always add characters, change settings, or lengthen the plot. Take, for example, the kindergarten class that wished to do a Christmas play. Since it was difficult to find a story or play with twenty-two parts, the children adapted one using Dr. Seuss' *How the Grinch Stole Christmas.* The play included a group of really rotten rats (five children) with one lead rat (dressed as a ragged Santa) who burst through a cardboard chimney to steal Christmas. The play also included four other children, the real Santa, the nine reindeer, and a mother and father. All twenty-two children had important roles. Reading the Dr. Seuss story helped the children understand the idea that would be created in the play. The Grinch was a superb model for the behavior of the rotten rats. All children had a speaking role through the use of a choral line that was repeated at key points in the play. One of the best parts of the experience was that no child had to play an ''added on'' part such as a tree or a bush.

FACILITATING INTEGRATION

Webs can be an immense help in developing integrated lessons. They allow one to step back and plan the big picture of a lesson prior to actually using it with children. In addition to planning, there are steps that can be taken within the lesson to further facilitate integration. Some of these ideas require the acquisition of materials to use in the lesson. Others focus on taking advantage of the things that happen within the lesson.

Recreating the Experience

Providing opportunities for children to recreate the learning enhances the understanding of the lesson. Providing inexpensive or no-cost materials can ensure that the learning or the story will be experienced again. Take, for example, a lesson in which Angela Grunsell's *At the Doctor's* was read. Providing a toy stethoscope, old white dress shirts, and bandaids can encourage the natural expansion of the story into dramatic play. Making some of these materials expands the story into art as well.

Another example might be Jean Johnson's *Postal Workers A to Z*. After the reading, children could be provided with a pile of old envelopes, stickers, an ink pad, and a rubber stamp. Milk cartons could be made into mailboxes, enabling the children to recreate the story. One of the purposes of free play is to allow children to try out the world from a safe harbor. It may be beneficial to allow children to engage in this activity prior to a field trip to a real post office.

Using Children's Interest

Use the motivation of the children to lead into another activity. Even if it wasn't the next activity planned, a high interest level can be a deciding factor in shifting the order of the day's activities. Perhaps the motivating factor was the reading of Donald Crews's book, *Freight Train*. If interest is high, the time is ripe to make different colored train cars as an expansion of the reading. Teaching shapes (of the cars) or counting (the number of cars) are additional expansions coming out of the initial motivation. A variety of fine motor activities could also be included in the construction of the paper train.

Robert McClung's *Animals that Build Their Homes* might provide inspiration for a matching game of animals with their homes. A listening activity could be used as well by having children identify the animals that make a particular sound. Clay or papier mache houses and animals might be used to integrate art with the other activities.

Bear's Busy Morning by Harriet Ziefert can be expanded by allowing children to dramatize the story with real teddy bears. Using doll clothes, this creates an enjoyable hands-on activity while also reinforcing the concept of getting dressed. Using velcro fasteners on the clothes enables very young children to engage in this activity. An alternative would be to have children role play the part of a bear using adult size clothing.

A Sense of Flexibility

It is important to keep a sense of flexibility. Even carefully made plans do not always work out as expected. Being flexible and being willing to use opportunities is an advantage when working with children. Without these skills, one misses the possibilities that are always presenting themselves. Keeping the original plan in mind is necessary, but one should not be a slave to it. Always be ready for the unexpected turns that the day may bring.

A frustrated reaction to a plan not working is detrimental. Children are quite forgiving when things don't work out. They also notice the reactions of adults since adults are their role models. It is important for both teacher and children to be willing to take healthy risks. Seeing the negative reactions of adults when things don't work out discourages this risk taking on the part of children. It is far better to model a proper response to life's minor disappointments. A calm or humorous remark is more appropriate. Demonstrating that one can always try again or do something else provides beneficial strategies for children to model.

LITERATURE USE IN INTEGRATED UNITS

Integrated units are often taught around a general theme or a key idea. These themes include the content for the lesson or unit. One may wish to develop a theme around a specific book. For example, Figure 4 illustrates a single book curriculum web developed around the theme of Ruth Sawyer's *Journey Cake, Ho!* The focus may also be in a content area such as science, social studies, basic concepts, or holidays. Selecting literature for each of these will be discussed. In addition to these, other units might be developed around literature, unique classroom projects, or nontraditional topics.

make many-sized (small, smaller, smallest) cakes—magnet fish for them

dramatic play—bake shop

stamp circle journey cakes—tempera paint designs

do story sequence cards

obstacle course—oven to house

make clay journey cakes and decorate with faces

make real journey cakes or pancakes

maze—oven to house

play "floppy frisbee" where it is the journey cake; if miss, sit down until next turn

dramatize the story; assign parts for *all*; use picture labels

Ruth Sawyer, *Journey Cake, Ho!* (New York: Viking, 1953).

flannel board re-telling

"The Farmer in the Dell" song

paper bag puppet of favorite character

Summer "slip 'n slide chase"; roll frisbee and child tries to slide and catch journey cake

visit a bakery or pancake restaurant

play flip the pancake (round potholder) in the frying pan; count times

read and compare "The Gingerbread Boy"

set up clay corner (rolling pins, pans, etc.)

"Farm Sounds," p. 80; more piggyback songs

make a cardboard journey cake; paint or color; cut into a puzzle

run with stick pushing hula hoops—have races

make journey cake paper plate masks

Figure 4.　Single book curriculum web. Courtesy Diana Comer.

Illustration by Robert McCloskey from Journey Cake, Ho! *by Ruth Sawyer.* ©
1953 by Ruth Sawyer and Robert McCloskey. © Renewed 1981 by David
Durand and Robert McCloskey. All rights reserved. Reprinted by permission of
Viking Penguin, a division of Penguin Books USA, Inc.

Science Units

When developing a unit on science, it is important to possess current information.
This should be included as a specific criteria when selecting books for use in the
unit. The teacher should read each of the books to be used ahead of time. Anticipating the questions that might be asked by children will help the teacher provide
better responses. Careful planning will help to make a content area theme a success. Webs can be particularly helpful. Figure 5 illustrates an integrated curriculum
web used to plan a unit on the ocean.

Various authors and some commercial publishing companies specialize in
science-related books. The books should, and usually do, contain an abundance of
age-appropriate photographs and illustrations. Certain field guides can be useful
as well. A field guide is a book used to identify things such as plants, birds, insects,
trees, animals, and clouds. It contains clear pictures and brief, descriptive
paragraphs of information.

Ruth Heller is one of many authors who have written in the area of science.
Her companion books, *Plants that Never Bloom* and *The Reason for a Flower,* are

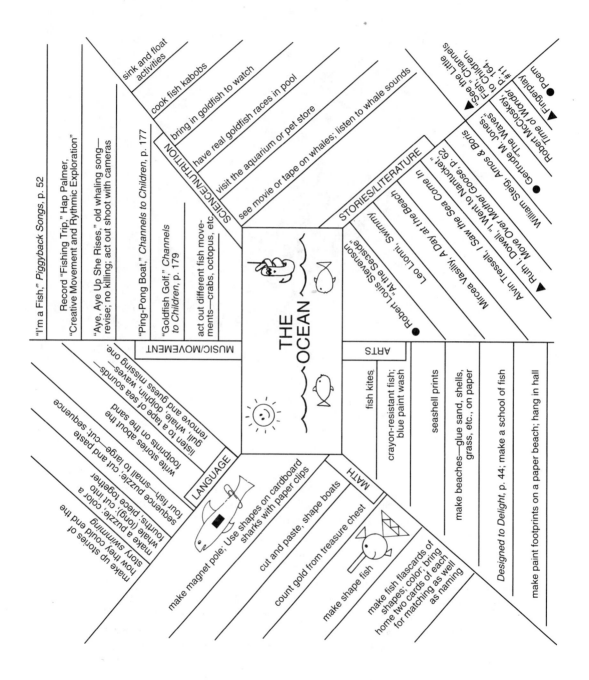

Figure 5. Integrated curriculum web. Courtesy Diana Comer.

beautifully illustrated. The information presented in each of them gives a clear and simple explanation for each title. Ole Risom's books, *I Am a Kitten* and *I Am a Puppy,* are excellent books to begin an increased understanding of each animal. Other aspects of animals are explored in Richard Scarry's *About Animals* and Aurelius Battaglia's *Animal Sounds.* Aliki (Brandenberg) has written a number of books on dinosaurs. The titles include *My Visit to the Dinosaurs, Dinosaurs Are Different,* and *Digging Up Dinosaurs.* They depict both the habits and lives of these prehistoric creatures. Archeological exploration, the process of discovering the remains of dinosaurs, is also covered.

Commercial publishers often provide a variety of books in science related areas. Usborne Publishing includes a nature series in its offerings. Topics addressed by its books include birds, butterflies, moths, flowers, and trees. Troll Publishing includes a wide assortment of science books appropriate for young children. They address many topics including the ocean, fish, clouds, trees, ponds, wind, alligators, crocodiles, whales, dolphins, and more. Books are grouped in a series aimed at particular age levels. As read-alouds, however, many of the books aimed at ages seven and up can be shared with younger children.

Goldencraft is another publisher that presents its books in age-related groups. The focus tends to be on animals and habitats. Included in the books are topics such as animal homes, jungles, birds, and mammals. Using some of the books from their higher series can be useful as well. Their completeness and ease of use allows the teacher to quickly answer a wide range of questions on a given scientific topic. National Geographic, Franklin Watts, and Mister Rogers' Neighborhood Books are also publishers that provide books related to science. They all possess unique features that enable a teacher to explore the topic more easily. Care has been taken in each to provide excellent photographs and clear illustrations on important points.

Social Studies Units

In selecting social studies related books, one must consider other criteria for selection. Social studies at the early childhood level generally consists of developing an understanding of self, family, community, health/nutrition, and social skills. These are all critical areas that demand that authors be perceptive and sensitive observers of humanity. Therefore, the best books for these issues are not necessarily found in a series of books. Books in a series are often written by a number of authors. As a result, the book is only as good as the author who wrote it. Since the literature about early childhood social studies concepts is often fictional, the writer becomes the critical component. Identifying authors who write with empathy and understanding on these issues becomes helpful in selecting books.

Beverly Cleary is a gifted writer who created the Ramona books. Readers and listeners quickly relate to the child in these books. Ramona encounters all of the typical childhood problems and emotions. The stories are entertaining and allow children to explore their own feelings and reactions to the problems encountered. The stories explore family relations, sibling rivalry, peer relations, beginning school, and understanding that people are different. Stan and Jan Berenstain,

This book and others like it can easily be integrated into a unit on the ocean, travel, or boats. Illustration from I Saw a Ship A-Sailing, Delmar Publishers Inc.

Rosemary Wells, Lois Lenski, Martha Alexander, and Russell Hoban are also excellent writers who address the same topics. Helen Buckley explores these areas and also includes some excellent work on grandparents in her writings.

Some writers take a different approach. Norman Bridwell's Clifford books explore the nature of love, even in the face of imperfections. Michael Bond also uses an animal, Paddington Bear, to portray social concepts. Children enjoy exploring the mishaps Paddington encounters in doing things in an individualistic manner.

There are, of course, many other authors and books that can be used to address these areas. Some are intended to address a specific problem, while others are not. Many books can be used simply to make a point or to begin a discussion about a social problem. Selecting such books is facilitated by a clear sense of the purpose of the overall unit.

Basic Concept Units

Basic concept units address some aspect of mathematics, language, the alphabet, and so forth. The purpose of literature in these units is to reinforce the learning of the concept, whether it be counting, spatial relationships, or a letter of the alphabet. Many of the books that might be selected for such a unit might not appear to have been written for that purpose. For this reason, it is important to have a wide knowledge of books and authors that might be appropriate.

Tana Hoban is an author who uses photographs to illustrate her texts. Her books have long been used to reinforce such concepts as pushing, pulling, and counting. Eric Carle's books are each imaginatively different. They are also quite effective in reinforcing concept learning with children. *My Very First Book of Colors* and *1, 2, 3 to the Zoo* are two of his books that have been used by early childhood educators for years. Jan Ormerod's books focus on movement concepts. Very young children are attracted by the large, bright illustrations and the simple texts. Among her titles are *Bend and Stretch* and *One Hundred One Things to Do with Baby*.

Donald Crews has made a substantial contribution to children's concepts with his books about buses, trains, and transportation. Mitsumasa Anno, Arnold Lobel, Brian Wildsmith, Richard Scarry, Tomie dePaola, Ed Emberly, and Dr. Seuss are all authors who have made innumerable contributions to this area of children's learning. Their books cover topics such as ABC's, planting a garden, shapes, numbers, seasons, and categorizing.

Holiday Units

Holidays are a celebration of life. They bring with them a sense of warmth, tradition, culture, and history. Each has the potential to increase understanding of the mutual humanity all people share. While no one wishes to offend children and families with holidays not celebrated in each child's home, learning that our culture is multi-ethnic and multi-religious is important. Since most holidays have some religious connotation perhaps it is best to inform parents about which holidays will be celebrated. If it is stated that the celebrations will not be religious, but rather explanatory in nature, there is less likelihood of a problem.

Parent involvement can be used to help with holiday celebrations. Parents can provide explanations of various celebrations to children from their knowledge of the holiday. This will help to integrate all children and their families in the educational process. It will strengthen the parent/child bond of the family as well.

It makes sense to become aware, early in the year, of the diversity of pupils in a class. This will enable the teacher to plan the holiday units to be celebrated throughout the year. Parents can be requested to share the customs and traditions of particular holidays early in the year. They can be helpful in explaining which traditions will be understandable and enjoyable to the children who may not be familiar with the holiday.

December is a major holiday season. It is advisable to combine Christmas, Hanukkah, New Year's Day, and Las Pasadas into a single unit friendship celebration. The activities can include decorating a friendship tree, playing with a dreidel, making candles and gifts, breaking a piñata, and perhaps a social activity. The social activity could be a gift to the community. Visiting a nursing home to sing songs or collecting donations for a food pantry would be appropriate. Tomie dePaola has written several books appropriate for this holiday. They include *An Early American Christmas, Baby's First Christmas, Christmas Pageant, Merry Christmas, Strega Nona, The Friendly Beasts,* and *Tomie dePaola's Book of Christmas Carols*. Other books include Tasha Tudor's *Take Joy: The Tasha Tudor Christmas Book* and *A Time to Keep,* Dick Bruna's *The Christmas Book,* Hilary Knight's *The Twelve Days of Christmas,* James Stevenson's *The Night after Christmas,* Steven Kroll's *Santa's Crash-Bang Christmas,* and Margaret Wise Brown's *Christmas in the Barn*.

Easter and Passover might be celebrated together as well. Activities might include an Easter parade, creating mosaics with colored egg shells, an Easter

Bunny visit, sharing a meal, hatching baby chicks, and making Easter bonnets. Easter books that might be used include Hans Wilhelm's *Bunny Trouble,* Charlotte Zolotow's *The Bunny Who Found Easter* and *Mr. Rabbit and the Lovely Present,* Margaret Wise Brown's *The Runaway Bunny,* and Adrianne Adams' *The Easter Egg Artists.*

A Mardi Gras festival might be just the thing to liven up a program toward the end of a long winter. A costume parade and samples of Cajun cooking could be included. Other popular holidays to consider include:

St. Patrick's Day–March 17
April Fools Day–April 1
Arbor Day–April 28
May Day–May 1
Rosh Hashanah (Jewish New Year)–September/October
Harvest Festival–(Jewish, Chinese, Asian)–fall
Halloween–October 31
Thanksgiving–November

Some less well-known holidays that might also be considered include:

Purim (Jewish Festival of Happiness)–March
Hina Matsuri (Japanese Doll Festival)–March 3
Now-Ruz (Iranian New Days)–March 21–23
Holi (Hindu Spring Festival)–spring
Song Kran (Buddhist New Year)–mid-April
Tangonosekku (Japanese Boy's Festival)–May 5
St. Lucia's Day (Candles and Lights)–December 13
Kwanza (African Harvest Festival)–last week of December

Other festivals and celebrations may include such themes as Groundhog Day, Dental Health Week, and Fire Safety Week. Resources that can be used to provide ideas for celebrating all of the festivals and holidays include books by Caroline Bauer;[4] Carol Beckman, Roberta Simmons and Nancy Thomas;[5] Bonnie Flemming and Darlene Hamilton;[6] Judy Herr and Yvonne Libby;[7] and Pat Short and Billee Davidson.[8] Additional children's books for holidays include Charlotte Zolotow's *Do You Know What I'll Do?* (Valentine's Day), Joan Anglund's *A Friend Is Someone Who Likes You* (Valentine's Day), Adrianne Adams' *A Woggle of Witches* (Halloween), Alice Dalgleish's *The Columbus Story* and *The Thanksgiving Story,* I. L. Peretz and Uri Shulevitz's *The Magician* (Passover), and Liza Donnelly's *Dinosaur's Halloween.*

[4] Caroline F. Bauer, *Celebrations: Read-Aloud Holiday and Theme Book Programs* (New York: H. W. Wilson, 1985).
[5] Carol Beckman, Roberta Simmons and Nancy Thomas, *Early Childhood Activity Guide for Holidays and Seasons* (Colorado Springs, CO: Channels to Children, 1982).
[6] Bonnie M. Flemming and Darlene S. Hamilton, *Resources for Creative Teaching in Early Childhood Education* (New York: Harcourt, Brace, Jovanovich, 1977).
[7] Judy Herr, Yvonne Libby, *Creative Resources for the Early Childhood Classroom* (Albany, NY: Delmar, 1990).
[8] Pat Short and Billee Davidson, *Special Things for Special Days: Holiday Ideas and Activities for Teaching Children Ages Five to Eight* (Santa Monica, CA: Goodyear, 1980).

Active involvement of children is a key to helping them understand new content no matter what the topic. Courtesy Diana Comer.

SUMMARY

Starting with literature and expanding its themes enhances the whole curriculum. Using literature as a solid foundation permits the teacher to have flexibility with planning. Integrating each of the content areas with literature brings a cohesiveness to the program and the classroom. It also lends stability, an important component of early childhood education. Yet, integration of content areas still allows wonderful things to happen in the classroom.

To achieve integration in the program requires careful planning. A planning process using webs helps the teacher choose the best activities possible to teach the concepts. Planning with a web allows one to consider and think about many choices. Planning allows time to gather the materials and ideas needed for creative and effective learning activities. Planning webs can be used in a variety of ways. Three types of planning webs used in this chapter were the literature web, the single book web, and the integrated curriculum web.

Both beginning and experienced teachers should frequently visit a children's library and spend substantial time looking at the books. Keeping notes of those books that are enjoyable and helpful is a good way to be organized for upcoming units. One might also watch children interact with the books and the library. This is an effective way to return to a child's level of thinking about literature. Both activities remind one of the choices to be made in planning creative lessons for children.

Simply browsing through books can generate ideas, thoughts, and memories as the illustrations, words, and characters pass by. Old friends jump out from books and delightful new ones draw the reader into their stories. Planning and integrating the program can be a fascinating process.

QUESTIONS FOR THOUGHT AND DISCUSSION

1. Explain the term "web" as it is used in program planning.
2. What is the difference between a literature web, a single book web, and an integrated curriculum web?
3. Defend or refute the following: It is better to create your own ideas for units rather than rely on someone else's.
4. What are the reasons for using an integrated curriculum with children?
5. Are there times when a teacher should not use an integrated approach with literature? Explain your reasons.
6. When might a teacher change or adapt a poem or rhyme for class use?
7. How can a teacher facilitate the integration of the curriculum?
8. Defend or refute the following: The use of a book series is never an appropriate approach because the quality is poor.
9. How might a field guide be helpful in early childhood education?
10. Which writers have written several books dealing with either family life or peer relations?
11. Identify a general theme and create an integrated curriculum web for that topic. Identify the level of the children for whom the unit is being planned.
12. Choose a topic and develop a literature web for it.
13. Develop a single book web for the preschool or kindergarten level.

CHILDREN'S BOOKS CITED

Adrienne Adams, *The Easter Egg Artists* (New York: MacMillan, 1976).

Adrienne Adams, *A Woggle of Witches* (New York: MacMillan, 1971).

Aliki (Brandenberg), *Digging Up Dinosaurs* (New York: Crowell, 1981).

Aliki (Brandenberg), *Dinosaurs Are Different* (New York: Crowell, 1985).

Aliki (Brandenberg), *My Visit to the Dinosaurs* (New York: Crowell, 1969).

Joan Anglund, *A Friend Is Someone Who Likes You* (New York: Harcourt, Brace, Jovanovich, 1983).

Aurelius Battaglia, *Animal Sounds* (Racine, WI: Western, 1981).

Margaret Wise Brown, *Christmas in the Barn* (New York: Crowel, 1949).

Margaret Wise Brown, *The Runaway Bunny* (New York: Harper, 1977).

Dick Bruna, *The Christmas Book* (New York: Methuen, 1964).

Eric Carle, *My Very First Book of Colors* (New York: Crowell, 1985).

Eric Carle, *1, 2, 3 to the Zoo* (New York: Collins World, 1969).

Donald Crews, *Freight Train* (New York: Penguin, 1985).

Alice Dalgleish, *The Columbus Story* (New York: Scribner's, 1955).

Alice Dalgleish, *The Thanksgiving Story* (New York: Scribner's, 1954).

Tomie dePaola, *Baby's First Christmas* (New York: Holiday House, 1988).

Tomie dePaola, *Christmas Pageant* (Minneapolis, MN: Winston, 1978).

Tomie dePaola, *An Early American Christmas* (New York: Holiday House, 1987).

Tomie dePaola, *The Friendly Beasts* (New York: Putnam, 1980).

Tomie dePaola, *Merry Christmas, Strega Nona* (New York: Harcourt, Brace, Jovanovich, 1986).

Tomie dePaola, *Tomie dePaola's Book of Christmas Carols* (New York: Putnam, 1987).

Liz Donnelly, *Dinosaur's Halloween* (New York: Scholastic, 1987).

Douglas Florian, *Discovering Frogs* (New York: MacMillan, 1986).

Angela Grunsell, *At the Doctor's* (New York: Franklin Watts, 1983).

Ruth Heller, *Plants that Never Bloom* (New York: Putnam, 1984).

Ruth Heller, *The Reason for a Flower* (New York: Grossett and Dunlap, 1983).

Jean Johnson, *Postal Workers A to Z* (New York: Walker, 1987).

Hilary Knight, *The Twelve Days of Christmas* (New York: MacMillan, 1981).

Steven Kroll, *Santa's Slam-Bang Christmas* (New York: Holiday House, 1977).

Robert McCloskey, *Time of Wonder* (New York: Viking, 1957).

Robert McClung, *Animals that Build Their Homes* (Washington, DC: National Geographic Society, 1976).

Jan Ormerod, *Bend and Stretch* (New York: Lothrop, Lee and Shepard, 1987).

Jan Ormerod, *One Hundred One Things to Do with Baby* (New York: Penguin, 1986).

I. L. Peretz and Uri Shulevitz, *The Magician* (New York: MacMillan, 1985).

Ole Risom, *I Am a Kitten* (Racine, WI: Western, 1970).

Ole Risom, *I Am a Puppy* (Racine, WI: Western, 1970).

Ruth Sawyer, *Journey Cake, Ho!* (New York: Viking, 1953).

Richard Scarry, *About Animals* (Racine, WI: Western, 1976).

Dr. Seuss (pseud. for Theodor Geisel), *How the Grinch Stole Christmas* (New York: Random, 1957).

James Stevenson, *The Night after Christmas* (New York: Scholastic, 1981).

Tasha Tudor, *Take Joy: The Tasha Tudor Christmas Book* (New York: Putnam, 1980).

Tasha Tudor, *A Time to Keep* (New York: MacMillan, 1977).

Hans Wilhelm, *Bunny Trouble* (New York: Scholastic, 1985).

Harriet Ziefert, *Bear's Busy Morning* (New York: Harper & Row, 1986).

Charlotte Zolotow, *The Bunny Who Found Easter* (Boston, MA: Houghton Mifflin, 1959).

Charlotte Zolotow, *Do You Know What I'll Do?* (New York: Harper, 1958).

Charlotte Zolotow, *Mr. Rabbit and the Lovely Present* (New York: Harper, 1977).

SELECTED REFERENCES

Roach V. Allen and Claryce Allen. *Language Experience Activities* (Boston, MA: Houghton Mifflin, 1976).

Bruno Bettelheim and Karen Zelan. *On Learning to Read* (New York: Vintage, 1981).

Bruce Joyce and Marsha Weil. *Models of Teaching* (Englewood Cliffs, NJ: Prentice-Hall, 1980).

Max van Manen. *The Tone of Teaching* (Portsmouth, NH: Heinemann, 1986).

8 Bibliotherapy: Using Books to Heal

he term bibliotherapy is made from two words. The first part of the word, "biblio," is a derivation of a Greek word referring to books. The second part, "therapy," is a derivation of a Greek word referring to procedures used to treat bodily disorders. Literally, bibliotherapy means the treatment of bodily disorders using books. While the term does include this definition, it has a much wider meaning. Bibliotherapy has come to refer to a process in which books are used to address a variety of physiological, developmental, and psychological concerns. Simply stated, bibliotherapy is the use of books, and the subsequent discussions about those books, to address a variety of concerns.

In order to make full use of bibliotherapy it is necessary to have certain understandings. First, of course, it is necessary to understand what bibliotherapy has come to mean in education. One should be aware of how to use it as well as its potential benefits. Finally, it is useful to have an understanding of both the concerns possessed by young children and an awareness of some of the books that may be helpful in addressing those concerns.

UNDERSTANDING BIBLIOTHERAPY

The use of bibliotherapy as a tool for teachers and librarians was recognized over a quarter of a century ago by educators David Russell and Caroline Shrodes.[1] They described bibliotherapy as a process in which the reader and the literature interacted. Taking a clinical approach, they felt bibliotherapy was a promising tool for assessing personality and monitoring adjustment and growth in individuals.

Years later Patricia Cianciolo published her beliefs using a less clinical perspective on how books can help the child.[2] She identified six areas in which books could provide positive help to children. Two of the areas addressed education and learning issues. Books could help children acquire information about human be-

---

[1] David Russell and Caroline Shrodes, "Contributions of Research in Bibliotherapy to the Language Arts Program," *School Review,* volume 58, September, 1950, pp. 335-392.
[2] Patricia Cianciolo, "Children's Literature Can Affect Coping Behaviors," *Personnel and Guidance Journal,* volume 43, May, 1965, pp. 897-901.

havior, including areas that were a current concern. Books could also help children come to an understanding of the phrase "heal thyself." That is, children learn that the answer to some problems must come from within. Two of the areas identified focused on the need to extend oneself. Through books, one can find interests outside oneself. Also, stories can be used to relieve conscious problems in a controlled manner. The last two areas focused on the use of books as problem solving tools. Books provide individuals with an opportunity to identify and compensate for conscious problems. That is, it is often easier to talk about a problem if it is someone else's problem. Finally, stories can illuminate personal difficulties and help one acquire insight into personal behavior. That is, a problem can be clarified by seeing it described by another person in a story. Betty Coody supports this view. She contends that bibliotherapy is based on the fact that readers are better able to view themselves through empathy with characters they meet in books.[3]

Books as Therapy

Charlotte S. Huck and Doris Young Kuhn provide a picture of how bibliotherapy can be used with children experiencing a variety of fears, anxieties, and worries associated with everyday life.[4] They identify the three processes of psychotherapy and suggest that they can parallel three stages of bibliotherapy. The first process is identification, in which there is an association of oneself with an individual found in literature. Secondly, there is catharsis, meaning the releasing of emotion. It is believed that by observing and identifying with a character in a story with a similar problem, one can gain some degree of relief from the stress and emotion caused by the same problem in one's own life. The third process is insight, in which one develops an emotional awareness of one's own motivations in dealing with a problem. That is, by observing and understanding how a character in a story deals with an emotion, one can better deal with the same emotion in real life.

This view can be helpful, since it provides a step-by-step procedure for using bibliotherapy with children. Teachers, parents, and others attempting to use bibliotherapy should use some caution, however. It is an appropriate tool for helping children approach minor anxieties associated with everyday life. When children have deeper psychological problems, they should be referred to other professionals who possess the appropriate training to deal with those difficulties.

The Chronically Ill Child

Bibliotherapy is an effective tool to use with children who are physically ill. Hospitals, clinics, and treatment centers throughout the country frequently use such an approach with their young patients. In Figure 1, Regina Houston describes the special considerations which one must have in using bibliotherapy with chronically ill children. She is the "Story Lady" in the pediatrics ward at the University of Massachusetts Hospital.

[3] Betty Coody, *Using Literature with Young Children* (Dubuque, Iowa: William C. Brown, 1983).
[4] Charlotte S. Huck and Doris Young Kuhn, *Children's Literature in the Elementary School* (New York: Holt, Rinehart and Winston, 1983).

Stories give readers experiences they haven't had in life. Books also acquaint the reader with different ways of looking at life. Watty Piper's *The Little Engine that Could* has inspired many young listeners to try their very best. It has given confidence to children even during the most difficult of times and in the face of the most adverse situations. The stories can help release tension and develop values. They can show one how to evaluate situations and how to solve problems. They do so by allowing us to observe the solutions reached by the characters in both ordinary and unusual situations. In so doing, books extend both a child's experience and world.

All people share the basic needs for food, clothing, shelter, and safety. Other needs which everyone has include the need for love, being part of a group, a positive self concept, and an understanding of what makes each of us special. Many of these needs can be partially met in books. Stories nurture the hopes and dreams of the child. They reinforce each child's uniqueness and provide courage and friendship.

Hospital-confined children have a special need for bibliotherapy. Children struggling with long-term illnesses find peace and solace in stories. Stories are comforting to the chronically ill child. The association lessens some of the trauma they are dealing with. Justin, a three year old, found a safe refuge in stories after his painful weekly injection. Another child, Benjamin, has used stories to come to an understanding that life has a beginning, a middle, and an end. Part of his regular out-patient visits to the hospital include a visit to the "Story Lady." It is an enjoyable and nonthreatening part of his visit. The story sessions are not an escape from pain for Benjamin. Rather, they are an important part of Benjamin's total medical program as explained to him by his doctor and his mother.

Pediatric physicians have observed children as being more relaxed during examinations after they have shared and experienced a story. The stories provide a therapeutic vehicle through which the child can deal with fears and doubts. They can both educate the child and facilitate the procedures which the child must endure. One of the greatest benefits, however, comes from the human interaction of the child and the reader. Through voice and body language, the reader can communicate a calmness and a warmth. This acceptance of children and their fears is invaluable to both the pediatric patient and the well child.

Parents, teachers, and others who share stories with the chronically ill child must have certain understandings. Such children have special needs which go beyond that of well children. Medications, phases of an illness, and healing processes can all affect behavior. One should take care to not misread or misunderstand these changes in behavior. Knowledge of a child's physical needs and problems is necessary for anyone using bibliotherapy with a chronically ill child. It requires interest and caring on the part of the reader. That is true for all children, of course. With the chronically ill child, it is critical.

Figure 1. "Books Heal." Courtesy Regina Houston.

BENEFITS OF BIBLIOTHERAPY

There are a variety of benefits derived from using bibliotherapy. The process can address a number of different needs a child may have in dealing with a difficulty. Obviously, some needs can be addressed better than others. The success of bibliotherapy depends on the child, the problem, and the situation in which biblio-

Comfort can be found in books and in sharing a teddy bear with a friend.
Courtesy Diana Comer.

therapy is used. The benefits discussed here include information, mutuality, empathy, options for action, and reaffirmation of life.

Information

The first benefit of bibliotherapy is the providing of information. Using books that address a particular problem often enables the child to gather accurate and reliable information in a subtle, nonthreatening manner. Educating children to the realities of the world and its problems provides a base of knowledge that they can rely on.

Many times children develop anxiety over a problem because they do not see the problem in its proper perspective. Education and the gaining of the truth that can come from books is helpful in destroying myths, misconceptions, and untruths. Problems often become much more solvable when they are seen correctly and understood by the individual facing the problem.

Mutuality

Mutuality refers to the experience of sharing. When children are confronted with a problem that is affecting them deeply, they often feel alone. They are frightened by the sense of isolation they feel. Discovering, through books, that others share the same problem reduces this sense of isolation. Coming to the understanding that one isn't the only one in the world with a particular problem can be an effective tool for coping with a problem.

Empathy

Empathy refers to the ability to share the feelings of another individual. Children are not necessarily born with this. A visit to most schoolyards will support the fact that children can be both cruel and thoughtless toward others whom they perceive to be different. Most often this cruelty is based on ignorance and fear. It may be that the other child dresses differently, looks different, or acts differently. The development of empathy is one of the most important things children can achieve. It places them firmly within the highest circle of humanity.

Books share the thoughts and feelings of others with their readers. Through books, children learn not only of their own worth but of the worth of others, even others who may not be like themselves. One might question whether this is truly the role of the educator. It cannot, of course, be otherwise. Achievement in academics without the development of character is of limited worth.

The teacher is in a unique position to address both character development and academic achievement. As a matter of fact, how can one ignore the importance of each within a classroom? One cannot meaningfully teach a group of children while some in the group are shunned and hurting. Group cooperation is impossible if some children avoid the child with cerebral palsy for fear of "catching it." The social relationships within a class have a direct influence on the productivity of the class. The teacher, by either addressing or ignoring these issues, determines whether or not the class will have a heart and a soul. Bibliotherapy is most effective when used by a teacher who is committed to addressing the whole child. Building empathy begins with seeing others as human beings with needs similar to our own.

Options for Action

When faced with a difficult problem, adults can often feel in a bind with no solution. Children are no different. They may be so focused on the problem that they are incapable of stepping back and seeing the situation in a larger framework.

Books provide opportunities to observe how others view a problem. They explore the various attempts the characters engage in to resolve that problem. Through books, children come to the realization that there are alternative ways for dealing with a problem. In discussing a story with a teacher or an adult, children can explore the situation and learn that choices can be made with most things in life. This is an important and healthy life skill.

Reaffirmation of Life

When faced with what appears to be a tremendous problem, the world can be a cold and frightening place. It is true that some bad things do happen in life. The world will never be perfect. Yet, there are many wonderful and beautiful things about life. There are some truly caring and loving people on this earth. There are flowers, birds, songs, and gorgeous sunsets. Children need to understand this when faced with problems. They need to be able to affirm that there are some truly beautiful things about life. This does not take away the problem; it merely helps put it in perspective.

Children are exposed to many of life's grim realities through television and the media. Unfortunately, the good things aren't deemed as newsworthy as the more sordid aspects of life. Children need to talk about the fears they have regarding some of the things they have seen. They often look to adults to help them affirm the positive aspects of their existence as people.

USING BIBLIOTHERAPY

Using bibliotherapy to address the problems and concerns of young children can be a powerful and effective tool. As with any activity or lesson to be used with children, planning will increase the effectiveness of the activity. In order to plan effectively, one must be aware of several factors surrounding the use of bibliotherapy. They include age-appropriateness, choice of books, effective strategies, and an awareness of the limitations of bibliotherapy.

Age-Appropriateness

The criteria for choosing age-appropriate books for bibliotherapy are similar to those used for choosing books for other purposes. One should be aware of the understanding children have at different developmental levels. One should also be aware of the types of concerns they have at different ages. These can vary, of course, but one can reasonably expect three-year-olds to have night fears, for example.

Adults need to realize that the fears children experience are very real to them. The best way to respond is with honesty and empathy. Children's fears need to be addressed without ridicule. While children's fears may not be totally overcome, coping skills and management of the fears can be established. A powerful aid to overcoming fear is an adult who is consistently accessible to the child and reinforces the concept that things are under control. This is true whether the child's fears are real or imaginary.

There are a variety of possible sources of concern for the young child. Some things such as parental separation, divorce, adoption, death, pregnancy, or the birth of a new sibling are centered around the family. Other concerns are more closely related to the child's ability to deal with the immediate environment. These may include friendship, illness, death, bullies, school, animals, moving, foster care, and self-worth. Still other fears may focus on world events. These may include nuclear war, crime, terrorism, and drugs. If the child initiates a discussion and describes a fear related to any of these, chances are that the fear is very real in the mind of that child.

Choice of Books

There is a wide variety of good books for meeting needs within most problem areas. The illustrations and text must be analyzed with the same criteria used to

Books can be a springboard to discussions about new babies and siblings.
Courtesy Delmar Publishers Inc.

select books for any use. Particular attention should be paid to the accuracy of the content and the style of delivery. A book that trivializes the problem or solves it in an oversimplified manner might not help a child to deal with reality. In bibliotherapy, the concept of reality is extremely important even though the books may be fictional.

Books that use either animals or people can be appropriate. Even though bears don't talk, the books by Stan and Jan Berenstain are effective in dealing with problems because the issues are realistic. The use of talking bears simply allows the child to look at a problem through another's eyes. Using books with animal characters can be especially appropriate when dealing with topics that are embarrassing to children. Children may find it difficult to deal with problems they find embarrassing. It is easier to talk about the animal in the book with the same problem.

To be effective, a book must communicate with children on their level. Children, like adults, do not like to be talked down to. When this is done, it often results in anger or an end to the communication. The story should also have a clear appeal. At an early point in the book the reader must be able to relate to the character and the situation. The message or theme of the book makes little difference if the story is not captivating enough to hold the child's interest.

Effective Strategies

Planning ahead will make bibliotherapy a more powerful tool. Using effective strategies will help as well. The most helpful strategies deal with such things as: 1.) informing parents; 2.) making decisions about when and how to use bibliotherapy; and, 3.) planning how to share the experience with children.

Research the Facts. It is important to have a good grasp of the information to be used. Only facts and real information should be used. Half truths and lies will only destroy credibility, no matter how well-intended they are. This is true whether the information comes from the literature or other sources. If the information is known ahead of time, it can be better tailored to the audience. Reviewing books and articles on the topic can suggest the best ways to introduce the subject and how much to introduce at each level.

Sensitive Sharing. When using bibliotherapy, one is providing help to both the child and the family. A child with a problem does not exist in a vacuum; such a child exists within a family. The family is most likely aware of the problem as well. Therefore, it makes good common sense to let parents know how the problem is being addressed. This can be done through meetings, telephone calls, or newsletters. The method of communication will depend on the type of problem. When working with children, it is helpful to anticipate all of the possible reactions children could have prior to beginning the lesson. By doing this, one can plan responses to these reactions. Such planning can help ensure that bibliotherapy will be carried on in a nonthreatening and supportive manner. As a result, children will be more likely to feel empowered by the experience.

Use Good Timing. Introducing bibliotherapy prior to the time that children are ready for it can mean failure. One should make certain that children possess a level of trust with the individual using the approach. Trust is something that builds up over time. It is inadvisable, therefore, to discuss physical or sexual abuse during the first week of school. Good timing must be used during the day as well. An adequate amount of time is needed to fully explore an issue. It is inappropriate to begin a session on new babies or racial issues at the end of the day or in the middle of a free play period. A time must be chosen when it is quiet and there will be an adequate amount of time: time to talk, time to listen, and time to internalize.

Integrate the Topic. No problem exists all by itself. Likewise, no solution exists in isolation. All of life is integrated with other parts of our existence. It is both logical and efficient to integrate the use of bibliotherapy with other parts of the curriculum. Many of the books one would use in a bibliotherapy session would be appropriate for other aspects of the curriculum as well. By integrating the understandings and issues, the learning is reinforced for children.

Long-Term Planning. In planning a long-term integrated curriculum, it makes sense to plan bibliotherapy in a logical progression of steps. For example, one might begin with self-concept, followed by family concerns, school concerns, and personal safety. Each of the latter topics builds on the previously introduced topics. A child's understanding increases when a logical order such as this is followed.

Remember the Role. There will always be the temptation to deal with issues that should be left to others. The teacher using bibliotherapy should keep in mind that the purpose is to shed light and understanding on some of the normal problems and fears children encounter as they are growing up. Serious mental and psychological problems should be referred to others with the appropriate training as soon as they are discovered. If a child is observed reacting with agitation or acting out behavior when a topic is discussed, the child should be talked to privately. A calm and supportive adult with gentle, nonthreatening questions is the most productive way to deal with a frightened child. If the child is not able to participate and continues to exhibit reactions that are noticeably different from those of other children, a parent conference is suggested. In meeting with the parents, it is important to listen to their understanding of the problem. When a mutual understanding of the problem is achieved, the best decision for the child can be made.

Maintain Flexibility. When working with young children it is always important to be flexible. With bibliotherapy, it is particularly important. One must be ready to shift gears, take an unexpected turn, or back up as the situation demands. While discussing a problem in a bibliotherapy session, it is a good idea to restate any questions a child might ask. This makes sure that everyone understands what is being sought. As this is accomplished, provide enough information to answer the question. Too detailed an answer could result in disinterest. One should always respond to a question, however. Avoiding a response of any kind to a question that was honestly asked is a poor choice. If an appropriate answer cannot be given, a response explaining that is still needed. In general, however, children will often ask simple and general questions prior to asking the real question that addresses a current problem or difficulty. Allow children time to build up to discussing their real concerns.

ADDRESSING THE CONCERNS OF CHILDREN

Young children often have different concerns than those of older children, adolescents, and adults. Sometimes what adults perceive to be the concerns of children seem to cause little difficulty for those children. The best way to learn of children's concerns is to ask or listen to them. Sometimes adults forget this, but it really does work. Indirect means such as reading a book and discussing it can also bring out the true concerns children possess. There is no best way to learn of a child's concern. Each individual sees things differently. Each child will use different approaches and coping strategies for dealing with problems.

In general, however, there are certain themes which include a range of the concerns and problems with which children are dealing. They are addressed here within the general categories of self, family, friends, other people, illness and death, and the world. This is not the only way of grouping these areas, of course. It is used here because it comprises an easily understood frame of reference.

Self

Am I as pretty as Jane? Does my ball bounce as well as the ball that Joe has? Will I always be short? Will Mom have time for me when the new baby arrives? These are only a few of the possible concerns of young children. While adults may see some of these problems as foolish, they are quite real to the child who wants to fit in with the rest of the world. The problems can be increased if other children learn about them and taunt the child with the problem. This can be the beginning lesson of the dark side of human nature.

Children need adults to bring light to this dark side of life. Having the entire group sit with a book related to the situation can enable everyone to think about their actions and the effect they have on others. Such a session can help to bring out the importance of feeling good about oneself.

There are a variety of books that can be used to explore this topic. Tomie dePaola's *Oliver Button Is a Sissy* explores the idea of being true to yourself and trying to do your best in your areas of interest. In *The Hating Book,* Charlotte Zolotow explores the emotion of hatred and its implications for those involved. The emotion of personal fear is explored in Phyllis Krasilovsky's *Scaredy Cat,* Morse Hamilton's *Who's Afraid of the Dark?,* Tony Ross's *I'm Coming to Get You,* Mercer Mayer's *You're the Scaredy Cat,* and William Joyce's *George Shrinks.* Concerns about being a competent person both at home and at school are addressed in Robert Kraus's *Leo the Late Bloomer,* Barbara Robinson's *The Fattest Bear in First Grade,* Phyllis Krasilovsky's *The Very Tall Little Girl,* Watty Piper's *The Little Engine that Could,* Patricia Reilly Giff's *Happy Birthday, Ronald Morgan* and Miriam Cohen's *First Grade Takes a Test* and *When Will I Read?.* In *Arnie and the Stolen Markers,* Nancy Carlson explores the themes of greed and guilt. Finally, Jane Yolen's wonderful book, *Sleeping Ugly,* does an exceptional job of dealing with the concept of physical attractiveness.

Family

The family continues to be seen as the basic social unit of society, but the twentieth century has brought many changes to it. Families are getting smaller and tend to be more spread out geographically. Separation, divorce, single parenthood, and extended families are more and more common. Children sometimes do not understand these changes, causing them to develop fears. Children wonder if they caused the divorce, whether Dad will ever come back, and whether they will be divorced by their families. They also worry about the mortality of parents, grandparents, and themselves.

The traditional causes of stress in families have never left. New babies, deaths, illness, sibling rivalry, unemployment, poverty and homelessness continue to create pressures on the young child. These aspects of family life put pressure on the entire family with a variety of results. The young child is the least able member of the family to deal with the fears these changes bring on. The fears and feelings overwhelm the verbal and coping skills of such a youngster. For this reason, bibliotherapy is particularly helpful. It will not solve all of the problems, but it will provide both a framework and some of the language necessary to understand the stresses.

Books dealing with family issues include Russell Hoban's *A Baby Sister for Frances*, Daniel Pinkwater's *The Wuggie Norple Story*, Cynthia Rylant's *When I Was Young in the Mountains*, Charlotte Zolotow's *Something Is Going to Happen*, Martha Alexander's *Nobody Asked Me if I Wanted a Baby Sister* and Susan Lapsley's *I Am Adopted*. Fathers are the focus of Beverly Cleary's *Ramona and Her Father*, Mercer Mayer's *Just Me and My Dad*, Robert Munsch's *50 Below Zero*, Patricia Quinlan's *My Dad Takes Care of Me* and Miriam Stecher's *Daddy and Ben Together*. Mothers are the focus of Joe Lasker's *Mothers Can Do Anything*, Vera Williams's *A Chair for My Mother* and Eve Meriam's *Mommies at Work*. The issue of illiteracy in the family is addressed in Eve Bunting's *The Wednesday Surprise* and Muriel Stanek's *My Mom Can't Read*. Siblings and sibling rivalry are the issue in books such as Judy Blume's *The Pain and the Great One*, Susan Bonners's *Just in Passing*, Nancy Carlson's *Harriet and Walt* and Kevin Henkes's *Sheila Rae, the Brave.*

Issues affecting the family can be explored in books as well. Poverty is the focus in Margot Zemach's *It Could Always Be Worse* and Barbara Shook Hazen's *Tight Times.* For a related problem, *Hotel Boy* by Curt and Gita Kaufman uses real photographs to illustrate the story of impending homelessness. Two excellent books on grandparents suffering from Alzheimer's disease are worth noting: Vaunda Micheaux Nelson's *Always Gramma* and Jonah Schein's *Forget Me Not.* Finally, imaginary fears are expertly dealt with in Mercer Mayer's *There's a Nightmare in My Closet* and Judith Viorst's *My Mama Says There Aren't Any Zombies, Ghosts, Vampires, Creatures, Demons, Monsters, Fiends, Goblins or Things.*

Friends

As children grow, they move from a focus on themselves to the need to be a part of a group. They want to extend their social interactions beyond their families. They seek friendships. This is a long process along a path that can have many obstacles and pitfalls. Since humans are social beings by nature, it is a path that all must somehow travel.

Adults often wince at what young children sometimes say and do to their friends. They can be alternately very loving and very hostile. Toddlers may hug each other one minute and bite each other the next. Preschoolers change best friends as though they are participating in a card game. Kindergarteners announce the beginnings and endings of best friendships as publicly as political campaigns announce endorsements. As a result, childhood friendships possess a combination of happiness, pain, and chaos. One can deal with these issues through discussion, understanding, and the use of bibliotherapy. It is through the reading of a story

Children have a variety of needs. Among these are learning about their world, active play, and the development of friendships. Courtesy Diana Comer.

that sounds familiar to the real situation that the best and most sensitive discussions will emerge.

Books that can be used to generate bibliotherapy discussions include Miriam Cohen's *Will I Have a Friend?*, Else Holmelund Minarik's *No Fighting, No Biting*, Stan and Jan Berenstain's *The Trouble with Friends*, Janice Udry's *Let's Be Enemies*, Joan Anglund's *A Friend Is Someone Who Likes You*, Kathryn Hitte's *Boy Was I Mad* and Marcia Brown's *Best Friends*. Two superb books on the subject of sleeping over at a friend's house are Kay Chorao's *Lester's Overnight* and Bernard Waber's *Ira Sleeps Over*. The joys of friendship are celebrated in James Marshall's *The Cut Ups*. The sadness of a best friend moving away is explored in Aliki's *We Are Best Friends*. The ups and downs of friendship are addressed in Arnold Lobel's *Frog and Toad Are Friends*, Nancy Carlson's *Witch Lady*, and Patricia Reilly Giff's *The Beast in Ms. Rooney's Room*.

Other People

Children try to make sense of the world. When things don't fit neatly into place in the child's mind, fear can emerge. Other people is a grouping that refers to people who for one reason or another may cause stress and fear in a child. It may be a child or neighbor the child sees but does not know. The stress and fear are usually caused by ignorance on the part of the child. Handicapped children in the classroom and ethnic minorities who may seem or appear to be different can cause anxiety. Children often exhibit fears of handicaps because they are afraid that they might be able to "catch it." Skin color, dress, and language that are not familiar can cause anxiety for both minority and nonminority children. Through bibliotherapy, children can learn that though people may have differences, they are all human beings. Bibliotherapy can help decrease ignorance and focus discussions on the common humanity of all people.

In *My Friend Jacob*, Lucille Clifton shows how understanding and love can transcend fears. In the story, a young, nonhandicapped black child and a mentally retarded white teenager develop a friendship. The difficult topics of race and retardation become secondary to the beautiful friendship that emerges. This is something to look for in a story: the importance of a good story should transcend the issue of accepting people who are different. A story focused primarily on the differences of the characters would not be as effective. The story must be universally appealing. Readers must be able to move themselves into the story because of the compelling nature of the tale.

There are many books that explore the concept of other people. Physical handicaps are clarified and explained in stories such as Lorraine Henriod's *Grandma's Wheelchair*, Curt and Gita Kaufman's *Rajesh*, Joan Fassler's *Howie Helps Himself*, Susan Jeschke's *Perfect the Pig*, and Berniece Rabe's *The Balancing Girl*. Visual handicaps are dealt with in Jack Ezra Keats's *Apartment Three*, Ada Litchfield's *A Cane in Her Hand*, Ellen Raskin's *Spectacles*, Miriam Cohen's *See You Tomorrow, Charles*, and Patricia MacLachlan's *Through Grandpa's Eyes*. Hearing handicaps are the focus of such books as Ada Litchfield's *A Button in Her Ear* and Jeanne Peterson's *I Have a Sister, My Sister Is Deaf*. Other handicaps and differences are addressed in Miriam Cohen's *First Grade Takes a Test* and *When Will I Read?*, Tomie dePaola's *Oliver Button Is a Sissy,* Charlotte Zolotow's *William's Doll,* Joe Lasker's *He's My Brother,* Susan Meddaugh's *Beast,* Mitchell Sharmat's *Sherman Is a Slowpoke,* and Harriet Sobol's *My Brother Steven Is Retarded.*

Books are also available that can help educate children about minority groups. Black Americans are the focus of books such as Barbara Winther's *Plays from Folktales from Africa,* Jack Ezra Keats's *The Snowy Day,* Lucille Clifton's *The Boy Who Didn't Believe in Spring,* and Arnold Adoff's *Black Is Brown Is Tan.* Books involving Hispanic Americans include *My Dog Is Lost* by Jack Ezra Keats and Pat Cherr as well as Wendy Kesselmann's *Angelita.*

Illness and Death

Illness and death are a part of life, but most people have a certain fear of both. For children who may be trying to understand each of these things, the anxiety may be greater. This topic can trigger powerful emotions, particularly if an individual is close to someone who is seriously ill or who has just died. For this reason, it is important to be particularly sensitive when dealing with these topics. The death of a classroom pet may provide an opportunity to explore this concept with a lower level of potential difficulty. On the other hand, the fears associated with medical and dental visits can be addressed quite readily with bibliotherapy.

The topic of illness is addressed in Barbara Kirk's *Grandpa, Me and the Treehouse,* Tomie dePaola's *Now One Foot, Now the Other,* H. A. and Margaret Rey's *Curious George Goes to the Hospital* and Paula and Kirk Hogan's *Hospital Scares Me.* Medical visits are dealt with in Harlow Rockwell's *My Dentist,* Lillian Hoban's *Arthur's Loose Tooth,* Alma Marshak Whitney's *Just Awful,* and David McPhail's *The Bear's Toothache.* The topic of death is explored in a sensitive manner in Alvin Tresselt's *The Dead Tree* and Judith Viorst's *The Tenth Good Thing about Barney.* Tomie dePaola deals with the death of a grandparent in an honest and straightforward manner in *Nana Upstairs, Nana Downstairs.*

The World

The world of children is the same as the world of adults, but children often perceive it differently. They have lived a shorter time, have not had the opportunity to study our world, and have not developed the mental capacities to comprehend the intricacies of modern life. However, children watch the news, listen to adults as they express their fears, and observe such things as pollution, crime, and homelessness in many neighborhoods.

Childhood Fears. Children have reason to have fears. In fact, some fear can be a healthy thing. Fear keeps one from engaging in dangerous activities and reminds one to use common sense. On the other hand, fear can be overwhelming if it produces stress beyond the point that children can effectively cope with. Many children develop fears about the great unknowns of the world. Adult responses to the problems of the world are very often too complex and sophisticated for young children to comprehend. When children are without satisfactory understandings of a major societal problem, they can turn to other solutions they see in the media of their childhood world.

The media, particularly television, often stresses a violent solution to problems. The values that children acquire as a result of this often run counter to the attitudes that one might like children to acquire. Commercial television programs and many of the toys aimed at children encourage violent and warlike play. It often makes adults uncomfortable, but there is a reluctance to interfere because it is just play.

Doug Lipman, a New England storyteller, has studied the issue of violent play modeled after the superheroes children observe on television. He conducts workshops on the topics for parents and teachers and shares his thoughts on the issue. He contends that one should look at the issue from the child's point of view in terms of the needs that the play is meeting. As those needs are met in other ways, the need to engage in superhero play will diminish. It is not necessarily desirable to totally eliminate this type of play. After all, there are many admirable heroes in life, song, and literature.

Causes of Pressure. According to Doug Lipman, there are six underlying emotional causes to superhero play. Since the play is usually a result of stress or pressure, children are affected in different degrees. The first stress is the fact that children sometimes feel powerless. Children need to possess a certain amount of power to feel competent. Adults can avoid power struggles and use the need for power to build independent skills. A second cause is a feeling of incompetence. Children need to constantly be made aware of the fact that they are loved and have much worth. Boys especially feel the expectation to be "super competent." Children need to be told that they can do many things well.

The other four causes affect the sexes differently. The third is the subtle societal understanding placed on boys that they may have to take command at any time. They often feel that they might not be able to meet the challenge. Fourth, boys quickly learn that they will be the agents and objects of violence. While there has been some enlightenment toward sex roles over the past decades, boys are aware that they will kill and be killed in wars and be involved in most of the violent crimes. The fifth cause is that boys are discouraged from dealing with their feelings. They are aware of the expectation that they "must be strong" and not "show that they are afraid." It is a tremendous burden, and one that is both unhealthy and unfair. The sixth and final cause relates to girls. Girls learn that they are often expected to remain dependent on males and that they will be treated as objects by males. Part of this message is given by the superhero play of boys. Girls learn that such play is the proper role for boys. The role of girls is different. Each of these causes is unhealthy for a child growing up in a society that is attempting to eliminate violence and sexist attitudes as a normal part of life.

Books for World Stresses. The world can be a highly complex and frightening place. To address some of the needs of children in this area, bibliotherapy can again be a powerful tool. Through books, children can learn facts and begin to deal with those facts through discussions with caring and sensitive adults. Books that address the issues of war include Judith Vigna's *Nobody Wants a Nuclear War* and Dr. Seuss's *The Butter Battle Book.* Another powerful book on the subject of war is the newly reissued *Faithful Elephants* by Yukio Tsuchiya. It is a somber reminder of the inhumanity and irrationality of war. Children and adults will both be moved by its message. Books on pollution include Dr. Seuss's *The Lorax* and Stan and Jan Berenstain's *The Berenstain Bears and the Coughing Catfish.* Other books suggested in other areas may be applicable for issues here as well.

SUMMARY

Bibliotherapy is a powerful tool at all age and grade levels. It can be effective with even very young children. Educators cannot ignore the emotions and feelings of children as they attempt to be a part of their environment. The understandings of children need to be clarified and expanded. It is only through that process that children will eliminate their ignorance and gain confidence in their ability to deal with the world.

There are many benefits to using bibliotherapy. The use of books to clarify misconceptions and to encourage discussion can lead the way to understanding and self-confidence. When children feel safe and competent, achievement in academics will be enhanced. While the benefits may not be immediate, the teacher or parent who uses bibliotherapy will help increase the likelihood of long-term benefits. Caution should, of course, be exercised when dealing with highly emotional topics and with children with severe psychological needs.

A variety of childhood concerns can be addressed with bibliotherapy. These include issues related to self, family, friends, other people, illness and death, and problems of the world. Finally, there are many books that can be used within the process. Any book used should be carefully selected. In addition to the regular criteria for using books, particular care should be taken with the content and presentation of books used in bibliotherapy.

QUESTIONS FOR THOUGHT AND DISCUSSION

1. What is bibliotherapy?
2. How does one know whether or not a book is age-appropriate for a child?
3. Why is it important that a book dealing with an issue be first and foremost a good story?
4. Briefly describe some of the emotional causes of superhero play.
5. If superhero play is not all bad, what is the role of the educator regarding this type of play?
6. Why should a teacher use caution when using bibliotherapy?
7. What are some of the benefits of using bibliotherapy?
8. What are some of the concerns of young children?
9. Fear can be both a benefit and a liability. When does it become a liability? When is it a benefit?

10. Briefly explain some of the strategies one should utilize with bibliotherapy.
11. List three different books for young children that deal with any of the following topics: divorce, poverty, war, sibling rivalry, death, illness, minority groups, and the handicapped.
12. Is parent notification and involvement important when using bibliotherapy? Why or why not?
13. Why expose a child to a book that deals with war?

CHILDREN'S BOOKS CITED

Arnold Adoff, *Black Is Brown Is Tan* (New York: Harper & Row, 1973).

Martha Alexander, *Nobody Asked Me if I Wanted a Baby Sister* (New York: Dial, 1971).

Aliki (Brandenberg), *We Are Best Friends* (New York: Mulberry, 1982).

Joan Anglund, *A Friend Is Someone Who Likes You* (New York: Harcourt, Brace, Jovanovich, 1958).

Stan and Jan Berenstain, *The Berenstain Bears and the Coughing Catfish* (New York: Random House, 1987).

Stan and Jan Berenstain, *The Trouble with Friends* (New York: Random House, 1987).

Judy Blume, *The Pain and the Great One* (New York: Dell, 1974).

Susan Bonners, *Just in Passing* (New York: Lothrop, Lee and Shepard, 1989).

Marcia Brown, *Best Friends* (Racine, Wisconsin: Golden Press, 1967).

Eve Bunting, *The Wednesday Surprise* (New York: Clarion, 1989).

Nancy Carlson, *Arnie and the Stolen Markers* (New York: Viking Penguin, 1987).

Nancy Carlson, *Harriet and Walt* (Minneapolis, Minnesota: Carolrhoda, 1982).

Nancy Carlson, *Witch Lady* (New York: Viking Penguin, 1985).

Kay Chorao, *Lester's Overnight,* (New York: E. P. Dutton, 1977).

Beverly Cleary, *Ramona and Her Father* (New York: Morrow, 1977).

Lucille Clifton, *My Friend Jacob* (New York: E. P. Dutton, 1980).

Lucille Clifton, *The Boy Who Didn't Believe in Spring* (New York: E. P. Dutton, 1973).

Miriam Cohen, *First Grade Takes a Test* (New York: Dell, 1980).

Miriam Cohen, *See You Tomorrow, Charles* (New York: Dell, 1983).

Miriam Cohen, *When Will I Read?* (New York: Dell, 1977).

Miriam Cohen, *Will I Have a Friend?* (New York: Macmillan, 1967).

Tomie dePaola, *Now One Foot, Now the Other* (New York: G. P. Putnam, 1981).

Tomie dePaola, *Oliver Button Is a Sissy* (New York: Harcourt, Brace, Jovanovich, 1979).

Tomie dePaola, *Nana Upstairs, Nana Downstairs* (New York: G. P. Putnam, 1973).

Joan Fassler, *Howie Helps Himself* (Chicago: Albert Whitman, 1975)

Patricia Reilly Giff, *The Beast in Miss Rooney's Room* (New York: Dell, 1984).

Patricia Reilly Giff, *Happy Birthday, Ronald Morgan* (New York: Viking Penguin, 1986).

Morse Hamilton, *Who's Afraid of the Dark* (New York: Avon, 1983).

Barbara Shook Hazen, *Tight Times* (New York: Viking Penguin, 1979).

Kevin Henkes, *Sheila Rae, the Brave* (New York: Viking Penguin, 1982).

Lorraine Henriod, *Grandma's Wheelchair* (Chicago: Albert Whitman, 1982).

Kathryn Hitte, *Boy Was I Mad* (New York: Parents Magazine Press, 1969).

Lillian Hoban, *Arthur's Loose Tooth* (New York: Harper & Row, 1985).

Russell Hoban, *A Baby Sister for Frances* (New York: Harper & Row, 1960).

Paula and Kirk Hogan, *Hospital Scares Me* (Milwaukee, Wisconsin: Raintree, 1980).

Susan Jeschke, *Perfect the Pig* (New York: Scholastic, 1980).

William Joyce, *George Shrinks* (New York: Harper & Row, 1985).

Curt and Gita Kaufman, *Hotel Boy* (New York: Atheneum, 1987).

Curt and Gita Kaufman, *Rajesh* (New York: Atheneum, 1985).

Jack Ezra Keats, *Apartment Three* (New York: Macmillan, 1983).

Jack Ezra Keats, *The Snowy Day* (New York: Vanguard, 1962).

Jack Ezra Keats and Pat Cherr, *My Dog Is Lost* (New York: Thomas Y. Crowell, 1960).

Wendy Kesselmann, *Angelita* (New York: Hill and Wang, 1970).

Barbara Kirk, *Grandpa, Me and the Treehouse* (New York: Macmillan, 1987).

Robert Kraus, *Leo the Late Bloomer* (New York: Simon and Schuster, 1971).

Phyllis Krasilovsky, *Scaredy Cat* (New York: Macmillan, 1959)

Phyllis Krasilovsky, *The Very Tall Little Girl* (New York: Random House, 1969).

Susan Lapsley, *I Am Adopted* (Scarsdale, New York: Bradbury Press, 1975).

Joe Lasker, *He's My Brother* (Chicago: Albert Whitman, 1974).

Joe Lasker, *Mothers Can Do Anything* (Chicago: Albert Whitman, 1972).

Ada Litchfield, *A Button in Her Ear* (Chicago: Albert Whitman, 1976).

Ada Litchfield, *A Cane in Her Hand* (Chicago: Albert Whitman, 1977).

Arnold Lobel, *Frog and Toad Are Friends* (New York: Scholastic, 1970).

Patricia MacLachlan, *Through Grandpa's Eyes* (New York: Harper & Row, 1980).

James Marshall, *The Cut Ups* (New York: Viking Penguin, 1984).

Mercer Mayer, *Just Me and My Dad* (Chicago: Goldencraft, 1977).

Mercer Mayer, *You're the Scaredy Cat* (New York: Parents Magazine Press, 1974).

Mercer Mayer, *There's a Nightmare in My Closet* (New York: Dial, 1968).

David McPhail, *The Bear's Toothache* (New York: Little Brown, 1972).

Susan Meddaugh, *Beast* (Boston: Houghton Mifflin, 1981).

Else Holmelund Minarik, *No Fighting, No Biting* (New York: Harper & Row, 1958).

Eve Miriam, *Mommies at Work* (New York: Alfred Knopf, 1961).

Robert Munsch, *50 Below Zero* (Toronto, Ontario, Canada: Annick, 1986).

Vaunda Micheaux Nelson, *Always Gramma* (New York: G. P. Putnam, 1988).

Jeanne Whitehouse Peterson, *I Have a Sister, My Sister IsDeaf* (New York: Harper & Row, 1977).

Daniel Pinkwater, *The Wuggie Norple Story* (New York: Four Winds, 1980).

Watty Piper, *The Little Engine that Could* (Eau Claire, Wisconsin: Hale, 1954).

Patricia Quinlan, *My Dad Takes Care of Me* (Toronto, Ontario, Canada: Annick, 1987).

Berniece Rabe, *The Balancing Girl* (New York: E. P. Dutton, 1981).

Ellen Raskin, *Spectacles* (New York: Atheneum, 1972).

H. A. and Margaret Rey, *Curious George Goes to the Hospital* (Boston: Houghton Mifflin, 1966).

Barbara Robinson, *The Fattest Bear in First Grade* (New York: Random House, 1969).

Harlow Rockwell, *My Dentist* (New York: Greenwillow, 1975).

Tony Ross, *I'm Coming to Get You* (New York: Dial, 1984).

Cynthia Rylant, *When I Was Young in the Mountains* (New York: E. P. Dutton, 1982).

Jonah Schein, *Forget Me Not* (Toronto, Ontario, Canada: Annick, 1988).

Dr. Seuss (pseud. Theodor Geisel), *The Butter Battle Book* (New York: Random House, 1984)

Dr. Seuss (pseud. Theodor Geisel), *The Lorax* (New York: Random House, 1971).

Mitchell Sharmat, *Sherman Is a Slowpoke* (New York: Scholastic, 1988).

Harriet Sobol, *My Brother Steven Is Retarded* (New York: Macmillan, 1977).

Muriel Stanek, *My Mom Can't Read* (Chicago: Albert Whitman, 1986).

Miriam Stecher, *Daddy and Ben Together* (New York: Lothrop, Lee and Shepard, 1981).

Alvin Tresselt, *The Dead Tree* (New York: Parents Magazine, 1972).

Yukio Tsuchiya, *Faithful Elephants* (New York: Houghton Mifflin, 1988).

Janice Udry, *Let's Be Enemies* (New York: Harper & Row, 1961).

Judith Vigna, *Nobody Wants a Nuclear War* (Chicago: Albert Whitman, 1986).

Judith Viorst, *My Mama Says There Aren't Any Zombies, Ghosts, Vampires, Creatures, Demons, Monsters, Fiends, Goblins or Things* (New York: Atheneum, 1977).

Judith Viorst, *The Tenth Good Thing about Barney* (New York: Atheneum, 1971).

Bernard Waber, *Ira Sleeps Over* (Boston: Houghton Mifflin, 1972).

Alma Marshak Whitney, *Just Awful* (London: World's Work, 1971).

Vera Williams, *A Chair for My Mother* (New York: Greenwillow, 1982).

Barbara Winther, *Plays from Folktales from Africa* (Boston: Plays, 1976).

Jane Yolen, *Sleeping Ugly* (New York: Coward McCann, 1981).

Margot Zemach, *It Could Always Be Worse* (New York: Scholastic, 1976).

Charlotte Zolotow, *Something Is Going to Happen* (New York: Harper & Row, 1988).

Charlotte Zolotow, *The Hating Book* (New York: Harper & Row, 1969).

Charlotte Zolotow, *William's Doll* (New York: Harper & Row, 1972).

SELECTED REFERENCES

Doris Brett, *Annie Stories* (New York: Workman, 1988).

Eileen Burke, *Early Childhood Literature: For Love of Child and Book* (Newton, Massachusetts: Allyn & Bacon, 1986).

Betty Coody, *Using Literature with Young Children* (Dubuque, Iowa: William C. Brown, 1983).

Charlotte S. Huck and Doris Young Kuhn, *Children's Literature in the Elementary School* (New York: Holt, Rinehart and Winston, 1983).

Margaret Mary Kimmel and Elizabeth Segel, *For Reading Out Loud!* (New York: Delacorte, 1983).

Jim Trelease, *The New Read-Aloud Handbook* (New York: Viking Penguin, 1989).

Using Commercial and Educational Media

lmost from the moment of conception children in America are confronted by various media. It is common practice to view prenatal children on an ultrasound screen. There have been many debates and arguments concerning the relationship of children with television, tape recordings, films, and other media. Since these media are here to stay, some of the arguments are moot. American families usually own at least one television set. Many of the programs depict violence, greed, and unrealistic pictures of life. Many households, and the number is increasing daily, also own video cassette recorders (VCRs), tape players, and compact disc (CD) players. Families receive newspapers and magazines in the home, go to movies, and see billboards along the highways. Increasing numbers of households possess personal computers. Because much of the media is presented for the purpose of earning revenue for advertisers, the quality is not always appropriate for children. The role of teachers and parents is to use the media effectively and to help children begin to make critical choices concerning the media.

MEDIA AND LITERATURE

One might wonder what all of this media has to do with literature. Actually there are two relationships between the media and literature, one friendly and the other adversarial. The friendly relationship is the blending of literature and media to provide more powerful learning experiences for children. Literature can give depth to the superficial aspects of media presentations by allowing children to learn more about a concept or an event. Media can be used to enhance a child's involvement with literature by increasing the use of the senses to experience a book. Media can also be used as a springboard for further discussion of a book.

The adversarial relationship occurs when the media overwhelms and takes the place of literature in the lives of children. Media will always be present in children's lives. It is up to parents and educators to control the media rather than letting the media control their children and themselves. If it is going to be a positive force in children's lives the use of media must be planned so that its best qualities are used to enhance the lives of children. Media can be valuable as an experience in its own right, but care should be taken to see that it is not used in place of literature, play, adult supervision, or the development of friendships.

Categories of media seem to be increasing rapidly. Hardly a day goes by when one does not hear about a new interactive video, laser disc, or innovative FAX machine use. However, the predominant media used with young children will generally include such things as television, audio tapes, films, filmstrips, magazines, newspapers, and computer programs. Each of these will be discussed. Care should be taken in selecting these materials. Therefore, criteria will be suggested. The focus will be on effectively using each of the media in conjunction with literature for the purpose of enhancing the experience of the story.

TELEVISION: SEEING THE WORLD FROM A CHAIR

There is no doubt about it: television can be a fantastic medium. From the comfort of an easy chair one can go on an African safari, attend a storybook wedding of a princess, take a shuttle into space, or participate in a bloody military skirmish in a third world country. The seemingly endless variety of experiences available through television is part of the problem. We simply watch too much television.

Negative Aspects of Television

By the time children enter kindergarten, they have watched 5,000 hours of television. Between the ages of three and seventeen, the average American child watches 15,000 hours. This is 2,000 hours more than that same child will spend in a classroom during those years. Prior to age 17, that child will watch 350,000 commercials and 18,000 acts of violence on television. Commercials aimed at children often encourage foods that are not nutritional. The acts of violence often depict a simplistic way of solving complex problems.[1]

The effect of large amounts of television viewing on school work has been established. The more children watch television, the lower their school achievement becomes.[2] Excessive television viewing also reduces a child's ability to have normal affective responses to such human problems as illness, intolerance, racism, and death.[3] There is a blurring of the lines between fantasy and reality that is clearly not in the best interest of children.

The shows offered and the commercials embedded within these shows are another problem area. The quality of television shows seems to have decreased.

[1] Paul Kopperman, *The Literacy Hoax: The Decline of Reading, Writing and Learning in the Public Schools and What We Can Do about It* (New York: Morrow, 1980).
[2] California Department of Education, *Student Achievement in California Schools, 1979–80 Annual Report* (Sacramento, California: Author, 1980).
[3] Frank Mankiewicz and Joel Swerdlow, *Remote Control: Television and the Manipulation of America* (New York: Times Books, 1978).

Our society appears to be more and more drawn to the flashy and the violent. Quality shows are removed and replaced with more violent fare. Much of this problem has to do with rating points, audience share, and advertising dollars.

During the past few years, a new low has been reached. Previously, children's toys depicting characters from a television show were created and marketed after a show had become popular. Currently, new shows are being programmed based upon the successful marketing of a toy. These include robots, dolls, and action toys. In effect, children who watch the shows are merely watching an ongoing half-hour advertisement.

Controlling Television Viewing

Most adults know that children watch far too much television. For that matter, most adults are aware that they themselves spend too much time watching television. There is a need to feel this awareness more deeply and to consider the effects of the problem. Following awareness, one must come to an understanding of some basic facts about television. Only then can an appropriate response be launched.

Awareness. To become aware of the seriousness of the problem requires closer study. To get a clearer view of the problem, several steps might be taken. First, one can obtain and distribute literature dealing with the problem of excess television viewing to teachers, caregivers, and parents. Such literature is available from several groups such as the National Education Association (NEA), Action for Children's Television (ACT), and the International Reading Association (IRA).

Secondly, collecting information on children's television viewing can be enlightening. This may be done by distributing television viewing recording charts, with boxes for half hour time slots and days of the week, to parents. By blackening a box for each half hour time slot a child watches a television show, parents will have a weekly picture of their child's television viewing. A chart with large areas of blackened time slots representing all of the time spent in front of a television set will have far more impact than anything that might otherwise be said.

Understanding. When one begins to realize some of the basic facts about anything, that individual is more able to take control and make better decisions about it. Young children need to develop an understanding of some of the basic facts about television in order to make decisions about it. An effective approach to this is the use of a video cassette recorder (VCR) to tape and stop various commercials and television shows. By stopping and discussing what is happening, children will begin to understand and take control. For example, advertising uses a wide variety of propaganda tricks to get consumers to buy certain products. By stopping to discuss the commercial, children will begin to understand what is happening. This kind of understanding will not lessen their trust in people. Rather, it will increase their trust in people who care about them. The understanding will also make them more aware of their own intelligence and their ability to make decisions. In addition, using language to discuss a problem will enhance their command over language.

Children can usually understand the concept of excess. What would happen if it rained all the time? What would it be like if the only things we ate were apples? The comparison can be made with television. What would it be like if we watched television all of our waking hours? What would it be like if there were no television? Like any diet or activity, children can learn that television can be a part of their life, but not the sole focus. Television can help us learn to cook, to draw, and to understand many things. It can be a wonderful machine. However, television is only a part of life. There are many other important parts as well.

Response. Awareness is helpful, but response is critical. Simply eliminating or drastically reducing television viewing will only partially solve the problem. When one activity is decreased, it is important to have healthy and wholesome alternative activities to fill the void that is left. If not, the activity will probably become one of children pleading to return to the original habit of watching television. Both Jim Trelease[4] and Marie Winn[5] have described programs for use when television viewing is either decreased or eliminated in the home. They describe a variety of family and independent activities that will broaden a child's vision and interests. Many of the ideas center around reading, literature, and family story times.

Part of the response to large amounts of television viewing can and should focus on the ability of people to understand what they are doing with their lives. It may be unrealistic to totally eliminate all television viewing for young people. It may not accomplish all of the things one might hope for anyway. For example, most people are aware of the violence exhibited on television and the reports of its effect on young children. However, eliminating all television violence will not eliminate all the fears, nightmares, and aggression children might experience. In her book, *The Magic Years,*[6] Selma Frailberg contends that these fears are a natural stage of human development. That is, children will develop them from a variety of sources.

This does not mean, of course, that unmonitored and indiscriminate viewing of television is acceptable. Rather, one's response should be to talk to and listen to children more. By attempting to understand the perspective of children, one helps children come to a better understanding of themselves. Better understanding leads to better control. This is true whether the topic is a story being read or a television program being viewed. By empowering children in this way, they become more able to make critical choices about many things as they grow. By seeing television for what it is, they become better able to make more critical choices concerning what and how much they will watch. In so doing, they will be better able to make choices about alternatives to television viewing.

Positive Aspects of Television

There have always been good quality television programs for children and there are still wonderful programs for children to watch. In the past, such shows as

[4] Jim Trelease, *The New Read-Aloud Handbook* (New York: Viking Penguin, 1989).
[5] Marie Winn, *Unplugging the Plug-in Drug* (New York: Penguin, 1987).
[6] Selma Frailberg, *The Magic Years* (New York: Charles Scribner's Sons, 1959).

"Ding Dong School," "Howdy Doody," "Captain Kangaroo," and "Kukla, Fran and Ollie" were favorites. "Captain Kangaroo" has been joined over the years by other quality children's shows such as "Mr. Rogers' Neighborhood" in celebrating the joys of children learning about the world. Fred Rogers, the show's main character, uses language, humor, and stories as integral parts of the program. He has also published a series of books for sharing between child and parent. The informative books, which do not talk down to children, cover such topics as daycare, doctors, and new babies.

"Sesame Street" evolved when the Children's Television Workshop turned market research into productive children's programming. Using Jim Henson's muppet characters and a diverse cast, "Sesame Street" provides learning experiences through a series of short segments that take into account the attention span of young children. This was one of the first programs for children to feature a multiethnic cast. Women, minorities, and the handicapped are all featured with realism and dignity.

Some programs focus directly on reading and quality children's literature. "Read-It" with John Robbins, produced by the Agency for Instructional Television, is such a program. Each day a story is read while illustrations are drawn on the screen. Prior to the ending of the story, children are asked how they think the story could end. The actual book and the author's name are revealed to the children at this point. They are encouraged to get the book and find out how the author ended the story.

"Reading Rainbow" also focuses directly on literature. During each program, one or more books are shared with the audience. The format expands the book through dramatization, animation, music, and personal responses to the story. After each book is presented, it is reviewed by children who share their personal responses to the book. The program has presented a variety of books from classical to contemporary. Among some of the selections are Ezra Jack Keats's *The Snowy Day,* Aliki's *How a Book Is Made,* Jane Yolen's *Owl Moon,* Tomie dePaola's *Bill and Pete Go down the Nile,* and Bill Martin Jr.'s *Knots on a Counting Rope.*

Commercial networks have also adapted several well known children's books for television. The quality of the presentations is uneven; some of the presentations ring remarkably true to the original story while others have been disturbingly altered. Cable television, through the Disney and Discovery channels, has tied several of its programs to literature. Again, the quality of the adaptations can vary.

Using Elements of Television

Because television can be a vehicle for learning, parents and educators can harness its power. By using selected television programs, parents and educators can reinforce basic concept skills, socialization skills, and self-esteem. Some of the thousands of commercials children watch can be used to teach about nutrition and critical decision making. By critically analyzing food commercials, children can learn about alternative snacks and nutrition. By analyzing toy commercials, children can make better decisions about whether they really need a particular toy.

The concept of developing their own programs can be appealing to children. A large cardboard box can become a television set on which children put their own shows and commercials. The spontaneous acting that will result during free play periods can reinforce language development. Brief skits and commercials, some based on stories they have read, will help children to recreate the experience of the story. The emphasis should not be on the excellence of the production. The main focus should be on the use of language within the experience.

AUDIOVISUAL MATERIALS

Audiovisual materials include records, cassettes, tapes, photographs, compact discs, filmstrips, slides, films, and the equipment needed to use them. Each can be used effectively to enhance the curriculum. A wide range of literature related to them is available as well. As a result, most audiovisual materials can be used to extend and enhance the literature used in the curriculum.

When using any audiovisual material to enhance a story, more planning time is needed to organize the presentation. The children may need more help in understanding what is happening than was apparent in the reading of the book. The reason for this is that the teacher may be less involved in the presentation. The machine may set the pace and timing of the presentation. As with all machines, a tape recorder or record player cannot detect a puzzled look on a child's face. For this reason, audiovisual materials should never replace the teacher, the parent, or the book. They should always be used to supplement the reading of the story.

There are a variety of sources to obtain audiovisual materials. Public libraries and elementary school libraries are both good sources. They usually have a variety of literature related materials. New materials may be purchased from a variety of commercial sources. Record companies and educational supply companies usually have catalogs offering their materials. In the case of films, many companies will rent the film for specified periods of time.

Criteria for Selecting Audiovisual Materials

Audiovisual materials that bring a book to another media need to be carefully screened. The film or filmstrip version of a story should neither diminish nor replace the original story. The illustrations, flow, and feeling of the story should possess the same impact as the initial reading of the story. Effective use of an audiovisual presentation should extend the reading and recreate the story for the child.

Some companies are more successful than others at maintaining this faithfulness to the original story. Weston Woods, for example, uses the complete texts of the book in their filmstrips. In their films, they use an iconographic technique instead of animation. In animation, illustrators create hundreds of pictures in order to produce movement in the films. The iconographic technique uses hundreds of photographs from the original book illustrations to produce the same effect. The photographs are taken at various angles and focuses to reflect the original illustrator's intent. This also enables the film to capture textual moods and actions.

The superiority of the iconographic technique does not diminish the value of a carefully crafted animated version of a story. Disney Studios has successfully produced animated versions of stories for years. The Disney stories, however, are often not faithful to the original texts. As a result, many of them seem to be new stories with lives of their own. It is still important for children to see and hear the original stories. This will add to the magic of the literature and broaden children's understanding of the story.

Infusing a desire to read and developing an enjoyment of literature are two very important objectives that parents and educators attempt to implant in young children. Selecting audiovisual materials should be done with these criteria in mind: The materials should enhance the original version of a story. They should be clear and coherent to the child. They should create or extend the magic of the original story. The original story should never be replaced by the audiovisual materials.

Using Audiovisual Materials

There are extensive audiovisual materials available in a variety of media. Records, tapes, and compact discs may present stories, music, or stories that include music. They may or may not be used with visuals such as the actual book. Films, videocassettes, and filmstrips contain a visual and sound recreation of a story. The costs vary greatly between and within each of these sources. The choice of any of these audiovisual materials should depend mainly on how well it fits into the overall objective for sharing or experiencing a story in the first place. When that is clear, a wide range of possible activities can be used in conjunction with the audiovisual materials.

Records and Tapes. Designating a specific quiet area of the room is helpful for using records and tapes. The area can serve for both instructional purposes and free play listening. Providing additional headsets enables several children to listen to a story at one time without filling the room with sound. Using a copy of the book with the recording is usually beneficial. Most recordings have a signal indicating the need to turn the page. Even if the children cannot read the words, they will become accustomed to the concept of words and the idea that language flows by turning the pages as the story proceeds. Excellent tapes of well known books include Margery Williams's *The Velveteen Rabbit,* Stephen Cosgrove's *Morgan Mine,* Matt Newman's (Adaptation) *Little Red Riding Hood*, and Ann McGovern's *Stone Soup.* In addition, classroom tapes can be created whenever the teacher reads a book. Children can relisten to these tapes as well.

Story tapes played at naptime can help children both relive the story and settle down for a quiet time. Some of the tapes may be made available for parents to sign out. In this way, parents could share the story with their children and enhance the experience with further discussion.

Films, Filmstrips, and Videocassettes. Filmstrips provide a wide variety of stories shown in still pictures on a screen. They usually come with a cassette that contains the sound and the story portion of the presentation. Excellent examples of books transferred into filmstrips include Arnold Lobel's *Mouse Soup,* Peggy Parish's *Amelia Bedelia and the Baby,* Claire Huchet Bishop's and Kurt Weise's *The*

Five Chinese Brothers and Norman Bridwell's *Clifford at the Circus.* Films enable one to turn the classroom into a small movie theater for the telling of a story. Other types of film can be used to create photographs and slides related to stories and the curriculum.

A videocassette is similar in function to a film, with the story shown on a television screen or monitor. Troll Associates publishes a variety of classic stories on videocassette including "The Brementown Musicians," "Little Red Riding Hood," "The Ugly Duckling," and "The Three Little Pigs." The cost of each of these varies greatly.

All of these media can be used for whole group presentations. Both the videocassette and the filmstrip projector can be used independently by many young children. The film projector cannot. As with records and tapes, these presentations should not replace the use of a book for the telling of stories. Rather, the presentation can and should be used to extend and enhance the story. For example, if fairytales are being used in the classroom, the concept can be extended with a recreation of some of the original stories on film. If a videocassette camera can be used, children in costume can recreate the stories as well.

Photographs and slides can be used to create books about any topic. Both original pictures and photographs of pictures from books and magazines can be used. The pictures can be used as starting points for original stories. Pictures of children enacting an entire story could also be used to develop a language experience story.

When creating with audiovisual equipment, it is best to consider a few things prior to the activity. Parents should always be informed. This is particularly true if the pictures will be used by the press. If parents don't wish their child to be included, the request should be honored without comment. Letting parents know ahead of time also gives them the opportunity to have their children look their best. If costumes or props are to be used, it allows parents enough time to acquire them.

Planning for the unexpected is recommended. This includes practicing with the equipment beforehand so that sufficient skill will have been achieved. It also allows one to realize that such things as additional lighting and extra extension cords are needed prior to the activity. Finally, a back-up plan should always be ready. Equipment may get lost or malfunction. Children get sick. An alternate plan can help achieve the goals of the project even when these problems occur.

MAGAZINES AND NEWSPAPERS

Magazines and newspapers abound in our culture. It is challenging, however, to find quality magazines that appeal to the interest of children. Likewise, it requires some creativity to develop appropriate uses for newspapers with young children. Figure 1 contains a summary of quality magazines appropriate for young children.

Cricket, Box 52961, Boulder, Colorado 80322, includes poetry and other writing by children (kindergarten to grade 4).

Ranger Rick, National Wildlife Federation, 1412 Sixteenth Street NW, Washington, D.C., includes material on nature and ecology (preschool to grade 2).

Scienceland, 501 Fifth Avenue, Suite 2102, New York, New York 10017, features vivid photography on science (preschool to kindergarten).

Sesame Street Magazine, P.O. Box 52000, Boulder, Colorado, features basic concept activities and stories (preschool to kindergarten).

Stone Soup, Children's Art Foundation, P.O. Box 83, Santa Cruz, California 95063, includes art, stories and poetry by children (ages six to thirteen).

Surprises, P.O. Box 236, Chanhassen, Minnesota 55317, includes activities for parents and children to do together (ages four to twelve).

Turtle, Children's Better Health Institute, P.O. Box 10003, Des Moines, Iowa 50340, includes poetry, stories, and games on health (preschoolers).

Your Big Backyard, National Wildlife Federation, 1412 Sixteenth Street NW, Washington, D.C. 20036, includes nature stories, activities, photographs, and recipes (toddlers and preschoolers).

Highlights for Children, 2300 West Fifth Avenue, P.O. Box 269, Columbus, Ohio 43272, includes stories, poems and activities by children (preschoolers and kindergarten).

Let's Find Out, Scholastic, 2931 East McCarty Street, Jefferson City, Missouri 65102, includes activities and games for holidays, seasons, and other topics (preschool to kindergarten).

Figure 1.   Magazines for young children. Courtesy Walter Sawyer.

Magazines and newspapers have a low cost, are filled with print, and contain many superb illustrations. It makes sense to use them as a resource for developing literacy with young children. To do this in conjunction with a literature program requires two things: First, one must have certain criteria for deciding to include newspapers and magazines. Secondly, one must develop a set of activities and strategies for effectively using them.

Criteria for Using Magazines and Newspapers

There are two basic criteria that should be considered. First, one must determine whether the magazine, article, story, or illustration supports the objective or purpose of the lesson or activity. Does it fit into the curriculum web for this lesson? Does it reinforce a concept that is being learned? Does it clarify the meaning of something the class is doing? Does it extend the learning in some way? The answers to these questions will help to determine how well the print media will support the purpose of the lesson.

Secondly, one must determine the suitability of the piece for children. Rather than focus on the appeal of the piece to the adult, one must see it through the eyes of children. What might be a stunning photograph to an adult might be too complex and vague to a child. A written text that might be fascinating to an adult might be too abstract and confusing to a child.

Using Magazines and Newspapers

In addition to the magazines listed in Figure 1, other magazines might be useful as well. While the texts might be inappropriate, the titles and photographs from other magazines might be helpful in reinforcing or extending a story or a concept. For example, sports magazines might contain illustrations and photographs for a unit on books dealing with sports and motor skills. Family magazines might include pictures of foods mentioned in the stories children are reading. Newspaper advertising headlines may contain words and phrases used in language development and story activities.

A variety of hands-on activities related to a story can be done with pictures and words cut from the pages of magazines and newspapers. Collages can be made from pictures of animals, foods, and shapes. Category charts can be constructed from pictures of houses, trucks, animals, or parts of the body. Sequences of a sports activity, a plant growing, or a cake being made can he cut out and mounted as a project. A series or set of related pictures can be displayed to children so that they can create their own story about the pictures. Games (e.g., "War," "Old Maid") can be created by mounting various types of pictures on index cards. Laminating any of these projects can protect them for long-term use.

COMPUTERS AND SOFTWARE

There are many arguments for using computers with young children: They live in an increasingly technological society. They have to know about computers when they enter school. Computers will give them a head start on reading. On the other hand, there are several arguments cautioning against the use of computers with young children. They take children away from social interactions. The software is often of poor quality: Children aren't ready to use a computer at such young ages. Each of the arguments on both sides of the issue may have some truth. The answers may vary depending on the age of the child.

It is important to have a clear idea of the issues and to make informed decisions about the amount of computer use in a literacy development program for young children. Jane Ilene Davidson offers a comprehensive look at the issues in her book, *Children and Computers: Together in the Early Childhood Classroom.*[7] The position taken in this chapter is that computers can be an effective tool to supplement and enhance literacy with young children. They must be used, however, as part of a carefully thought out plan that considers the child's development, the purpose for using the computer, and the software that will be used.

Criteria for Computer Use

The criteria for using computers must address child development, the purpose of the computer use, and the software selected for use.

[7] Jane Ilene Davidson, *Children and Computers: Together in the Early Childhood Classroom* (Albany, New York: Delmar, 1989).

Child Development. The child's development will have an effect on the ability to use the keyboard and other peripheral devices of a computer. According to Rosalind Charlesworth,[8] fine motor development generally follows gross motor development. The eye-hand coordination that might be helpful to use a computer effectively may not mature until the age of six or seven. One might, therefore, question the appropriateness of having children work independently at a computer terminal.

On the other hand, if the teacher manages or guides the use of the keyboard while the children view the screen, there may be ample reason for using certain programs. This does not mean that children should not be allowed to touch a computer. Development takes place over a period of time. Opportunities to experiment and manipulate parts of the environment can and should be provided. Realistic expectations must be accepted, however, when children are given control of a computer.

Purpose. The purpose of using a computer should be legitimate. One might have as a purpose the simple notion of exposing children to a powerful technology. While that may be a valid purpose, it is not necessarily part of a literacy program. If the purpose is to drill young children on letter and number identification, it is at odds with current thought on developing literacy with children. Such drill tends to take children away from the social interactions and the opportunities to recreate stories and events that are important to language development. Such drill can also lead to a belief that language and reading are monotonous and boring activities.

Computer use can coincide with a contemporary view of literacy development when it is used to reinforce and enhance the development of literacy in a social context. This can be done in several ways. As noted above, the teacher can control or guide the use of the keyboard while children interact with each other and the program on the screen. The teacher guides the group so that the technology is used as a means to create and recreate language and stories in meaningful ways. The teacher can also provide opportunities in which pairs of students interact with each other as well as the computer in order to accomplish a task. Guidance is a key to providing effective opportunities for computer use with young children.

Software. There is a great deal of poor quality software available. It tends to require little more than rote responses from children. In effect, this type of software does little more than duplicate a ditto sheet or a workbook page on an electronic screen. One should seriously question using an expensive piece of electronic equipment for a task that can be accomplished just as easily with a pencil and paper.

The software selected might better be used to encourage the development of original stories or to recreate stories the child has experienced. Creative art programs and simplified word processing programs are available for this purpose. This approach will more closely coincide with contemporary thought on literacy

---

[8] Rosalind Charlesworth, *Understanding Child Development—For Adults Who Work with Children* (Albany, New York: Delmar, 1987).

development. It will also provide an experience for the child that is much more meaningful than the simple recall of rote information.

Computer Use

It is best to use the computer as a means rather than an end. Learning about computers is important for nearly everyone, but it is not absolutely essential that children acquire this familiarity in early childhood. The focus in an early childhood education program should be on using the computer as a means to enhance literacy development. While children might be allowed to actually use the computer, it can be a more powerful tool when the teacher guides children in a language development activity while using the computer.

For example, a computerized version of a previously read story can be explored through a computer program. Several titles are already available. They include Margery Williams's *The Velveteen Rabbit* and H. A. Rey's *Curious George Goes Shopping, Curious George in Outer Space* and *Curious George Visits the Library.* Additional titles are also becoming available. A language experience approach (LEA) story can be created as an original piece on the computer. A previously read story can be recreated on the computer using the words of the children. Scholastic's "Bank Street Writer," using enlarged letters, can be used for this purpose. An alternative word processing program that could be used is "Muppet Slate" by Henson Associates and Sunburst Communications. Designed for young children, it combines words and pictures in a word processing format. The major point with these approaches is that the language and the understanding of the story are the focus, rather than the computer. This coincides with the major purposes and objectives of a literacy curriculum for young children.

SUMMARY

The commercial media is a major influence in the lives of young children. It brings forth a constant stream of new ideas and images. Children, however, need to grow at their own pace. They are often not able to discriminate between the important, unimportant, truthful, and deceptive images they find before them. They are exposed to television, audiovisual materials, newspapers, magazines, and computer software. The question isn't whether children should or should not be exposed to this; it will happen anyway. Rather, the question for teachers and parents is how to control the amount, the timing, and the use of that media exposure.

Appropriately introduced and used, commercial media can support the development of literacy in young children. Introduced too soon and in inappropriate amounts, it can leave a child confused about many aspects of reality. Teachers and parents need to decide how to use the media for their own purposes rather than for the purposes the media may have developed. While television can be a tremendous problem if overused, there are constructive purposes that it can support. The same is true for audiovisual materials, magazines, newspapers, and computers. Adults must develop appropriate structures for their effective use. The key ingredients include understanding the development of the child, developing clear purposes for media use, and carefully selecting the appropriate media for those uses.

QUESTIONS FOR THOUGHT AND DISCUSSION

1. What are some of the dangers of overusing the media?
2. What are some of the positive aspects of television?
3. What are some of the negative aspects of television?
4. Why is it important to have alternative activities available when television viewing is decreased or eliminated?
5. What are the criteria for effectively using television with young children?
6. Describe an activity in which television can be used to support the development of literacy.
7. What are the criteria for effectively using audiovisual materials with young children?
8. Describe an activity in which audiovisual materials can be used to support the development of literacy.
9. What are the criteria for effectively using print media with young children?
10. Describe an activity in which print media can be used to support the development of literacy.
11. What are the criteria for effectively using computers with young children?
12. Describe an activity in which computers can be used to support the development of literacy.
13. Television viewing is not the sole cause of nightmares and childhood fears. How can violence on television affect a young child?
14. What is the appropriate role of computer technology in the early childhood program?

CHILDREN'S BOOKS CITED

Aliki (Brandenberg), *How a Book Is Made* (New York: Crowell, 1986).

Claire Huchet Bishop and Kurt Weise, *The Five Chinese Brothers* (New York: Coward-McCann, 1938), tape by Weston Woods, Weston, Connecticut.

Norman Bridwell, *Clifford at the Circus* (New York: Scholastic, 1981).

Stephen Cosgrove, *Morgan Mine* (Los Angeles, California: Price/Stern/Sloan, 1984).

Tomie dePaola, *Bill and Pete Go down the Nile* (New York: Putnam, 1987).

Ezra Jack Keats, *The Snowy Day* (New York: Viking, 1962).

Arnold Lobel, *Mouse Soup* (New York: Random House, 1983).

Bill Martin, Jr., *Knots on a Counting Rope* (New York: Holt, 1987).

Ann McGovern, *Stone Soup* (New York: Scholastic, 1986).

Matt Newman (adapt.), *Little Red Riding Hood* (Chicago, Illinois: Society for Visual Education, 1980).

Peggy Parish, *Amelia Bedelia and the Baby* (New York: Enrichment Materials, 1983).

H. A. Rey, *Curious George Goes Shopping* (Allen, Texas: DLM, 1983).

H. A. Rey, *Curious George in Outer Space* (Allen, Texas: DLM, 1983).

H. A. Rey, *Curious George Visits the Library* (Allen, Texas: DLM, 1983).

Margery Williams, *The Velveteen Rabbit* (Mahway, New Jersey: Troll, 1988), computer program by Sunburst Communications, Pleasantville, New York.

Jane Yolen, *Owl Moon* (New York: Philomel, 1987).

SELECTED REFERENCES

California Department of Education, *Student Achievement in California Schools, 1979–80 Annual Report* (Sacramento, California: Author, 1980).

Rosalind Charlesworth, *Understanding Child Development—For Adults Who Work with Children* (Albany, New York: Delmar, 1987).

Jane Ilene Davidson, *Children and Computers: Together in the Early Childhood Classroom* (Albany, New York: Delmar, 1989).

Selma Frailberg, *The Magic Years* (New York: Charles Scribner's Sons, 1959).

Susan Haugland and Daniel Shade, *Development Evaluations of Software for Young Children* (Albany, New York: Delmar, 1990).

Paul Kopperman, *The Literacy Hoax: The Decline of Reading, Writing and Learning in the Public Schools and What We Can Do about It* (New York: Morrow, 1980).

Frank Mankiewicz and Joel Swerdlow, *Remote Control: Television and the Manipulation of America* (New York: Times Books, 1978).

Neil Postman, *Teaching as a Conserving Activity* (New York: Delacorte, 1980).

Wilbur Schramm, Jack Lyle and Edwin B. Parker, *Television in the Lives of Our Children* (Stanford, California: Stanford, 1961).

Jim Trelease, *The New Read-Aloud Handbook* (New York: Viking Penguin, 1989).

Marie Winn, *Unplugging the Plug-in Drug* (New York: Penguin, 1987).

CHAPTER

10

Involving the Community

Every community, large and small, contains a wonderfully rich variety of resources. Young children can and should learn about these resources. From late infancy through the kindergarten years, children are fascinated by the world around them. By using this intrinsic motivation, one can enrich the lives of children by using the people and places found in the community. It may be a visit to a library, auto repair shop, or a bank. It may be a visit from a farmer, a nurse, or a bookstore owner. Whatever the occasion, community involvement can be combined with literature and the educational program for children.

In viewing a community, it may be helpful to see it in several different ways. First of all, a community contains people and places. The people have many different jobs and the places have many different roles. The buildings have been constructed to serve a variety of purposes. Some buildings are like big empty boxes that can be used for a variety of things such as a store, an office, or a business. Other buildings have specific designs and contain specialized equipment so that they can be used as a police station, church, or hospital. Another way of viewing the community deals with determining how it can best be used with children. Is it best to bring the children to the community? Or should the community be brought to the children? Actually, both approaches can be effective depending on the situation. Each approach will be explored here.

PLACES TO GO: EXPLORING THE COMMUNITY

A field trip is always an exciting part of an education program, and should be seen as an integrated part of the program. Since it can be such a powerful learning experience, it makes good sense to plan a field trip within an integrated program. Literature can easily be correlated with such parts of the program. Depending on the community, the possibilities are wide and varied. Each place visited will be important in developing the schemas that children will use to continue to make sense of the world. Libraries, museums, parks, zoos, banks, theaters, and municipal service buildings are all appropriate field trip destinations. Before attempting such a visit, a sound field trip plan should be developed.

Field Trip Planning

In order to have a successful and effective field trip, it is necessary to attend to both the trip details and the learning details. Ignoring either of these can result in an experience that is either less meaningful or unsafe for the children.

Trip Details. When taking a group of children into the community, safety has to be a constant thought. If it is planned ahead of time, the trip should go more smoothly. One should always make arrangements with the people at the destination and have an understanding of what the experience should be like for the children. Planning trips for warmer weather, early fall or late spring, eliminates the need to focus on extra clothing, weather related closings, and driving conditions. Parental permission slips, children's name tags, and car assignments are all details that must be attended to as well. When it is a walking field trip, safety concerns for crossing streets and not getting lost must be addressed.

Learning Details. One should question a field trip to the firehouse if the trip is being planned simply because it is only a block away. If closeness is the main reason for the field trip, it may be more of an entertainment experience than an opportunity for learning. With careful planning of integrated units, it is not difficult to choose both appropriate field trip destinations and appropriate literature to share before, during, and after the trip. Appropriate literature will help children anticipate, enjoy, and recreate the experience. In doing this, the children will receive the greatest benefit from the experience.

Libraries

In any program that views books and literature as important to child development, visits to libraries quickly come to mind. Nearly all communities have libraries with long visiting hours. Even when this is not the case, or when there is only a weekly bookmobile, it is worth the effort to make arrangements for such an experience. Library visits can have several important outcomes: First, children can learn that libraries are one of the few places that have a major focus on books. Secondly, they can become aware of the enormous variety of books. Finally, children can learn that libraries are places of learning that go well beyond books. Good stories to introduce the library to children might include Anne Rockwell's *I Like the Library* or Elizabeth Levy's *Something Queer at the Library.*

Learning to Love Books. From late infancy on, it is possible for children to understand the rules of book friendship. The librarian, as an expert in books, can reinforce the understandings that children have been taught about taking care of books. While children may already see parents and teachers modeling the appropriate care of books, the librarian's teachings will help reinforce these ideas. Other concepts, such as not writing or coloring in books, can also be reinforced. Children often do not distinguish between coloring books and those that are not meant to be drawn in.

MARCHING FEET

by Rachel Mahood   Illustrated by Daniel Sylvestre

Any field trip could be preceded by a book to set the tone for the adventure.
Courtesy Delmar Publishers Inc.

By contacting the librarian ahead of time, other concepts about book care might also be addressed. The idea of seeing a book as a friend is helpful. As one is kind to friends, one should be kind to books. This includes keeping pages straight, not spilling things on books, keeping them safe, and keeping them dry. Other concepts about a book might include the ideas of enjoying it, sharing it, and returning it to the library when it is due. Librarians often wish to explain to children the importance of not replacing books on shelves once they have been taken. It is better to let the librarian make sure the book gets back to the correct spot so that others can find it.

A World of Books. Libraries are special places within the community. One will see many different kinds of people in the library: young, old, rich, poor, men, women, and children. Those people are all there because libraries have books and resources for everyone.

Gone are the days when librarians tried to make the library a place of absolute silence. Today, children talk quietly about a project in the library and even listen to the librarian reading a story out loud. There are programs for toddlers and

Introducing children to the library has become easier since libraries have set up inviting children's sections. Courtesy Diana Comer.

preschoolers. Libraries sponsor films and puppet shows related to children's books in order to encourage children to use the library. Summer reading programs, craft hours, cooking, singing, and dramatic storytelling are all a part of a modern library program.

Adults can model the benefits of using the library and knowing the librarian. By having a library card, one can take home wonderful stories to be read during the week. By asking the librarian, one can find out about new books by a favorite author or about a favorite topic.

More than Just Books. Libraries house more than books. They contain videotapes, filmstrips, films, records, magazines, and historical records. Local historical information can be most interesting to children, particularly those whose families have been living in the community for a long time. By using the historical records, one can find the answers to many fascinating questions: What was it like to live in the community one hundred years ago? Were there Indians? Was it unsettled land or a village? Were there buildings? Was our school here then? Posters, maps, and photographs can often be found in the library to answer many of these questions. This activity can be a springboard to future field trips and for developing language experience stories about this topic.

Out of a search of historical records, heroes can emerge. The library can help children learn about the sacrifices and accomplishments of people who lived and

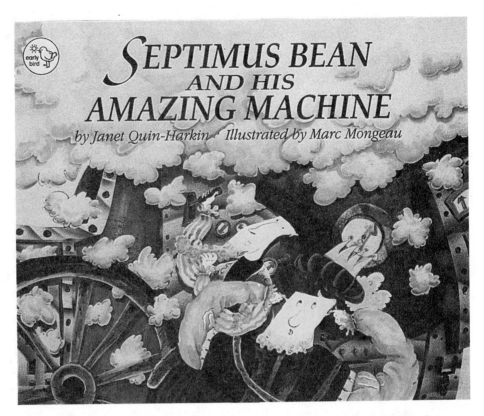

A trip to a science museum can be made more fun by using books that explore and extend current technology. Courtesy Delmar Publishers Inc.

worked in the community many years ago. Once this knowledge emerges, it can lead to other activities. The children might be able to visit the childhood home of the individual or have a descendant of the individual visit them.

The library is a very versatile place. It has a tremendous variety of resources about nearly any topic. Librarians are willing to assist visitors and groups in locating information and materials. The library is a place that children can use for many purposes.

Museums, Parks, and Zoos

Museums, parks, and zoos offer unparalleled opportunities to extend and enrich the lives of children. They are special places that compress much of life into a framework that one can experience in a matter of hours. Each of these places has a character of its own. Museums may focus on art, science, natural history, technology, and so forth. Some specialized museums may recreate colonial villages. Parks may feature different terrains, trees, and gardens. Different zoos may contain some similar animals. However, many zoos specialize in birds, monkeys, reptiles, or large cats. Some places such as planetariums and aquariums don't fit into either the museum or zoo category. However, each can be used to create powerful learning experiences for young children. Most of these resources have a designated education coordinator who can help make a field trip a most beneficial experience for young people. Each of these places has a role that can be integrated with literature in the curriculum.

Literature can be used before, during, and after a field trip. As a way of encouraging students to stay together as a group on a field trip, one might read Miriam Cohen's *Lost in the Museum* prior to the trip. While going through an art museum with a group of children one may wish to pause for a story about a visit to an art museum. Laurene and Marc Brown's *Visiting the Art Museum* describes a family visit to an art museum. The idea of paintings in an art museum coming to life is explored in two different books. A Renoir and a Rousseau are among five old masterpieces that come to life in James Mayhew's *Katie's Picture Show*. This theme is explored further in *The Incredible Paintings of Felix Clousseau* by Jon Agee. A natural history museum field trip might include dinosaur books by Aliki.

The books used do not have to be set in a museum or a park. Rather, books should be selected with the aim of learning in mind. For example, one might simply wish for children to learn about some of the animals, insects, and plants found in the area. In this case, books such as Millicent Selsam's *Backyard Insects* would be appropriate. Another good example of this type of book is Bianca Lavies's *Lily Pad Pond*. It contains stunning photographs of a woodland pond ecosystem. The sequence showing a tadpole developing over time into a frog totally captivates young children. Sharing of this type of literature during the field trip can greatly enhance the children's learning and understanding. Museum shops often carry related books and artwork that could be used in discussions before and after the museum visit. Large museums usually operate a children's shop that could become part of the field trip experience.

Places Serving the Community

A community cannot exist without a variety of services. Some services like fire and police protection are an absolute necessity, while others like stores are more of a convenience. Still others such as movie theaters are there solely to entertain. Each place, however, can add to the quality of life in the community. The people working at these places have a variety of interesting jobs and their work is important to the community. By understanding this, children can develop a better understanding of the community. The places serving the community can basically be divided into two groups: commercial and public service.

Commercial Locations. Places that exist to earn money for a profit constitute commercial locations. This includes banks, stores, newspaper buildings, theaters, florists, some hospitals, and so forth. Children can understand the importance of these places to the community because they often know people who work at such places. An understanding of these places will help children to better comprehend the books they might read about commercial locations.

Meeting some of the people who work at commercial locations and learning about the work they do is helpful. It might be possible to have one of the workers read a related story to the children. Books such as *Zoo Song* by Barbara Bottner and *Orchestranimals* by Vlasta van Kampen and Irene C. Eugen are appropriate not only at a zoo but at a symphony concert hall as well. Books that could be read in conjunction with a field trip to a store include *The Supermarket Mice* by Margaret Gordon, *The Storekeeper* by Tracy Campbell Pearson, *Pig Pig and the Magic Photo Album* by David McPhail, and *The Pizza Monster* by Marjorie Sharmat and Mitchell Sharmat. When visiting transportation related businesses, books to be shared might include *Freight Train* by Donald Crews, *Trains* by Gail Gibbons, and Anne Rockwell's books: *Planes, Cars, Big Wheels, Trains* and *Trucks*.

Public Service Locations. In addition to the businesses found in the community, many services are provided through the work of public and private agencies. These services are often aimed at providing protection to residents, maintaining good health, and responding to the religious needs of the population. The places that provide these services are quite varied, making them fascinating field trip destinations. They include water filtration plants, fire houses, police stations, hospitals, clinics, dental offices, weather stations, law offices, courthouses, churches, and so forth. The buildings often contain specialized equipment that performs important jobs related to the safety and health of the community. The people who work in these places are often quite willing to explain the importance of their work in the community.

There is a wide variety of books that can be used in conjunction with a field trip to a public service location. When visiting a fire house, one might read *Fire* by David Bennett or *Fire Engines* by Anne Rockwell. *Curious George Visits a Police Station,* one of a series of books by Margaret Rey and A. J. Shalleck, might be appropriate for use during a visit to the police station. Other books in this series follow Curious George as he visits an aquarium, restaurant, circus, hospital, and laundromat. A visit to a church or synagogue might include a reading of *Cathedral Mouse* by Kay Chorao.

Whenever a field trip has been scheduled, it is important to acknowledge and thank the people responsible for making it possible. Sharing a copy of a language experience story developed by the children after the trip is a thoughtful gesture. A thank you note might also be accompanied by photographs or children's drawings of the visit. Inviting radio, television, or newspaper reporters and photographers to accompany the children on these field trips is still another way of demonstrating the importance of the occasion.

PEOPLE TO SEE

Although it is not possible to arrange field trips to every place one would like children to visit, it is not always critical that children see the actual location. Many times the people and the jobs they perform are more important. In these situations, the experience might be more meaningful if a person with an interesting or specialized job made a visit to the class. People are often flattered and quite willing to devote the time to such an activity. They can explain their jobs, demonstrate a piece or two of the equipment they use in the job, and perhaps read a story about their job to the children.

Parents of children can be recruited for these activities. Most likely, they will represent a number of different occupations and resources. Parents may be the most overlooked group of people as positive contributors to learning within an educational program. It is critical, therefore, to maintain frequent and effective communications with parents concerning the program. In this way, they will be better able to support it and contribute to it. Other sources of classroom visitors may include representatives from community businesses and service organizations.

Involving Parents

Parents often seek ways in which they can become actively involved in the education of their children. Parental involvement in both the literature and the content parts of the program can benefit parents, children, and the program. By making arrangements for parental inclusion in the program, children see other adults who model the importance of books. This helps children see how books are related to life. In addition, children are usually delighted with and proud of the fact that their parents are visiting the classroom.

It is important to be sensitive to the fact that some parents cannot participate. This may not be because they don't wish to take part. Some jobs and employers can't or won't allow parents to take the time to participate in their children's classrooms. When this occurs, other family members should be invited. Older siblings, aunts, uncles, and grandparents often represent a further source of people willing and eager to contribute to the education of children.

Careful planning of a parent visit will contribute to the success of the event. Inviting a parent to participate early or late in the day can help them arrange the visit around their work schedule more easily. Day of the week, inclement weather, time of the year, and refreshments are all factors that need to be considered when planning parent participation. Notices and time schedules can aid both the parent, teacher, and the program. With careful planning, the program will not be overscheduled. Planning will also help to ensure that such things as notices and thank you notes are not overlooked. Developing a schedule for parent participation well in advance can help the planning for all involved. Keeping other parents informed about what is happening in advance can also be a benefit. They may be able to attend the program or further discuss the visitor and the ideas presented with their children. Both can enhance the program and the learning.

As with any effective part of the program, literature and books can be integrated with a parent visit. If parents are visiting the program to explain their jobs as bakers, lawyers, plumbers, or auto repair technicians, having them share a related story can enhance the visit. The story may be one selected by the teacher or the parent. Resources could be shared with parents beforehand to aid them in selecting an appropriate book. For example, a copy of one of the resource books by Jim Trelease[1] or Dorothy Butler[2] could be sent home two weeks before a planned visit

[1] Jim Trelease, *The New Read-Aloud Handbook* (New York: Viking Penguin, 1989).
[2] Dorothy Butler, *Babies Need Books* (New York: Atheneum, 1985)

by parents. In this way, parents could carefully consider a number of stories and choose the one they feel best supports the ideas they will talk about. Parents may also have children's books at home that were purchased because they were related to their employment.

Involving parents in education in this manner is a positive approach because it integrates them into their children's education. Parent involvement also makes use of a valuable resource: the work lives of the parents. Most parents, of course, are willing to help with the usual tasks of helping the school. These include baking cookies, supervising field trips, and helping at school parties. By including parents in the actual education program, however, they are provided the dignity and status that they more truly deserve.

Communicating with Parents

The key to an effective parent involvement program is communication. Parents must be aware of what is happening in the education lives of their children. They need to know what is happening in the classroom, how they can help in the classroom, and what can be done at home with their children. This goes beyond the usual notices about the topic being studied this month and the recommendation that parents read with their children. Those kinds of communications, while well intended, are too general to be of much guidance.

This does not mean that a total home instructional program must be prepared to back up what is being done in the classroom. This would simply put an unhealthy amount of pressure on children. Rather, if parents have a better idea of the topics being studied, why they are being studied, and the related books that they may wish to share at home, they would be in a better position to be involved. The idea is not to place pressure on anyone. The focus is on providing parents with enough information to be actively involved. If this occurs, they will be able to help make their children's educational life more meaningful.

Notes and Newsletters. Formal and informal parental communications are a primary source of information. They can be used to notify parents about more specific topics to be studied, the classroom visitor's schedule, meeting notices, and special projects for which supplies are needed. Newsletters can also be used to suggest books and stories related to the program.

Questionnaires and Surveys. Questionnaires and surveys can be distributed separately or they can be part of a newsletter. Either way, they help to foster two-way communication. By requesting information and opinions, parents are given an opportunity to provide input about their needs and potential contributions. Information that they might provide could include classroom visits they would be willing to make, hobbies they could demonstrate, areas of concern, and activities in which they would like to be involved.

Community Representatives

In many cases, representatives of the community may be identified from the ranks of the parents of children in a program. When this is not the case, businesses,

A classroom visit by a weather announcer could include any one of a number of books about storms. Courtesy Delmar Publishers Inc.

municipal departments, service organizations, and charitable foundations may be contacted as potential resources. The choices of whom to seek should be based upon the educational program and the learning goals for the children. Requesting a visit from an individual who happens to be available may not be worthwhile. While it may be entertaining, if the visit has nothing to do with the program it may become merely a diversion.

Individuals selected for classroom visits may represent the same types of organizations one might visit on a field trip. The key is to include a diversity of visitors who can focus on specific areas of the program. They may be bankers, nurses, musicians, construction workers, office workers, or dentists. As such, the books that they may choose to share with the children will be equally diverse. A lawyer may use Peter Spier's *We the People* while a nurse might use *All about Me* by Melanie Rice and Chris Rice. A dentist might choose to share Bernard Wolf's *Michael and the Dentist,* while a television weather announcer might read Mary Szilagyi's *Thunderstorm.* A 4-H representative or farmer might choose to read Brenda Cook's *All about Farm Animals.*

Classroom visits require the same careful planning as a field trip. Making arrangements early helps all involved. A thank you note accompanied by illustrations or a copy of the language experience story developed by the children after the visit is usually appreciated by the guest. Including announcements in the parents' newsletter before and after a visitation is beneficial. It enables parents to extend the learning through discussion and by listening to their children tell about the experience.

SUMMARY

Most communities have a wealth of resources that can be useful to an early education program. The resources may be somewhat different from place to place, but such things as fire houses and restaurants are usually common to all. Since learning often depends on the development of background knowledge and an understanding of the world, it is beneficial to include the resources of a community in the educational program. Using literature to enhance this part of an integrated curriculum can extend the learning of the children.

A community can be seen as including places and people. The places that make up a community are diverse, including everything from libraries to stores to churches. The people of the community reflect that diversity. In most communities one will encounter a variety of workers in such fields as banking, fire protection, music, and dentistry. Whether one takes the children to the place of work or brings the workers to the children, much will be learned. That learning can be enhanced, both before and after the experience, through the use of appropriate related literature.

Parents can be an outstanding source of support for field trip coordination and classroom visitations. A key component of tapping this resource is effective two-way communication. Such communication enables both parents and teachers to understand the concerns and needs of the children. Through this sharing, more effective instruction and learning can be planned.

QUESTIONS FOR THOUGHT AND DISCUSSION

1. What are some of the ways in which young children can learn about their community?
2. Why should field trips be planned as part of an integrated educational program?
3. Why is it important for young children to learn about their communities?
4. What are the two major areas to be considered in field trip planning?
5. When and why should literature be used in conjunction with a field trip?
6. What are some of the things children can learn from a field trip to a public library?
7. How should one select the books to be used in conjunction with a field trip?
8. Why can a class visitor sometimes provide an experience that is just as meaningful as a field trip?
9. How can parents as class visitors contribute to the educational programs of young children?

10. Why is effective communication important to successful parent involvement in the educational program?
11. How can parent/school communication be made more meaningful?

CHILDREN'S BOOKS CITED

Jon Agee, *The Incredible Paintings of Felix Clousseau* (New York: Farrar, Straus and Giroux, 1988).

David Bennett, *Fire* (New York: Bantam, 1989).

Barbara Bottner, *Zoo Song* (New York: Scholastic, 1987).

Laurene Krasny Brown and Marc Brown, *Visiting the Art Museum* (New York: E. P. Dutton, 1986).

Kay Chorao, *Cathedral Mouse* (New York: E. P. Dutton, 1988).

Miriam Cohen, *Lost in the Museum* (New York: Dell, 1979).

Brenda Cook, *All about Farm Animals* (New York: Doubleday, 1989).

Donald Crews, *Freight Train* (New York: Scholastic, 1989).

Gail Gibbons, *Trains* (New York: Holiday House, 1987).

Margaret Gordon, *The Supermarket Mice* (New York: E. P. Dutton, 1984).

Bianca Lavies, *Lily Pad Pond* (New York: E. P. Dutton, 1989).

Elizabeth Levy, *Something Queer at the Library* (New York: Delacorte, 1977).

James Mayhew, *Katie's Picture Show* (New York: Bantam, 1989).

David McPhail, *Pig Pig and the Magic Photo Album* (New York: E. P. Dutton, 1986).

Tracy Campbell Pearson, *The Storekeeper* (New York: Dial, 1988).

Margaret Rey and A. J. Shalleck, *Curious George Visits a Police Station* (New York: Scholastic, 1989).

Melanie Rice and Chris Rice, *All about Me* (New York: Doubleday, 1987).

Ann Rockwell, *Big Wheels* (New York: E. P. Dutton, 1986).

Ann Rockwell, *Cars* (New York: E. P. Dutton, 1984).

Ann Rockwell, *Fire Engines* (New York: E. P. Dutton, 1986).

Ann Rockwell, *I Like the Library* (New York: E. P. Dutton, 1977).

Ann Rockwell, *Planes* (New York: E. P. Dutton, 1985).

Ann Rockwell, *Trains* (New York: E. P. Dutton, 1988).

Ann Rockwell, *Trucks* (New York: E. P. Dutton, 1984).

Millicent E. Selsam, *Backyard Insects* (New York: Four Winds, 1983).

Marjorie Sharmat and Mitchell Sharmat, *The Pizza Monster* (New York: Delacorte, 1989).

Peter Spier, *We the People* (New York: Doubleday, 1987).

Mary Szilagyi, *Thunderstorm* (New York: Bradbury, 1984).

Vlasta van Kampen and Irene C. Eugen, *Orchestranimals* (New York: Scholastic, 1989).

Bernard Wolf, *Michael and the Dentist* (New York: Four Winds, 1980).

SELECTED REFERENCES

Dorothy Butler, *Babies Need Books* (New York: Atheneum, 1985).

Susan Hill, *Books Alive!* (Portsmouth, New Hampshire: Heinemann, 1989).

Jim Trelease, *The New Read-Aloud Handbook* (New York: Viking Penguin, 1989).

And they all lived happily ever after . . .

APPENDIX A
Publishers and Suppliers

Books

Annick Press, Firefly Books, 3520 Pharmacy Avenue, Unit 1-C, Scarborough, Ontario, Canada, M1W 2T8

Atheneum Books, Division Macmillan Publishing Company, 866 Third Avenue, New York, New York 10022

Avon Books, 1790 Broadway, New York, New York 10019

Ballantine Books, Division Random House, 201 East 50th Street, New York, New York 10022

R. R. Bowker Company, 205 East 42nd Street, New York, New York 10017

Bradbury Press, Division Macmillan Publishing Company, 866 Third Avenue, New York, New York 10022

Children's Book Council, 67 Irving Place, New York, New York 10003

Children's Press, 1224 West Van Buren Street, Chicago, Illinois 60607

Children's Television Workshop, 1 Lincoln Plaza, New York, New York 10023

Clarion Books, Division Houghton Mifflin Company, 1 Beacon Street, Boston, Massachusetts 02108

Coward-McCann, Division G. P. Putnam's Sons, 200 Madison Avenue, New York, New York 10016

Crowell, Division Harper & Row, 10 East 53rd Street, New York, New York 10022

Crown Publishers, 225 Park Avenue South, New York, New York 10003

Delacorte, Division Doubleday & Company, 245 Park Avenue, New York, New York 10167

Dell Publishing Company, 1 Dag Hammarskjold Plaza, New York, New York 10017

Dial Books, Division E. P. Dutton, 2 Park Avenue, New York, New York 10016

Doubleday & Company, 245 Park Avenue, New York, New York 10167

E. P. Dutton, 2 Park Avenue, New York, New York 10016

Farrar, Straus & Giroux, Division Harper & Row, 19 Union Square West, New York, New York 10003

Four Winds, Division Macmillan, 866 Third Avenue, New York, New York 10022

Golden Books, Division Western Publishing Company, 1220 Mound Avenue, Racine, Wisconsin 53404

Greenwillow, Division William Morrow, 105 Madison Avenue, New York, New York 10016

Grosset & Dunlap, Division G. P. Putnam's Sons, 200 Madison Avenue, New York, New York 10016

Harcourt, Brace Jovanovich, 1250 Sixth Avenue, San Diego, California 92101

Harper & Row, 10 East 53rd Street, New York, New York 10022

Hill & Wang, 19 Union Square West, New York, New York 10003

Holiday House, 18 East 53rd Street, New York, New York 10022

Holt, Rinehart & Winston, 151 Benigno Boulevard, Bellmawr, New Jersey 08031

Houghton Mifflin, 1 Beacon Street, Boston, Massachusetts 02108

Alfred Knopf, Division Random House, 201 East 50th Street, New York, New York 10022

J. B. Lippincott, Division Harper & Row, 10 East 53rd Street, New York, New York 10022

Little, Brown and Company, 34 Beacon Street, Boston, Massachusetts 02106

Lothrop, Lee & Shepard, Division William Morrow, 105 Madison Avenue, New York, New York 10016

McGraw-Hill, 1221 Avenue of the Americas, New York, New York 10020

Macmillan Publishing Company, 866 Third Avenue, New York, New York 10022

William Morrow, 105 Madison Avenue, New York, New York 10016

Mulberry Books, Division William Morrow, 105 Madison Avenue, New York, New York 10016

Pantheon Press, Division Random House, 201 East 50th Street, New York, New York 10022

Parents Magazine Press, Division E. P. Dutton, 2 Park Avenue, New York, New York 10016

Philomel Books, Division G. P. Putnam's Sons, 200 Madison Avenue, New York, New York 10010

Prentice Hall, 1230 Avenue of the Americas, New York, New York 10020

Price, Stern and Sloan, 360 North La Cienega Boulevard, Los Angeles, California 90048

Puffin Books, Division Viking Penguin, 40 West 23rd Street, New York, New York 10010

G. P. Putnam's Sons, 200 Madison Avenue, New York, New York 10010

Raintree Publications, 330 East Kilbourn Avenue, Milwaukee, Wisconsin 53202

Random House, 201 East 50th Street, New York, New York 10022

Scholastic, 2931 East McCarthy Street, Jefferson City, Missouri 65102

Scott Foresman, 1900 East Lake Avenue, Glenview, Illinois 60025

Charles Scribner's Sons, Division Macmillan, 115 Fifth Avenue, New York, New York 10003

Simon & Schuster, 1230 Avenue of the Americas, New York, New York 10020

Troll Associates, 320 Route 17, Mahwah, New Jersey 07430

Viking Penguin, 40 West 23rd Street, New York, New York 10010

Franklin Watts, 387 Park Avenue, New York, New York 10016

Western Publishing, 1220 Mound Avenue, Racine, Wisconsin 53404

Albert Whitman, 5747 West Howard Street, Niles, Illinois 60648

Workman Publishing, 708 Broadway, New York, New York 10003

Book Clubs

Walt Disney Music, Discovery Series, Department 5W5, 5959 Triumph Street, Commerce, California 90040

Firefly Book Club, Scholastic, 2931 East McCarthy Street, P.O. Box 7503, Jefferson City, Missouri 65102

Parents Magazine Read-Aloud Book Club, 1 Parents Circle, P.O. Box 10264, Des Moines, Iowa 50336

Seesaw Book Club, Scholastic, 2931 East McCarthy Street, P.O. Box 7503, Jefferson City, Missouri 65102

Sesame Street Book Club, Golden Press, 120 Brighton Road, Clifton, New Jersey 07012

Dr. Seuss and His Friends, The Beginner Readers Program, Department ZBU, Grolier Enterprises, P.O. Box 1797, Danbury, Connecticut 06816

Troll Book Club, 320 Route 17, Mahwah, New Jersey 07498

Trumpet Book Club, P. O. Box 604, Holmes, Pennsylvania 19043

Weekly Reader Children's Book Club, 4343 Equity Drive, P.O. Box 16613, Columbus, Ohio 43216

Big Books

Delmar Publishers, 2 Computer Drive West, Albany, New York 12212

Goldencraft-Children's Press, Western Publishing, 5440 North Cumberland Avenue, Chicago, Illinois 60656

Learning Well, Department DF, 200 South Service Road, Roslyn Heights, New York 11577

Random House, Department 436, 400 Hahn Street, Westminster, Maryland 21157

Rigby, P.O. Box 797, Crystal Lake, Illinois 60014

Scholastic, P.O. Box 7501, 2931 East McCarthy Street, Jefferson City, Missouri 65102

Wright Group, 10949 Technology Place, San Diego, California 92127

APPENDIX B
Caldecott Medal Winners

DATE	TITLE	AUTHOR/ILLUSTRATOR
1938	*Animals of the Bible*	Helen Dean Fish/Dorothy P. Lathrop
1939	*Mei Li*	Thomas Handforth
1940	*Abraham Lincoln*	Ingri and Edgar Parin D'Aulaire
1941	*They Were Good and Strong*	Robert Lawson
1942	*Make Way for Ducklings*	Robert McCloskey
1943	*The Little House*	Virginia Lee Burton
1944	*Many Moons*	James Thurber/ Louis Slobodkin
1945	*Prayer for a Child*	Rachel Field/Elizabeth Orton Jones
1946	*The Rooster Crows*	Traditional/Maud and Miska Petersham
1947	*The Little Island*	Golden MacDonald/Leonard Weisgard
1948	*White Snow, Bright Snow*	Alvin Tresselt/Roger Duvoisin
1949	*The Big Snow*	Berta & Elmer Hader
1950	*Song of the Swallows*	Leo Politi
1951	*The Egg Tree*	Katherine Milhous
1952	*Finders Keepers*	William Lipkind/Nicholas Mordvinoff
1953	*The Biggest Bear*	Lynd Ward
1954	*Madeline's Rescue*	Ludwig Bemelmans
1955	*Cinderella, or The Glass Slipper*	(Trad.) Charles Perrault/Marcia Brown
1956	*Frog Went A-Courtin*	ed. John Langstaff/Feodor Rojankovsky
1957	*A Tree Is Nice*	Janice May Undry/Marc Simont
1958	*Time of Wonder*	Robert McCloskey
1959	*Chanticleer and the Fox*	(Adaptation) Geoffrey Chaucer/Barbara Cooney
1960	*Nine Days to Christmas*	Marie Hall Ets and Aurora Labastida/Marie Hall Ets

1961	*Baboushka and the Three Kings*	Ruth Robbins/Nicolas Sidakov
1962	*Once a Mouse*	Marcia Brown
1963	*The Snowy Day*	Ezra Jack Keats
1964	*Where the Wild Things Are*	Maurice Sendak
1965	*May I Bring a Friend?*	Beatrice Schenk DeRegniers/Beni Montresor
1966	*Always Room for One More*	Sorche Nic Leodhas/Nonny Hogrogian
1967	*Sam, Bangs & Moonshine*	Evaline Ness
1968	*Drummer Hoff*	Barbara Emberly/Ed Emberly
1969	*The Fool of the World*	Arthur Ransome/Uri
1970	*Sylvester and the Magic Pebble*	William Steig
1971	*A Story–A Story*	Gail E. Haley
1972	*One Fine Day*	Nonny Hogrogian
1973	*The Funny Little Woman*	(Retold) Arlene Mosel/Blair Lent
1974	*Duffy and the Devil*	Harve Zemach/Margot Zemach
1975	*Arrow to the Sun*	(Adaptation) Gerald McDermott
1976	*Why Mosquitoes Buzz in People's Ears*	(Retold) Verna Aardema/Leo and Diane Dillon
1977	*Ashanti to Zulu: African Traditions*	Margaret Musgrove/Leo & Diane Dillon
1978	*Noah's Ark*	Peter Spier
1979	*The Girl Who Loved Wild Horses*	Paul Goble
1980	*Ox-Cart Man*	Donald Hall/Barbara Cooney
1981	*Fables*	Arnold Lobel
1982	*Jumanji*	Chris Van Allsburg
1983	*Shadow*	(Translation) Blaise Cendrars/Marcia Brown
1984	*The Glorious Flight: Across the Channel with Louis Bieriot*	Alice and Martin Provensen
1985	*St. George and the Dragon*	(Retold) Margaret Hodges/Trina Schart Hyman
1986	*The Polar Express*	Chris Van Allsburg
1987	*Hey Al*	Arthur Yorinks/Richard Egielski
1988	*Owl Moon*	Jane Yolen/John Schoenherr
1989	*Song and Dance Man*	Karen Ackerman/Stephen Gammell
1990	*A Red-Riding Hood Story from China*	Lon Po Po/Ed Young (illustrator and translator)

APPENDIX C
Best Selling Children's Books

The following are the all-time best selling children's hardbound books in the United States, according to Publishers Weekly:

1. *The Tale of Peter Rabbit* by Beatrix Potter
2. *Pat the Bunny* by Dorothy Kunhardt
3. *The Littlest Angel* by Charles Tazewell
4. *The Cat in the Hat* by Dr. Seuss
5. *Green Eggs and Ham* by Dr. Seuss
6. *The Children's Bible*
7. *The Real Mother Goose* illustrated by Blanche F. Wright
8. *Richard Scarry's Best Word Book Ever* by Richard Scarry
9. *One Fish, Two Fish, Red Fish, Blue Fish* by Dr. Seuss
10. *Hop on Pop* by Dr. Seuss

Index